Praise for *An Apostate's Gu*

"This book is three things at once: a very good introduction to witchcraft and magic, a moving account of a personal journey, and—most remarkably—an effective guide to finding personal freedom."
—**RONALD HUTTON**, historian and author of *The Witch* and *The Triumph of the Moon*

"An extraordinary blend of personal narrative and practical wisdom.... Each chapter is rich with information, from understanding the role of spirits to the importance of community in witchcraft, all presented in an accessible and engaging manner. The exercises are thoughtfully crafted, inviting readers to actively participate in their own journey of liberation and empowerment.... Matthey's compelling work stands out as a heartfelt and enlightening guide, offering a beacon of hope and a rich source of inspiration."
—**MAT AURYN**, bestselling author of *Psychic Witch* and *Mastering Magick*

"It's not enough to walk away from a bad religion. True healing requires finding something good and helpful to replace the void left behind.... The empowerment, acceptance, and joy Moss found are available to anyone who will follow the steps in this straightforward and easily accessible guide."
—**JOHN BECKETT**, Druid and author of *The Path of Paganism*

"A deeply personal look at finding power and connection in witchcraft, designed to help others find their own footing on this often-ephemeral path.... The exercises, meditations, and spells allow the reader to incorporate the book's message in practical ways and offer tangible methods to address the wider issues of overcoming and resetting past harmful spiritual beliefs. A unique and important addition to any witch's library."
—**MORGAN DAIMLER**, author of *Fairycraft* and *Living Fairy*

"Moss writes so beautifully on a topic not often discussed.... This book feels like the supportive rock amidst the crashing waves.... It truly feels like a friend sharing their experiences and lending their wisdom and warmth."
—**ELLA HARRISON**, author of *The Book of Spells*

"A deeply personal work engendering a sense of power and triumph for finding one's way out of the mire of organized religion. Relatable on so many levels, *The*

Apostate's Guide to Witchcraft is a song of joy, empowerment and victory, a reminder of our own worthiness and connection to the sacred. This will be an important book for all those who find their way to its powerful healing magic."
—**COBY MICHAEL,** author of *The Poison Path Herbal*

"*An Apostate's Guide to Witchcraft* sings sincerely with personal knowledge and experience, welcoming the newcomer into a witch's world of healing, growth, and remembering. ... A sheer joy, mixed with beautiful tears. Healing and honest."
—**FIO GEDE PARMA,** author of *The Witch Belongs to the World*

"Moss Matthey has written an inspirational book that takes the reader on a journey of freedom. ... I wish this book was available when I first escaped the thorny clutches of the church. ... It is full of exercises to heal, hold, and transform yourself into the witch you wish to become."
—**ANNWYN AVALON,** author of *Water Witchcraft*

"A timely road map for those who are just beginning their quest for freedom, and those who have walked this path for many years. ... Examining the potential role of witchcraft for those leaving restrictive birth faiths, Matthey takes us on a journey through various areas of the modern witchcraft movement."
—**BEN STIMPSON,** author of *Ancestral Whispers*

AN APOSTATE'S GUIDE TO WITCH CRAFT

About the Author

Moss Matthey (Wales, UK) was an active, indoctrinated member of a fundamentalist Christian cult for two decades before he found Witchcraft and broke free. This newfound spirituality helped him heal and experience true freedom. Now he speaks at A Festival for Pagans and Witches and the Centre for Folklore Myth Magic. He was also filmed as a member of the Coven of the Red Serpent for a Welsh-language documentary. Visit him at MossMatthey.com.

To Write to the Author

If you wish to contact the author or would like more information about this book, please write to the author in care of Llewellyn Worldwide Ltd. and we will forward your request. Both the author and publisher appreciate hearing from you and learning of your enjoyment of this book and how it has helped you. Llewellyn Worldwide Ltd. cannot guarantee that every letter written to the author can be answered, but all will be forwarded. Please write to:

Moss Matthey
℅ Llewellyn Worldwide
2143 Wooddale Drive
Woodbury, MN 55125-2989
Please enclose a self-addressed stamped envelope for reply,
or $1.00 to cover costs. If outside the U.S.A., enclose
an international postal reply coupon.

Many of Llewellyn's authors have websites with additional information and resources. For more information, please visit our website at http://www.llewellyn.com.

AN APOSTATE'S GUIDE TO
WITCH CRAFT

FINDING
FREEDOM
THROUGH
MAGIC

MOSS MATTHEY

LLEWELLYN
WOODBURY, MINNESOTA

An Apostate's Guide to Witchcraft: Finding Freedom Through Magic Copyright © 2024 by Moss Matthey. All rights reserved. No part of this book may be used or reproduced in any manner whatsoever, including internet usage, without written permission from Llewellyn Worldwide Ltd., except in the case of brief quotations embodied in critical articles and reviews.

FIRST EDITION
First Printing, 2024

Book design by Christine Ha
Cover design by Shannon McKuhen

Llewellyn Publications is a registered trademark of Llewellyn Worldwide Ltd.

Library of Congress Cataloging-in-Publication Data (Pending)
ISBN: 978-0-7387-7711-5

Llewellyn Worldwide Ltd. does not participate in, endorse, or have any authority or responsibility concerning private business transactions between our authors and the public.

All mail addressed to the author is forwarded but the publisher cannot, unless specifically instructed by the author, give out an address or phone number.

Any internet references contained in this work are current at publication time, but the publisher cannot guarantee that a specific location will continue to be maintained. Please refer to the publisher's website for links to authors' websites and other sources.

Llewellyn Publications
A Division of Llewellyn Worldwide Ltd.
2143 Wooddale Drive
Woodbury, MN 55125-2989
www.llewellyn.com

Printed in the United States of America

For my Coven,
who helped me find my path

And for my partner, Brett,
without whom this journey would never have started

Contents

Exercises

Acknowledgments

There are many people who guided me on my journey and helped this book come into being. To all the other people who left cults and shared their stories with me, I owe a debt of gratitude. Your kind words and support kept me going through the most difficult times, and these words would not exist without you. To all the Witches and Pagans I have met, who have ignited inspiration in my soul and helped my practice in myriad ways, I owe the same debt. I would not have the practice and spirituality I do without your kind and patient support.

Diolch yn enwedig i Mhara Starling, *i* Matthew Lewis, *ac i* Kristoffer Hughes. Your passion for the beautiful land of Wales is contagious, and having the opportunity to converse in the language of this place and share in that passion with you has left an indelible mark on my soul. Thank you for the many moments of inspiration; I hope the words contained in this book do them justice.

Special thanks are reserved for my family. For my partner, Brett, who saved more than one draft from the bin and brought me back from the brink of abandoning this project on many occasions: thank you for your eternal patience, for the inspiration we have shared, and for the passion you have for Witchcraft and the Welsh Marches. It is no secret that I would not be a Witch without you. You have shaped my life in more ways than I can ever hope to express. For all those who chose me over the cult, who left and kept me in their lives, you know who you are. I am deeply grateful to have you in my life and will always treasure the moments we share. For my father, who taught me the value of the world around me, and for my mother, who has done more for me than I can ever repay. I love you all.

Also, thank you to Heather, Hanna, and the editing team. Without you, this book would not exist. Thank you for always being in my corner and for the invaluable feedback every step of the way.

Finally, I want to acknowledge the many authors, podcasters, YouTubers, and other Pagans who share their knowledge and experience in various ways, including the many covens and individuals who have shared their time and inspiration with me. It is a great privilege to share a small part of this conversation with you all. And of course, the Unicorn Pin Cushion. You know what you did.

Foreword

Witchcraft has always, within my personal perception, been a path of empowerment and transformation. Over the years I have spent practicing, organising community events, attending festivals and gatherings, I have witnessed the blossoming of people who approached this path after a tempestuous past. It is rather magical indeed to witness someone grow into their most authentic, most unapologetic selves.

I still remember the first day I met Moss Matthey. It was during a moot that I had organised. A *moot* is a gathering of local Pagans, Witches, and spiritually inclined people. Held in the centre of the city I lived in at the time, it was a scorchingly hot day—or at least scorching within a British context. Here in the UK, our buildings rarely have air-con, and so our indoor gathering was moved to the venue's outdoor area. There, beneath the branches of a beautiful fig tree, as the summer sun set and the birds hovered around us, magical people began filtering in.

Against the backdrop of a red summer sky, the most delicious of discussions began. A group of likeminded people began discussing, debating, and sharing elements of their own personal practices and experiences.

Moss was a quiet one. He attempted to hide behind his partner as he filed his way in, though of course this would never be possible considering he is over six feet tall. Beyond his height, he also had a face that seemed to imply he knew some hidden, arcane things. Quite intimidating, even to me. He barely spoke that meeting, and I could tell he was taking it all in and was potentially a tad overwhelmed. I had no idea at the time what his past entailed.

Over many moons Moss began attending the events and classes I ran regularly. Soon, I was less intimidated by him and more intrigued. He hinted at a past that was restrictive and abusive. And so, in response to that, I began making it ever more clear just how welcoming, transgressive, and free of a space this magical path of ours was.

I did not grow up within the dogma of a restrictive faith. My parents were agnostic at best, claiming they believed that something beyond the physical, tangible world existed, but that they weren't quite sure what that something was. I never attended church, beyond the odd school event, wedding, or baptism I was invited to. I was never christened, and the Bible was nothing more than a book to me.

Despite this, I did grow up queer. I knew from a very young age that I did not fit into the neat little boxes society attempted to cram me into. From as young as I can remember being able to form thought, I made clear that my gender expression and identity did not match the expectations that were laid upon me from birth. Despite having parents that were not part of any religion so to speak, one parent in particular struggled immensely with my queer identity, so much so that he became my first and most terrifying bully.

I hid who I truly was for many years, attempting to keep the peace. It wasn't until I escaped the abuse he had subjected me to as I toddled off to university in England that I finally found the courage to come out as transgender.

Witchcraft played a vital role in my journey to becoming my most authentic self. It was among magical friends on darksome nights that I felt I was truly free. I could break free of the judgment, abuse, and ridicule I was so often subjected to as I danced under starry skies with Witches donning cloaks and robes.

Whilst my experience is not identical to the experience of growing up in a fundamentalist, restrictive environment, I can relate to the idea of feeling broken, wrong, unseen, a burden, and a disappointment. And perhaps that is what initially helped Moss and me to "click" as friends. We related to one another and could see the power present in stepping out of the shadow of expectation and condemnation.

Within no time, Moss flourished in our little groups. Eventually we would gather outside of the scheduled events, and we would become good friends. When I initially put out the feelers of wanting to start a coven or working group of my own, Moss was one of the first to excitedly agree to join me on such a venture. And now here we are.

Within the pages of this book, you will hear Moss's story—a story of one person's journey into accepting themselves fully whilst consistently shadowed by the influence of a restrictive, fundamentalist belief system. But beyond Moss's personal story, which I am certain many will be able to relate to, he also introduces you to the magic, empowerment, and, most importantly, joy of Witchcraft as an embodied, fulfilling spiritual practice.

You will read about the ways in which embracing magic can aid us in connecting on a more visceral level to our culture, our community, and the spirits that reside in this world alongside us, as well as how a magical mindset can offer us a new perspective on divinity.

I believe this book will prove useful not only to those tentatively taking their very first steps into the world of Witchcraft and magic, but also to those who are seasoned practitioners. Moss's insights into the power of narrative storytelling, the importance of community, and new ways to perceive certain aspects of our life and upbringing are truly captivating.

Throughout the exercises and nuggets of information woven into this work, you will also come across hints toward the new tradition we are building together, a tradition rooted in the very culture both Moss and I were raised in— Welsh culture. And yet, none of these practices mentioned are in any way limited to those who share our cultural heritage. As queer Witches, as Witches who value the power of authenticity and communal support, these exercises will aid you in finding the very transgressive and empowering potential of Witchcraft and magic.

Moss acts throughout the book as a considerate, sensitive, and nurturing guide. The way out of the dense forest of self-doubt and uncertainty that the restrictive, narrow thinking of our previous lives may have left us in can seem treacherous and fill us with dread. However, this book offers a light at the end, a guiding beacon which can act as a piggyback out of that dense, foggy wood onto a path much easier to navigate. May this book inspire you and aid you on your path to becoming. I am glad to have met Moss and to be a mentor as he paves his own way. And now, you too can be led down a similar path of empowerment and enchantment.

—Mhara Starling, author of *Welsh Witchcraft*
Founder of the *Sarffes Goch* Coven

Introduction

Our ancestors had a lot to say about journeys. If they had to travel, they made efforts to do it in a way that would bring them home safely and successfully. They carefully planned their routes, setting out at the right time and on the right day. Countless folk beliefs and charms grew out of the idea that a journey is sacred and that it must be well planned and respected.

Possibly the most important part of a journey was the beginning: that liminal point where anything could happen and the outcome was still up in the air. It was important to start with your best foot forward, not focusing on the uncertainty or distracted by what might go wrong, but with an eye to the future and a certainty that you would succeed. In fact, folklore tells us that one of the worst things you could do when setting out was to look back toward home, for that was sure to bring bad luck.

This book is a journey, one which starts in a fundamentalist Christian cult but ends somewhere far more joyful. And so, much like our ancestors would begin their travels, this book starts on a hopeful note and with an eye to the future. Rather than being rooted in the past and the distressing things that dwell there, we first look to our destination: Witchcraft.

I am a Witch, and this is the world that welcomed me so warmly. It helped me step into my power and find community and a spiritually satisfying path, and it gave me a deep sense of connectedness to the world around me. I believe the journey here is one of hope and joy, and through the pages of this book, I invite you to walk it with me.

One of the great joys of life is that we can grow together and find inspiration in one another. I could not have journeyed from cult to coven without the many people who guided me or spoke to my soul with their own stories. Those moments of connection were crucial every step of the way, and it is my hope that, no matter where you are in life, you can find something that speaks to you here. Much like the travellers of old would have gathered around the fire and shared their tales, we can sit here together and share a moment of connection along our intersecting paths. As you read my story, I also hold space for yours.

When we share our stories, we start to realise that we are not alone. We find our people—those who are happy to make space for us, to help us carry what ails us, and to help us step ever more into our power. The shame and hurt we carry drops away, even if only for that brief shared time. The most powerful moments I have experienced as a Witch are those when my life has been touched by someone else's story, or when my story has touched theirs. This sense of connection is a magic deeper than any other.

Witchcraft

Let's begin by looking to Witchcraft. Often, people are frightened when it's mentioned. When you hear the word *Witch*, what images does it conjure up?

Perhaps you think of an old crone riding along on a broomstick, cackling away into the night. Or maybe you think of superheroes who use their powerful magic to defeat their enemies. If you have been raised in certain mainstream religions, you may think of demonic or even Satanic pacts. Or, if you are more historically minded, you might think of the great tragedy of the witch hunts and the thousands of innocent people tortured and killed for the alleged crime of Witchcraft.

These images are burned into our collective consciousness and showcase the range of meanings this word might conjure up. Who isn't afraid when they first hear of the wicked Witch hiding in the forest? She is a creature of nightmares found in countless stories and often used to frighten children.

Being born and raised in Germany, I was especially familiar with this character from the fairy tales of my home. It is no surprise that Germany would preserve this image of the Witch so ferociously, having a notorious reputation for the sheer amount of Witchcraft persecutions that occurred there. It is estimated that around 25,000 people were killed as Witches in Germany alone.[1] The fear of Witches and the suffering heaped on the accused was intense.

....

1. Johannes Dillinger, "Germany—'The Mother of the Witches,'" in *The Routledge History of Witchcraft*, ed., Johannes Dillinger (London: Routledge, 2021), 94.

But does that have anything to do with what it means to be a Witch today? It may surprise you that a practicing Witch today has very little to do with these malevolent creatures of legends, and even less with the pyrotechnics of Hollywood. On the whole, we don't live in gingerbread cottages and lure children into the woodlands, and only partially because of how inconvenient that would be. And since Witchcraft isn't criminalised in much of the Western world anymore, there is little danger of being burned alive either.

This book showcases how I made the transition into Witchcraft and the freedom I found here. As you may have noticed by now, I haven't always been a Witch. I was stuck in a fundamentalist Christian cult for two decades, paralysed by fear, obligation, and guilt. I was ashamed of my identity and felt completely powerless. I gained so much by stepping into the world of Witchcraft, and that is what I hope to show through these pages.

However, this book is not an attack on Christianity or a teardown of any doctrine. Throughout this book, I talk about my experiences in a group I now describe as a cult. The term *cult* is very vague and very broad. I explain why I use it a little later, but essentially it allows anyone who has come from a controlling or traumatic religious experience to relate to one another. While this book is meant for anyone, I especially hope those who have been through the experience of controlling religion will find it helpful. However, I believe there are parts of this journey that anyone who has been through, or is thinking of, a change of faith can relate to. Therefore, my focus will be on the freedom Witchcraft brings rather than any particular practices I have escaped.

I also don't claim to have found the one true faith. Witchcraft is one of many valid spiritual paths, and I'm sharing it not to convert anyone, but to share the joy and freedom I have discovered.

This is also not an academic book. I reference scholars throughout that inform my beliefs and practices, but they do not justify them. The practice of a Witch is not trapped on dead pages; it is alive and in the moment, and spiritual beliefs do not need academic validation.

Through these pages I will introduce you to a world of magic and spirits, where queerness is celebrated and sin does not exist. I will tell you how I left a cult and the lessons I learned along the way. Culture and community will be celebrated through folklore, myth, and folk magic. We may even take a detour into theology and philosophy, though hopefully it won't be too boring. Above all, we will celebrate the joy and freedom of Witchcraft.

Apostacy

But first, a small detour. Since the word *apostate* is a big part of this book, it's important I explain what I mean. Whenever I heard the word *apostate* from the cult, I knew my fate was sealed. It was inevitably followed by an attack on my character or a reminder that God would soon destroy me. Whenever it was invoked, I knew I would not get a fair hearing. It was designed to shut me down and to attack my character rather than the substance of my argument. To be an apostate was the worst thing you could possibly be, or so I was expected to believe.

It was not until I became an apostate myself that I discovered there were two definitions—that the meaning I had been taught was not the widely accepted one. To the wider world, an apostate is simply someone who has renounced their faith. It is a descriptor that could be applied to anyone who leaves one belief system for another. It is therefore not an inherently negative thing, even if it is often invoked in negative ways. Neither is it indicative of a person's character.

However, the cult had other ideas. To them, an apostate was the ultimate traitor, a deranged and dangerous individual. They were servants of Satan, often described as "mentally diseased." I sat through many sermons eagerly awaiting the time God would destroy all the shameless apostates and their corpses would litter the earth. This distorting of language itself is a telltale characteristic of a cult.

How would one go about becoming an apostate by this definition? It was not by leaving the religion. That was bad, but it was not apostasy. No, to achieve this level of sin you had to do the unthinkable—speak out against the organisation. It is a word to demean and discredit whistleblowers, to attack them and avoid taking any kind of responsibility. The worst, most unforgivable thing a person could do was be open about the bad way they were treated. The word *apostate* was redefined exclusively to stop people from speaking out and to easily dismiss them if they did.

One reason this book exists is because I am so dangerous millions of people are forbidden from speaking to me. Merely reading this book could cause them to be kicked out of their faith and shunned. I will let you be the judge of whether the contents are truly so radical. I am an apostate in both senses of the word and wear this label with pride. I have renounced my faith and speak very openly about my experiences while I was trapped there. However, this book is mostly presented from the perspective of someone who has found the wonderful world of Witchcraft. Rather than focusing on who I am an apostate to, this book focuses on where I am now and is informed by the experience I have been through.

What's the Point of Witchcraft?

Christianity is defined by sin and waiting for the next life. However, Witches are not defined by our mistakes, nor do we believe in sin. That is probably the biggest difference that's immediately apparent. Removing sin from the equation also removes the shame that comes with it, leading to a free and celebratory spiritual path that is also practical. But there are also some other major differences that are immediately apparent.

Witchcraft is *decentralised*. This is a word I use frequently throughout this book, and it simply means there is no doctrine at the core of what we believe. We're not built around some sacred text or priesthood that tells us what to do or think. The practice and spirituality of every single Witch is unique to them.

In my opinion, the purpose of life is to indulge ourselves in the mystery. Witchcraft is one pathway into that mystery and allows us to immerse ourselves in it. I couldn't teach you the one true religion if I wanted to, because I don't think it exists. The river of spirit and mystery is constantly flowing, and we can simply find our small piece of it. Witchcraft gives me that, as it does for lots of others on this journey.

Many people think there is a long lineage of Witches stretching deep into the past. Unfortunately, that's not very likely. Most traditions of Witchcraft are a rather modern invention. However, that's not to say we don't have any roots. The long, unbroken history we have is in finding power in myth, in folklore, and in magic. It is in innovation, in finding magic in the moment. We are the explorers and experimenters, those who find power in the most unlikely of places. This is not restricted to any one tradition but expressed in a beautifully diverse world of modern Witches from many different paths.

As you read further, you may notice I seem to use the words *Paganism* and *Witchcraft* quite interchangeably. This reflects my personal practice, which is rooted in Paganism—that is, a non-Christian, nature-based faith. It is important to note, though, that not all Pagans are Witches, and not all Witches are Pagan. However you identify is valid, but my path is that of a Pagan Witch. A nice way to visualise this is by imagining a forest. Where many religions are like a single tree which branches out, Paganism is like a forest. There are many trees growing from many traditions, but we all share the same space. Witchcraft is one tree in the forest of Paganism, at least to me.

How to Use This Book

This is also not a Bible of Witchcraft. I'm not going to tell you every possible way to practice, nor am I going to teach you everything you need to know. No book could do that. This is simply a beginning informed by my own experiences, and a taste of what Witchcraft can be. It is also a book of philosophy and opinion, some of which you will likely disagree on. That's completely fine; it would be strange if you agreed with everything. However, when those passages arise, I challenge you to ask yourself why you disagree. I don't say that because I want to convince you of my point of view. If we all thought the same, life would be rather boring. No, I challenge you simply to think rather than shutting down immediately. Some of my best thoughts have come from writing I disagreed with, as it challenged me to defend my position and refine my belief.

There are a series of exercise and journaling prompts in these pages. If you feel comfortable doing so, I encourage you to at least try them. In so doing, you are not committing to the path of Witchcraft. You are always free to change your mind. Think of these exercises simply as samples, little bites to see if you like the taste. If not, you can stop anytime you like. Witchcraft is a craft; it exists in the doing, so please do get involved and see if it works for you.

This book is also informed by my experiences as a member of a queer coven. Therefore, it also contains brief insights into things I have learned on my journey with my closest friends and magical partners in crime. These insights show how my own thinking has evolved as well as the things I have learned from this wonderful community. While I will refer to the practices of my coven, some of them have been a little altered, and the majority are simple exercises that don't approach the deeper mysteries of our tradition. In addition, I offer some exercises from my personal practice, informed by both my Welsh and German identity.

If this is your first step on the Witch's path, then don't rush. Take your time, experiment, and see what works for you. There is no finish line and no prize for getting there first. Some of your best experiences and most treasured memories will come from the exploration and the journey. So sit back, enjoy the ride, and welcome to the magical world of Witchcraft.

Chapter 1
Finding Witchcraft

When I tell people I am a Witch, it inspires a range of reactions, as I'm sure you can imagine. My favourites are those from people who knew me in my past life as a devout Christian preacher, even if only for the priceless facial expressions. I have to pick some people back up off the floor again before I attempt to explain—if they don't run away terrified first, that is.

The truth, however, is that there are many conflicting ideas about what it means to be a Witch in the modern world, even among Witches themselves. That is because Witchcraft is a loose term, encompassing a wide variety of paths and beliefs. Further complicating the situation is the amount of misinformation and fearmongering that exists around the idea of being a Witch, which all makes it incredibly difficult to explain. To do so, you have to clear up the myths and then find a definition broad enough that any Witch can find something of themselves in it. Since I enjoy a challenge, I'll attempt just that here.

The Myths

A whole book could be written about the myths that have grown around the idea of Witchcraft, but this is not that book. However, I have personal experience with some of the more common myths from within fundamentalist Christianity and will address some of those here.

Witches Are Devil Worshippers

This is a deeply rooted myth that is stoked by many fundamentalist churches and cults. I heard this more times than I can count, repeated in sermon after sermon. The Christian idea of Witchcraft is nothing like the reality of the experience, as I can personally attest. Divinity is incredibly nuanced within the practice of a Witch, and different Witches will work with different pantheons. Though it is far more complex than I can fully discuss here, the myth of devil worship is perhaps fuelled by the fact many traditions work with a deity known as the "Horned God," and people latch onto this concept and project their idea of the Christian devil onto it. Again, the truth is far different. Professor Ronald Hutton, a historian of Paganism, perhaps puts it best when he writes that the description of Witches merely as devil worshippers "can only be sustained by those who firmly believe that any deity or deities except their own must automatically be demonic."[2]

Witchcraft Is Evil

This myth often follows hot on the heels of the idea that Witchcraft is demonic. However, I'm discussing it separately, as this allegation usually refers to what Witches do, not who they worship. The idea that Witches exist only to work evil and curse people with all manner of terrible ills has been thrown around for centuries. A famous example is the *Malleus Maleficarum*, or the *Hammer of Witches*, first published in 1487, which made all manner of claims about the evil of Witches.[3] While the Witches of today are completely different than the Witches described in the *Hammer*, the myth stuck, and many still believe that we are agents of evil. However, the question must be asked: Which is truly evil? The people who carry the title of *Witch,* or the lies stoked by fundamentalist religious teachings that led to an estimated 40,000–50,000 innocent people being killed?[4] In fact, it is the term *witch hunt* that invokes ideas of oppression today, and outdated ideas of the "evil witch" are best left in the past.[5]

Witchcraft Is Contagious

This myth is the idea that seeing Witchcraft or magic in movies, on TV, or in books will corrupt you somehow. It always makes me chuckle a little, as it

....

2. Ronald Hutton, *The Triumph of the Moon: A History of Modern Pagan Witchcraft* (Oxford, UK: Oxford University Press, 2001), 407.
3. Robin Briggs, *Witches & Neighbours: The Social and Cultural Context of European Witchcraft*, 2nd ed. (Oxford, UK: Blackwell Publishers, 2002), 65.
4. Gordon Napier, *Maleficium: Witchcraft and Witch Hunting in the West* (Stroud, UK: Amberley Publishing Limited, 2017), 228.
5. Wolfgang Behringer, *Witches and Witch-Hunts: A Global History* (Cambridge, UK: Polity Press, 2004), 10.

sounds a lot like contagious magic, or the idea that just being near something can cause it to influence you. We need look no further back in history than the Satanic panic of the 1980s and the fear it provoked that consuming any media depicting Witchcraft would contaminate you. This is a fear that fundamentalist Christian denominations today continue to stoke, claiming that consuming media containing magic will cause untold harm to an individual.

The truth is that Witches don't proselytise, much less force people to take part. We don't need to. Our path is our own, and it doesn't matter who else walks it. The only hint of truth in this myth is that Witchcraft is such a freeing and joyous path that many who find it do choose to stay, but not because they have been influenced or coerced.

Witchcraft Is Just Fantasy

I didn't really experience this final myth while I was in the cult. Rather, it's one I mostly experienced after becoming a Witch myself. Because of the concept of the Witch in books and on TV, there is an idea that those who claim to be Witches today are just playing pretend. This is quite a modern myth, arising with the Age of Reason that dismissed all ideas of magic. For millennia, magic was an accepted part of everyday life. Only over the last couple of centuries have ideas of Witchcraft been completely fictionalised.

However, nothing could be further from the truth! Modern Witchcraft has very little in common with the exaggerated portrayals across the media. For modern practitioners, it is an enlightening and empowering spiritual path, a deeply personal and important part of our life.

The Reality of Witchcraft

Now that I've cleared up a handful of myths, let's talk about what modern Witchcraft actually is. Again, the concept of Witchcraft is very broad, and there are many different paths, but each path does seem to have something in common. Within my own practice and the practices of many Witches I have spoken to at various festivals and events, there are four common threads that seem to run through. These threads are spirituality, community, empowerment, and connection.

Spirituality

While Witchcraft today often involves connection to the Divine, the idea of spirituality goes far deeper than that. Society often equates spirituality with the belief in some form of omnipotent god, and many Witches will have a relationship with some form of divinity. However, there are also Witches who identify as atheist or agnostic, and this is a completely viable approach to Witchcraft.

To the Witch, spirituality is a deepening of the world. It is the appreciation that there is more to reality than that which is immediately apparent to our senses, that there are deeper mysteries to be explored. It is a belief in beings and forces that exist alongside our physical world, and that we can interact with those forces. This may be in the form of gods, but it may also be spirits that are not above us but exist as equals. I have yet to meet a Witch who does not believe in this deeper dimension to life, even if it is not always expressed in the same words.

Within my own practice as a native Welsh practitioner, I find this easiest to understand through the concept of *Awen*. This is an incredibly important concept in Welsh poetry and spirituality, being the source of inspiration and prophecy that flows through the bardic tradition, and is described by Kristoffer Hughes as "the most sacred and all-encompassing spirit of Celtica."[6] Awen is not treated as a divinity that must be appeased or worshipped, but as a spirit or force that flows through us. In fact, the root word of Awen basically means "to blow." It is breathed into us, and we can breathe it into the world.[7] It is the very force of inspiration that moves the poets and the artists, the wisdom in all living things. The poem "Angar Kyfundawt" from the Book of Taliesin claims that Awen is brought forth from the depths.[8] It is a deeper dimension to existence, a force that connects us to something greater and enriches our existence. To connect with Awen is not inherently to worship or even believe in a god, but it is certainly a spiritual experience.

....

6. Kristoffer Hughes, *From the Cauldron Born: Exploring the Magic of Welsh Legend & Lore* (Woodbury, MN: Llewellyn Publications, 2012), xix.

7. Patrick K. Ford, *The Celtic Poets: Songs and Tales from Early Ireland and Wales* (Belmont, MA: Ford & Bailie, 1999), 38.

8. Marged Haycock, *Legendary Poems from the Book of Taliesin* (Aberystwyth, Wales: CMCS Publications, 2007), 119.

Exercise: Recognising the Awen

This exercise is a brief introduction to one spiritual concept in modern Witchcraft traditions. It does not ask you to do any magic, simply to think about a time you may have experienced a spiritual dimension of life.

Materials:
• A quiet place to sit and think
• Your thoughts

Directions:
Take a moment to sit down and be still, then think about a time you felt really inspired. It may have been to create a work of art, compose a poem, or write a song, or it may have been as simple as cooking a new meal or mixing a new drink. As you hold the memory of that experience in mind, think about these questions:

• How did that moment of inspiration feel? Try and engage your senses and truly embody the memory.
• Did this feel like a completely mundane moment, or was there some sense of "moreness," almost as if the inspiration was breathed into you?
• Can you bring that feeling back into your body now?
• Are there any other moments in your life when you felt connected to some deeper aspect of existence?

Sit with these questions and allow yourself to explore them. The simple act of quiet contemplation can be spiritual in and of itself.

Community

As humans, we are inherently social. We rely on connection to others, seeking it out wherever we can. Even the most introverted among us will have a network of friends we can turn to when needed. Modern society seems more connected than ever, with more and more people living in big cities and social media being easily accessible. Counterintuitively, though, rates of loneliness are increasing year on year and contributing to a range of health issues.[9] People are more isolated than ever, even as the world seems all the more connected.

Witchcraft may not fix this issue, but it can certainly help. Walking this path automatically connects you with others who are doing the same, and you immediately have something in common. I have been attending Witchcraft events for several years now, and seeing people who have only just met talking like they've known each other for years always brings me joy. There is something special that comes with embracing the spiritual and magical side of life, and helps connect you with others who have a similar worldview. The sense of distance that seems so prevalent in society melts away, and you connect with those around you as your authentic self, as the 1996 film *The Craft* puts it, "With perfect love and perfect trust."[10]

The community aspect of Witchcraft was particularly striking to me. As I'll discuss later, being in a cult is a very social experience. Your community is used against you to control you. They judge and report back, keeping your behaviour in check. This does not exist within Witchcraft, and finding a community, a coven, that simply accepted me was a breath of fresh air.

An Introduction to My Coven

Imagine a warm evening as summer nears its end. The sun lingers in the sky, casting a golden glow across the world as a gentle breeze tames the comfortable heat. You are stood in the centre of an ancient city, encircled by walls built millennia ago. Half-timbered buildings are all around, with most dating back centuries.

As the sun continues its steady descent, you make your way to a small spiritual shop, hidden away on the ancient rows. You pass through the doorway and are welcomed by the strong scent of incense and the shimmer of crystals

....

9. Susanne Buecker, Marcus Mund, Sandy Chwastek, Melina Sostmann, and Maike Luhmann, "Is Loneliness in Emerging Adults Increasing Over Time? A Preregistered Cross-Temporal Meta-Analysis and Systematic Review," *Psychological Bulletin* 147, no. 8 (August 2021): 787–805, https://doi.org/10.1037/bul0000332; John T. Cacioppo and Stephanie Cacioppo, "The Growing Problem of Loneliness," *The Lancet* 391, no. 10119 (February 2018): 426, https://doi.org/10.1016/S0140-6736(18)30142-9.
10. Andrew Fleming, dir. *The Craft*, 1996; Culver City, CA: Columbia Pictures.

as you rush through to a garden hidden in the back. You settle under the leaves of a fig tree, sitting around a cauldron simmering gently, the smoke filling your nose with a burst of rosemary and lavender.

Soon others arrive, and the courtyard is bustling with people here for one purpose. You are attending your first moot, and everyone is here to grow and learn. You settle your nerves, and the evening begins.

The previous description is almost exactly how my journey into Witchcraft began. I was a little afraid taking this first step. I had been taught Witchcraft was evil and demonic. But I managed to swallow that fear, and I set out on a path that would change my entire life.

The moot was hosted by Mhara Starling, who went on to write the phenomenal book *Welsh Witchcraft: A Guide to the Spirits, Lore, and Magic of Wales*. Over time, it grew into something a little more. Alongside my partner, I started to work magic and attend further discussions with Mhara and a small group of dedicated practitioners. We began to meet weekly at minimum, and quickly realised a more formal arrangement would help us in our workings.

We were all inspired by the lore and magic of Wales and realised that there was no practice that reflected our worldview and perception of magic and ritual. Throughout many conversations, we shared our thoughts on magic and the nature of the universe, and I took those conversations and proposed we do something new. Drawing heavily on the Welsh bardic tradition, we created new ritual structures and practices. We began to call ourselves Bardic Witches, fusing the path of the modern-day Witch with the inspiration of the ancient bards.

I share this story because it helps show the power of community within the world of Witchcraft. A handful of practitioners from different streams came together and began to develop something new. If you choose to follow this path and the coven you want doesn't exist yet, be the one to create it. And if a coven is too formal, attend a moot or join a forum. There is a rich and vibrant community out there for all who want to take part.

Empowerment

The world we live in can often make us feel powerless. Life in a cult certainly did that for me, teaching that I had absolutely no power and must rely on God for everything in my life. But even less-extreme circumstances can make you feel completely restricted: The daily grind of having to work for people who don't value you and having to appease faceless corporate bosses. Having laws passed that steal your freedom and autonomy by a government you didn't vote for. Feeling unsafe walking down the street simply for living as your authentic self. These are not some fringe events but an everyday lived reality for many of us.

While Witchcraft may not always solve these problems, it offers us a way to feel empowered and reclaim some control over our lives. By being part of a community that values and accepts you exactly as you are, you get a sense of peace and empowerment, but this path goes far deeper.

Throughout this book, I often refer to Witchcraft as a practice. That is because it goes beyond something you believe. It is a craft—something you *do*. The doing often happens in the form of magic, a force I will discuss in greater depth in chapter 3.

But magic is not merely some tool to effect change. It is a thread that ties us back through history, to people who for centuries have practiced very similar traditions to those we utilise today. The magic of the modern Witch is built on a very rich foundation, constructed by generations of practitioners and innovators. They were not all called *Witches*. Most, in fact, were not. Some were astrologers, mystics, occultists, Freemasons, or ceremonialists. But all helped build up the traditions we build our practices around today. The history of magic is deep and enriching, and connecting to that in your own practice can be a very spiritual experience. Being able to draw on this potent force is certainly an empowering and exhilarating part of the Craft.

The power of Witchcraft comes from the community it offers. It flows through the rich ancestral streams you are tied back to. More than anything, it crackles through you in magic, both everyday and extraordinary.

Connection

Connection may sound like community, but it goes a little deeper. Most streams of Witchcraft today are inherently animistic. That means they believe that all things on earth have a spirit, and that human life is not elevated above the rest of the natural world, but living alongside a thriving ecosystem of living, feeling beings.

It is hard to feel connected in a world encased in concrete, where the only living thing often seems to be the humming of the wires. But the Witch sees beyond the world that humans have constructed. We see that even the dandelion forcing its way through the cracks is alive and inspirited, a blazing reminder of what we must never forget. No matter how advanced we become as a society, we are never above nature. We are connected to her; we live alongside her, and to neglect that is to invite disaster.

This philosophy is not only spiritual but also deeply practical. Our mother is being destroyed and polluted at an unprecedented rate. We are killing our very home because so many seem to believe we are somehow above the natural world. But to the Witch and any other animist, we know this is insanity. We need connection with the world around us more than ever, and I believe this is one of the greatest gifts of the Witch.

Exercise: Embracing Nature

It is not difficult to feel connected with nature, but in this busy world, we often forget to take a moment to truly feel that. This exercise asks you to simply be still and feel, to embrace the spirit of the world around you.

Materials:
- Your body
- *Optional but encouraged:* An outdoor space

Directions:
This exercise is best done by stepping outside to be somewhere in nature that means something to you. However, it can just as easily be performed anywhere. A houseplant or a blade of grass forcing its way through the sidewalk can be just as effective. If nowhere is available or safe for you to access, then envisioning the vitality of nature can also work. Hold a picture in your mind of a place in nature you love or a plant that speaks to you in some way.

As you sit with or visualise nature, take a moment to remind yourself that this is a living thing. We are passengers on a spinning rock bursting with life. Feel the energy of your surroundings or visualisation and allow yourself to reach out to it. This may not feel completely natural; we are so often cut off from the world around us.

Think of the feeling you have when there is another person in the room with you, even when you cannot see them. Can you get that feeling from this experience?

Remind yourself that as you sit and breathe, so too do the plants you sit with or visualise take in the carbon dioxide from your breath and release oxygen that you need to live. You exist in a delicate balance, relying on this inspirited being simply to be able to live.

Appreciate the sense of connection that brings. You do not exist in a vacuum. Whether you believe the plant you sit with or visualise has a spirit or not, you need them to exist. Your very life is inextricably tied to the green world around you. On a purely physical level, you are connected.

How does that make you feel? Really bring your attention to that sense of connection. What emotions does it inspire?

You may find it helpful to write about how you feel, but the main thing is to take a moment and appreciate your connection to, and place in, the living, breathing world around you.

Bringing It All Together

Hopefully this information has helped you get a sense of what it means to be a Witch today. There are no easy answers or boxes we neatly fit into, but there are threads and ideas that tie it all together. I find it helpful to imagine those threads like the source of a river high up in a mountain. Take a moment to picture it with me.

The water is perfectly clear and almost seems to glow. You instinctively sense it is powerful. This same water has carved out valleys and levelled mountains. You decide to follow it down the mountains and are surprised to see more sources on your descent, all adding to the stream. There are too many for you to count, each as pure and clean as the other.

Soon the stream becomes a raging river, and you sense that without each and every source contributing, it would not be here. You decide to continue following it, and as you go, you notice the river start to branch off in several different directions. You follow one of the branches and notice it continues to be fed by smaller tributaries. Soon you lose count of all the splits and branches, but still you follow. When the river reaches the sea, you glance around and see some of its many siblings all reaching the same destination.

There is no one source, nor is there one tradition. It is a vast network of many sources and many branches. All mix on their journey and add to each other. Each river, in some way, is fed by the others and draws on a variety of sources. Some are shared; some are unique, but all are alive and urgent. The same water flows through them all. The rivers press ever onward, growing, changing, and feeding into each other, patient in the knowledge they will all one day reach the sea.

Ultimately, Witchcraft is a treasure trove of practices, a wonderful and rich tradition many have drawn upon. It is a beautiful collection of lore and beliefs, of stories and lessons passed down from our ancestors, of knowledge embedded in blood and bone. It is the birthright of anyone who wishes to walk this path, for a spiritual yearning is a part of the human condition we all share. This path also bridges the old ways and the new, helping bring back lessons that should never have been forgotten. The Witch is the custodian of the earth, in tune with her rhythms and beholden to them. We care about our world, breathe with her, and seek to make a difference in the moment however we can.

Each practice is nourished by streams reaching deep into the past but exists in the here and now. A personal definition of the *practice* of Witchcraft that resonates with me is "A new way of doing old magic." We are fed by many magical paths, but what we do today is meant for today.

The Witchcraft I practice is not some hidden esoteric cult. It is freely shared knowledge synthesised into an everyday practice that emphasizes connection, forged out of the stories, myths, and legends that bind us all together. It draws on the knowledge contained in this folklore to form a rich and deeply personal cosmology and celebrates the magic and power of the bardic arts. The Witch knows something need not be factual to hold wisdom, rather that mythology may teach us deep truths about the human experience and the magic of the universe.

This is an increasingly radical act in a world devoted to the empirical and measurable. To see the truth in the lie is to turn the world upside down, and it is in this liminal paradox that the Witch may find their power.

The Most Important Reason

With all that in mind, if someone asked me why I was a Witch and I could give only one answer, it would be joy. Above all else, I am a Witch because it truly makes me happy and is a spiritually satisfying path for me. I'm not trying to proselytise Witchcraft here. There's no point, and honestly, I've done enough preaching to last a lifetime. If Witchcraft doesn't make you happy, then there's no reason to do it.

As a spiritual path, it must speak to you and resonate with your spirit. If it doesn't make you feel connected and fulfilled, it probably isn't for you, and that's okay. This journey isn't about salvation. If it doesn't resonate with you, you don't have to do it. There are no consequences. This is only the path for you if you choose it and keep on choosing it. You are always free to change your mind, and can return to it whenever you want.

Witchcraft makes my heart sing. What I will preach is the value of finding a spiritual path that does spark that joy for you, whatever that path may be. Find what makes your heart sing and follow it. If you find that you feel drawn to this path too, that's amazing. If not, that's also great, but I hope you can find something of value here anyway. Life is about finding the things that make us feel connected and bring us joy. This is mine. I hope it helps you find yours too.

Starting Your Own Journey

One of the first things I recommend is creating a journal. Books have a long history of being associated with magic and Witchcraft.[11] This is especially true in Welsh culture and preserved in the folklore and history of the *Llyfr Cyfrin*.[12] Welsh magical practitioners were renowned for possessing tomes of magical wisdom, often possessed by some spirit that granted them power. A famous

....

11. Owen Davies, *Grimoires: A History of Magic Books* (Oxford, UK: Oxford University Press, 2010).
12. Mhara Starling, *Welsh Witchcraft: A Guide to the Spirits, Lore, and Magic of Wales* (Woodbury, MN: Llewellyn Publications, 2022), 40.

story is that of John Harries, a conjuror whose magical book was said to unleash a horde of demons when opened.[13] This is similar to the idea of a Wiccan Book of Shadows but is a little older in origin.[14] However you choose to relate to this idea, the concept of a book to collect your thoughts, rituals, and magic exists across many traditions of Witchcraft.

Exercise: Creating and Dedicating Your Llyfr Cyfrin

To create your own magical journal, you must first choose a notepad. This may be something very mundane or it may be highly ornate. John Harries, mentioned earlier, was rumoured to have a Llyfr Cyfrin that was incredibly ornate, bound in thick leather and wrapped up in heavy chains. It may even be something you choose to create yourself and could be as simple as a ring binder into which you gather all your thoughts and workings.

Whatever you decide on, it must be something that speaks to you and that you can work with throughout the course of this book (and possibly beyond).

Materials:
• The notepad you have chosen
• A pen

Directions:
Once you have settled on a book, it is time to dedicate it to its purpose. To do this, set the book on a table in front of you and place your hand upon it. Feel what you intend to use it for. If it feels right, perhaps say it out loud. The important thing is to know and feel that this book is set apart; it serves a purpose, and you will honour that purpose.

13. Kate Bosse-Griffiths, *Byd y Dyn Hysbys: Swyngyfaredd yng Nghymru* (Talybont, Wales: Y Lolfa, 1977), 40.
14. Doreen Valiente, *The Rebirth of Witchcraft* (Ramsbury, UK: The Crowood Press, 2016), 51.

You may choose to write that purpose on the first page. Perhaps something like "This book is dedicated to exploring the path of Witchcraft and accepting whatever I may find there." Do whatever feels right. Remember, this is not a commitment to practicing Witchcraft, merely to giving yourself the freedom to explore.

There is an incantation contained within some German printed magical books that was designed to protect them from copyright theft and curse anyone who stole what was contained inside. I offer it to you here to copy into your own books, but also in the hope that it will offer its protection to my own:

Mirathe saepi Satonich petanich Pistan ytmye higarin ygcirion temgaron-aycon, dunceas cafliacias satas clacius Jacony hàslhaya yeynine Stephatitas beaae lud Doneny eya hideu reu vialta cyc vahaspa Saya Salna bebia eucy yaya Elenche na vena Serna.[15]

Keep the book close at hand as you read this book, and if anything speaks to you, I encourage you to note it down. Sometimes the simple act of writing can spark further thoughts or change the way you think about something. There are also journaling exercises throughout this book that your newly dedicated Llyfr Cyfrin will be perfect for. You may even wish to go back and record your experiences from the exercises in this chapter.

---

15. Ulrich Jahn, *Hexenwesen und Zauberei in Pommern* (Breslau, Germany: W. Koebner, 1886), 34.

Chapter 2
How to Leave a Cult

A frog wakes up one day to find their pond has changed. Rather than the lone weeping willow and reeds dancing on the breeze, they are surrounded by shining metal walls stretching sharply upward. The murky water they call home is replaced by clean, pure water that allows them to see straight down to the shining floor. Everything seems very unfamiliar but not too threatening. If anything, it seems a little safer. The water is clear, and there isn't a predator in sight.

The frog floats a while, contemplating their new surroundings. As they do, the water begins to become a little warmer. At first it is barely noticeable, but soon it feels like a warm, relaxing bath. Our froggy friend finds themself washed in a wave of calm and relaxation. The pond back home was never like this, only cold and murky. They float there quite content, allowing their legs to spread out and the heat to course through their body.

As they float, the heat increases even more, but they barely notice in their relaxed stupor. Hotter and hotter and hotter, until they boil to death with a smile on their face. They do not fight or resist. There is no attempt to escape. They do not notice the danger until it is far too late.

Had they been plunged into boiling water to begin with, they would not have been so resigned. The danger would be clear. They would frantically claw their way out the pot, craving the cool, tranquil pond they call home. The gradual introduction of danger makes it far less noticeable.

This story has been used for a long time to highlight the danger of gradually changing circumstances. While not scientifically accurate, it is nonetheless a powerful metaphor that we can all learn from.

Being in a cult is a lot like the experience of our tragic frog friend. People join something they think is healthy and spiritually satisfying and don't notice the destructive influence slowly being increased. They are suddenly surrounded by new people who offer amazing promises of community and salvation. Who wouldn't want to be around smiling, happy people who seem to have a genuine interest in you? And who doesn't want to believe in a long and happy future? The problems begin as the harmful and controlling teachings are slowly introduced, and this is something anyone can fall victim to.

This leads to an important point: Very few people know they're in a cult. It's not something anyone knowingly joins, and cults are experts at deception and hiding their more sinister teachings until it's too late. Even if you do start to question, great effort is put into keeping you there, with all manner of controlling techniques designed to stop you from being able to leave. The majority of cults believe they serve some higher purpose or know the secrets of salvation, and all manner of evil can be committed in the name of the "greater good." For example, one of the mantras of the cult I left was "Discipline is love," frequently invoked to justify brutal shunning practices that ripped families apart. But before we go any further, it's probably best to explain what I mean when I use the word *cult*.

What Is a Cult?

We are all vulnerable to social influence. Where we shop, what we eat, what we wear—these are all to some degree affected by the society we live in. The multibillion-dollar advertising industry is testament to just how powerful influence can be. However, this is not an inherently negative thing. Think about the successful anti-smoking or healthy eating campaigns that have been run, or the initiatives to clean up the environment. Most would argue these are noble efforts to change people's behaviour in positive ways, but problems arise when influence is used in *destructive* ways.

Cults prey on our basic human needs for community and acceptance. They offer hope and salvation, but these are twisted into chains of control. Anyone can be taken in because they promise to give us something we all want. Destructive influence is used by cults to keep people dependent on them and obedient to the authority they represent.[16] Steven Hassan, a renowned cult expert, has developed a model for identifying this cultlike influence that he calls

....

16. Steven Hassan, *Combatting Cult Mind Control: The #1 Best-Selling Guide to Protection, Rescue, and Recovery from Destructive Cults*, 30th anniversary edition (Newton, MA: Freedom of Mind Press, 2018), 82.

the BITE model. This stands for "behaviour control," "information control," "thought control," and "emotional control."[17] I use the word *cult* to describe a group or organisation that employs all four of these methods of destructive influence. I'll discuss this model briefly, but I highly recommend you read Hassan's work if you would like to know more.

Behaviour Control

Behaviour control is all about what you are allowed to do. It might include what films you are allowed to watch, what clothes you are allowed to wear, who you are allowed to spend time with, or how you spend your free time. Bodily autonomy may also be overruled by this behaviour control, for example in the banning of blood transfusions or extreme rules around sex and sexuality. If you don't follow the "rules," there are often punishments, which may vary in severity. The most extreme form in the cult I left was strict shunning, with all contact being cut off from someone who steps out of line, and members, including close family, not being permitted to say hello or even wave to them in the street. I am still subject to these shunning practices, with all the people I knew and grew up with who remain in the cult forbidden from associating with me in any way. What makes the shunning even worse is that all association with people outside the cult is extremely discouraged, to the point of being effectively banned. Those who are cast out are left without family, without friends, and without any kind of support system, since they were never allowed to build an external support system.

Information Control

Information control is all about what you are allowed to know. It usually involves certain sources of information being banned; in some cases, this means any information from outside the cult is off limits. This type of control is crucial in deceiving people, keeping them cut off from any kind of knowledge that would allow them to see through the lies and begin to question what they are being taught. Information is also rationed to potential recruits, giving them only a small part of the picture and gradually introducing the more controlling practices over time. If

17. Hassan, *Combatting Cult Mind Control*,114–24.

you make sure people don't have access to all the information, you make it a lot easier to manipulate and deceive them.

Within the cult, I was not allowed to do any outside research or read anything critical of the group. That kind of information was branded as "apostate," and to read it was just about the worst thing you could do, and a "sin" worthy of disfellowshipping—that is, being thrown out and shunned. The risk was not worth the extreme consequences.

Luckily for me, I saw fiction as a little bit more of a grey area. While it would be frowned on, it usually wasn't considered apostate. One novel in particular made it through: *Small Gods* by Sir Terry Pratchett. I had a deep love for the Discworld series and devoured them voraciously, but none affected me quite as much as the story of a god slowly dying from lack of belief and the oppressive organisation that had grown around him.[18] Looking back, this novel started my journey to leaving. Its powerful lessons were disguised in the Trojan horse of narrative, and once they got in, there was no stopping them. By reading fiction, I learned how to think and learned more than I have from any academic text.

Thought Control

Thought control is all about changing the way you think. It is often subtle and nuanced and becomes so automatic you don't even realise it's happening. It usually involves being taught to police your own mind—that there are good thoughts and bad thoughts, and you have to fight and get rid of the bad. Those bad thoughts are usually doubts about the organisation or criticism of the leadership. Rather than face these thoughts, you are taught to suppress them. A healthy spirituality is not afraid of doubt but sees it as an opportunity to learn and explore. Only a truly fragile belief system cannot tolerate any level of questioning.

Another subtle method of thought control is us-vs.-them thinking. You are taught you have "the truth," that every other belief system is inherently a lie. You are taught outsiders are "worldly," that they are inferior and corrupted. Everything that comes from the outside is automatically a lie spread by "worldly" people to discredit "the truth." You don't have to think about it; it is an automatic process. You are almost taught a new language that separates you from

....

18. Terry Pratchett, *Small Gods: A Novel of Discworld* (New York: Random House, 2008).

the world and people around you, which also makes the other forms of control easier to enforce.

Emotional Control

Emotional control is all about manipulating how someone feels. The mantra mentioned earlier—"Discipline is love"—is a good example of this. It redefines what love is and forces you to conform. Within many cults, the same is true about happiness. You are instructed that you must be the happy people. You know the true secrets of the universe are on the path of salvation. Crucially, other people must *see* you are happy. If they see anything else, it reflects badly on the cult, so always be smiling and remember you are one of the happy people. The negative emotions must be buried or at least hidden from public view.

The control starts out seemingly harmless in the form of love bombing. This is when a new recruit is showered with affection and praise, visited regularly, and made to feel special and a part of the group. The problem is that this is merely a manipulation. Once the recruit commits and leaves behind their previous community, the love bombing slows down, and the next stage begins.

Within the ex-cult communities I am part of, this fear, obligation, and guilt is usually known as mental FOG—a term coined in the book *Emotional Blackmail* by Susan Forward and Donna Frazier. That is, fear of imminent destruction or discipline, obligation to always be doing more, and the guilt of being "sinful," never good enough, and never doing enough. These three factors in combination create an emotional haze that blinds you to the truth. You are controlled through your emotions without ever having a moment to realise it. The fear keeps you from ever questioning, because you are taught God will literally kill you if you ever leave. The obligation keeps you too busy even if you could overwhelm the fear, and the guilt keeps you constantly paralysed, stopping you the moment you get close.

Why the Word *Cult?*

Now that I've discussed some of the identifying factors of a cult, I will take a moment to discuss the word itself. The term *cult* can be a little controversial, sometimes used to attack any new religious movement, sometimes even levelled toward Witchcraft itself. It is a vague term and can be misused. In fact, because of how vague it is, cults will often give their own definition to "prove" they are not one. So why am I using the word?

I believe this is a word for survivors. It is a powerful way for us to relate to our own experiences. There are a huge number of cults out there, and having a word that tells someone the experience you've had without re-traumatising yourself by having to go into the details is enormously helpful. I don't think the language survivors use to relate to their experience should be policed, and to do so is simply to continue the harm the cult initiated. I will also never insist anyone else use this word. I personally find it helpful, especially in relaying my experience. If you do not, feel free to substitute *high-control religion* or *undue-influence group* whenever you read it in these pages.

In addition, the word *cult* is a warning label for people who might otherwise be taken in by these groups. At the very least, it gives you pause and asks you to do a little more research, even if the group ends up not being one. Remember: a healthy spirituality is not afraid of questions. Research should always be encouraged, especially when first joining anything!

However, I do want to be clear that this is not a word that should be used to attack. When we throw the word *cult* around to describe anything we don't like, we diminish it and play into the narrative of harmful groups. And those who are in a cult do not know they are in a cult, so to attack them simply feeds into the persecution complex and is more likely to push them back toward the group. In my opinion, *cult* is very much the word of the survivor, and it is a word for an organisation, not for an individual.

In fact, if you do attack members, you're doing exactly what these groups want. Many of these organisations teach that the outside world is cruel and wicked and that they should expect to be persecuted by these wicked people since they are different and know "the truth." This is especially true of cults that engage in preaching campaigns. Preaching is a notoriously ineffective recruitment method. It's about sending people out and setting them up to have a bad reaction so that when they come back to the safety of the group, they can share the experience and reinforce how much better they are than the corrupt world. If you react with anger, you are doing exactly as the cult wants, you are playing your part in reinforcing the indoctrination. Kindness is not the response they expect. Even a kind but firm "no" is better than a reaction that reinforces the idea they are a persecuted people.

A Quirky Reputation

One thing that makes cults successful is their reputation management. Many groups will spend large sums of money pursuing defectors through the courts or trying to bury negative news coverage. They seek to hide their more abusive practices like shunning, often directly lying about them. They create a quirky reputation as harmless evangelists, those strange people that knock on your door now and then. Those who have left are painted as bitter and twisted, branded as "apostates" corrupted by the devil and only seeking to do harm. It is a powerful way to avoid scrutiny.

The truth, however, is that these groups are often extremely harmful. The cult I left banned blood transfusions, forcing countless individuals to die on the operating table, or worse still, forcing them to let their children die. They were inherently misogynistic and homophobic, teaching that women are inferior to men and cannot be allowed to teach, and that they must be submissive to their husbands. Queer people were told they must change who they were or they would be destroyed in the fast-approaching Armageddon, since God only approves of monogamous heterosexual relationships. Higher education is discouraged to the point of being effectively banned. All these "sins" are ruthlessly policed, with any offenders being cast out and subjected to intense shunning practices that leave them completely isolated. There are many other harmful policies from the cult I left, but this book is not about how terrible these groups can be. The point is that there is genuine harm occurring. People are being forced to bury parts of themselves or even put their lives in danger on pain of social punishment. There is also the mental torment of being taught they will be imminently destroyed.

My Story

I was raised as one of Jehovah's Witnesses. From my earliest years, I attended a minimum of two weekly meetings and was taught their doctrine as an unquestionable truth. Core to that doctrine is the belief that life on earth as we know it is imminently going to end in an event known as *Armageddon*. I was taught to be constantly in expectation of this event, when God would wipe out the majority of humanity so the faithful few could live in paradise forever. The only way to survive was to follow all the rules carefully. Any violations had to be reported to the "elders," the cult version of priests, immediately. This included a moral imperative to report anyone else you found out had "sinned," as then they could be disciplined and wouldn't be killed at Armageddon. If saving their life wasn't enough to guilt you into reporting your friends, you were also told that if you didn't report them, you became a "sharer in their sins," and simply by your knowledge would be destroyed too.

I truly believed what I was taught, since I didn't know any better and was banned from doing any outside research. Besides, most of my family were members, and if I ever left, they would be instructed to shun me, as would all my friends. It was the perfectly engineered social blackmail—no outside friends were allowed, and all those you did have would cut you off immediately if you ever left. Questioning was never a valid option, and so I never did.

The problems began when I realised I was gay. I spent hours praying, begging God to make me straight. I learned to hate everything I was, certain I would be destroyed because of this defect inside me. Many nights throughout my teens I cried myself to sleep, convinced God had abandoned me, that I was disgusting and weak. Obviously, I wasn't trying hard enough to change. I truly believed that I deserved to die.

Eventually, I started bargaining with myself. As long as I never had a relationship, never acted on my disgusting feelings, then it would all be okay. I confided in a few close friends to keep myself accountable and was met with a limited acceptance. It was okay with them as long as I never did anything about it. God would fix me after Armageddon, then I could have a relationship. I just had to fight my sinful impulses until then. I tried harder, invested myself deeper into the cult, even getting to the point of delivering sermons to the congregation.

Burying a huge part of my identity didn't work for long, however, and it soon caught up with me. I "gave in to temptation," and like a good, indoctrinated cult boy immediately reported myself. As an act of "kindness," I was shown mercy. Rather than be subject to a "judicial committee," a process by which my actions would be judged by three elders who could then cast me out, I was told to meet with all the elders in groups of two and be told how disgusting my actions were, while being interrogated with incredibly personal and shaming questions. The humiliation nearly broke me, but sadly it still took me five years to actually leave.

The self-hatred caught up with me quickly, however. I fell into a deep depression, which also manifested in physical pain. I rarely left the house. Armageddon was just around the corner, or so I kept being told, and when it arrived, I knew God would kill me. The worst part of the indoctrination is I truly believed I deserved to die and deeply hated myself. The way indoctrination can turn you against yourself is terrifying.

Eventually I managed to break free from the mind control, but not because of my sexuality. As I mentioned earlier, I loved reading fiction. I thought it was simply an escape, but the whole time it was teaching me how to think. I started to reason on things and commit the cardinal sin of "independent thinking." What eventually got through was the realisation that if the cult doctrine was true, it would lead to an unprecedented genocide. Billions would be killed for a handful to survive. That thought was the gateway for further doubts, and once the floodgates opened, there was no stopping them.

Even with this realisation, actually leaving was not easy. I believed I would lose everyone—that my friends were fully indoctrinated and would abandon me without question, as would my family. For months I tore myself apart, my doubts growing but the indoctrination still rooted. Eventually I realised that losing everything was the only way I could actually live. I left, and everything fell into chaos, but from the chaos, I built something new. I built a life of my own with people who love me for me. It took time, and there were months I thought I would never make it, but the life I have now is better than anything I dared dream of. My greatest joy is that, after a period of shunning me, some of my family left too, eventually choosing their relationship with me over the indoctrination. It took some time, but now I am truly living the best life ever.

Exercise: Lighting a Candle for Your Past Self

Candles have been used in Witchcraft for a long time. In fact, the magic of candles is used across religious and secular traditions. Churches will often have spaces for lighting a candle for a dead loved one or to accompany a prayer, and they have a central role in many birthday traditions. They have equally wide uses in Witchcraft, but this exercise focuses on using a candle to honour and accept a part of yourself.

Materials:
- A quiet space to be by yourself
- A small white candle
- A lighter or matches
- *Optional:* Some paper and a pen or pencil if you want to write your dedication

Directions:

The purpose of this exercise is to honour the part of yourself that got you through some really difficult times. For me, this exercise is a powerful way to honour the part of myself that was stuck in a cult and taught to hate himself, but it works well to appreciate the part of you that got you through any difficult situation. I perform this exercise regularly, as I carried a lot of shame from my time in a cult, and some days that still comes back. This is designed to soothe that shame and celebrate the strength that carried me through an extremely difficult experience.

Take yourself to a quiet space where you feel comfortable. Take a few moments to simply be in the moment and calm your breathing. When you feel ready and comfortable, place your candle in front of you. At this point, you can either speak out loud or write a dedication to the part of yourself you want to honour. I have included the following dedication, but this is only an example, as this exercise is incredibly personal. It is important to truly feel the dedication, to believe the words, and that is why I cannot create it for you.

Dedication:

I light this candle for my past self, who was not allowed to be who he really was. I honour him and celebrate his courage. I thank him for the difficult choices and sacrifices he made so that I may live my life today. I remember the pain and suffering he went through for my sake and praise his strength. Though he felt lost, he found a path and dared to walk it. He was trapped and still fought for my freedom, going through hell for us, and I offer him my deepest gratitude. I light this candle in his honour and offer him nothing but love, healing, and heartfelt thanks.

In his loneliest moments, I wish him the knowledge of all that will come. I take his shame and remind him of his courage. I hold him and tell him it all gets better. May I always have the courage he showed. May I always have the strength he needed to carry all he did and fight onward. May I always honour the part of me that faced so much and kept going.

Once you have spoken or written your dedication, light your candle. Sit with it as it burns and allow yourself to replace shame with appreciation, celebrating the qualities that got you through truly difficult times. Allow the candle to burn and take this time to embrace yourself. I will often wrap my arms around myself, offering myself the unconditional love my past self so desperately needed. Sit with yourself for as long as you need and know that you are truly loved.

How to Leave

I can't give a detailed plan for how to leave a cult; the best I can offer are the lessons I have learned from my own experience. Everyone will go through their own journey when leaving a cult, and often, factors outside of your control will interfere with plans you do make. This is especially the case when people are cast out and shunned. The change is often sudden and unexpected, almost impossible to plan for. However, I have gathered some suggestions here that I would offer to anyone who is planning to leave a cult or high-control group.

One thing I have also noticed is that these suggestions can be helpful in a range of circumstances. Those who are experiencing a difficult transition from one faith to another or who may be struggling with cultural or family changes may also find something helpful here.

Analyse Your Beliefs

A cult will tell you what to believe; you don't ever have to question it. In fact, questioning is expressly forbidden. There is a type of cold comfort in that kind of certainty, but reality is a little more complicated. Now *you* have to figure out what it is you actually believe. This is a step that is likely to take a long time, quite possibly the rest of your life, so there isn't any rush to figure it all out.

Just be open to questioning and enjoy the journey. For me, this journey led me to Witchcraft, but I still regularly question my beliefs. A healthy spirituality can cope with scrutiny, and in my experience, questions are exciting rather than scary.

This step is especially important when you are first leaving. Are you bringing any of the harmful beliefs with you? Indoctrination is a really difficult thing to work through and is likely to take years to unpack. Now is a good time to read widely, especially all the books that were banned, or do whatever research comes naturally to you. Podcasts by experts and ex-members were really helpful for me, as were documentaries.

Figuring out what you believe, what resonates with you, is a lifelong process. It also asks something of you. Learn as much as you can, read widely, think critically. Independent thinking is amazing, not something to be afraid of.

Plan Your Escape

By design, leaving a cult isn't easy. If you do it suddenly, you may find yourself completely without a support system, possibly even without a job. Many cults encourage you to work for members, and when you leave, that job goes too. It's tempting to rush into getting out, especially if you have strong ethical objections to the harmful things the cult does. However, rushing now will make it a lot more difficult in the long run.

Plan what you need to put in place to get the softest possible landing. Are you financially dependent on anyone in the group? Then it's a good idea to make a plan for how you will financially survive when you leave. This may involve a level of deception, pretending you still believe. As uncomfortable as that may be, remember the cult has been deceiving you the entire time. Planning ahead can make the transition far easier when you do pull the plug.

As tempting as it may be, try not to tell anyone about your plans. Remember that they feel a moral responsibility to report you, and just having doubts can be enough to activate the shunning process.

Build a Support System

Cults thrive on social blackmail. Leaving is highly likely to mean you lose your support network. If possible, try and make new friends before you take the plunge. Using social media really helped me; I was able to come out to friends online and experience genuine acceptance. Before I could make new friends locally, my online connections were an essential lifeline.

Try reaching out to local support groups, or even other members who left before you did. This can be difficult if you have been shunning them, but they know the social control and pressure you've been under. I have been really happy to reconnect with several friends who left since I did. However, respect that some people will want to leave that part of their life behind and may not want to reconnect. There are loads of amazing people out there; you just have to reach out and take the first step.

Read Other People's Stories

One thing that helped me break through the indoctrination was seeing through the lies they told about people on the outside. Cults love telling you that ex-members' lives fell apart and that the world outside has nothing to offer. Find stories that disprove that. I personally know dozens of happy, successful ex-cult members, and their experiences offered me hope when I was first leaving. Those same stories were an anchor as I started to rebuild my own life.

Focus on Yourself

You can't force anyone else to leave a cult, or even to accept that they are in a cult. As you are first leaving, focus on getting yourself out. You cannot save anyone except yourself, and as much as it hurts, you will have to leave people behind. Your safety and welfare are the highest priority.

Take some time to decide what you would like to do next. For me, that was going to university, since it was forbidden in the cult. I wanted to do something for myself and my personal development. Find that for yourself. Personal projects are really important, giving you something to work on and a way to meet new people.

Minimise Contact

This may seem obvious; however, getting some physical distance is important to escape the echo chamber of indoctrination. This isn't some kind of reverse shunning, just taking some time away to gather your own thoughts. If you are still planning your escape, be careful that this doesn't tip anyone off. Most people will eventually shun you, but some may keep contact in the hopes of bringing you back. Set strong boundaries about what you will tolerate; the fear and guilt are difficult enough to shake off without anyone reinforcing them to try and make you come back.

As hard as it is, and as rude as you may feel, going cold turkey is the best option. Maintaining contact will only make it more difficult in the long term; however, this is best decided on a case-by-case basis.

Focus on Your Strengths

Cults want you to believe you're worthless and that you can't trust yourself. You may well feel ashamed that you believed for so long, or struggle to trust your own judgment. There will likely be an element of grief for the life and people you have left behind. Now is the time to focus on the strength you have shown. Remember that few people make it out; you have done something amazing and deserve to celebrate yourself. This ties in to prioritising yourself, but if you work on learning new skills, you will have even more to celebrate. Believing you are good enough and being proud of yourself are radical acts that help tear down the indoctrination.

It is also helpful to think about the strengths you may already have or that you learned in the cult. For example, I was trained in public speaking by the cult, a skill that I now use in the world of Witchcraft. Using those skills as you build your new life can be particularly empowering.

Reach Out for Professional Support

In my opinion, this is the single most important step you can take when leaving a cult. I still see a therapist down to this day. Having someone to check in with when you struggle or something triggers a memory of the indoctrination is invaluable. Being in a cult is traumatic, leaving even more so, and having help from someone qualified is a real lifeline. However, it is important to be honest with any counsellor or therapist you may see about your experience, and it is helpful to find someone who has experience with cults or other forms of spiritual abuse.

Know that people may not understand your experience, or they may seek to defend the cult, which invests heavily in reputation management. This can also apply to professionals, and if someone isn't the right fit, that's okay. Just don't give up; find the person or group that is a good fit for you.

Exercise: Protecting against Restrictive Ideologies

I would like to end this chapter with a brief exercise that is designed to put up some protection against restrictive and harmful ideologies while also asking you to think about your own belief system. It is a simple visualisation exercise but can be very powerful if practiced regularly. Simply shifting your mindset into one of openness and curiosity after leaving a restrictive environment is incredibly liberating.

Within German folk magic, the pentagram is seen as a powerful protective symbol. In the play *Faust* by Goethe, it has the power to restrain demons, and in some German traditions it is still used as an alternative to the crucifix.[19] Within some streams of ceremonial magic, the pentagram is used in visualisations for cleansing and protection, for example in the Lesser Banishing Ritual of the Pentagram. This exercise draws on that protective association.

Materials:
• A comfortable, relaxed space

Directions:
Take a few moments to slow your breathing and make yourself feel comfortable. When you are ready, close your eyes and allow yourself to simply be in the space you inhabit. Once you are relaxed and it feels right to do so, visualise a glowing pentagram forming in front of you. Beyond the pentagram are the restrictive beliefs and ideologies you have left behind. It acts like a wall, separating you from beliefs that once caged you.

Within this space, take a moment to reflect on what you believe now. Are you restrained or controlled by it in any way? You are in a space of safety and freedom, able to question without consequences. The pentagram protects you from any unwelcome or intrusive influence. Allow yourself to approach your beliefs with curiosity, explore freely and allow any

19. Johann Wolfgang von Goethe, *Goethe's Faust*, parts 1 and 2, trans. Albert G. Latham (London: J. M. Dent & Sons, 1912), 66.

questions to form. You do not need to answer them now, but bring them back with you after the visualisation and allow yourself to explore them.

Once you have created this free and safe space, repeat the following affirmations, and with each word, see the pentagram burn a little more brightly:

I set my intention to follow a path of freedom and curiosity.
Harmful and restrictive ideologies are not welcome on my journey.
I will not be caged by someone else's beliefs.

Feel the truth of these affirmations flood through your mind. When you feel ready, bring yourself back to the room and open your eyes, knowing that you have set this intention. Affirmations work particularly well when practiced regularly, putting in the time and work.[20] You may find it helpful to record the affirmations in your Llyfr Cyfrin and return to them whenever you find it useful.

Clearing the FOG

Leaving is only step 1 in your recovery journey. Deconstruction can only really begin once you're out of the physical environment of the cult. Despite being out for many years, I am still unpacking the experience. It definitely gets easier with time, but leaving a cult is an extreme experience that leaves a mark. Give yourself the time and love you need to heal and fight against the residue of indoctrination. Fear, obligation, and guilt are hard habits to break, and it's easy to feel like you aren't good enough or aren't doing enough. The truth, however, is that simply by walking your own path, you are doing enough. You *are* enough; it really is that simple, even though you might need a reminder from time to time.

For me, finding the path of Witchcraft helped clear some of the mental FOG, and it's a big reason why I'm so passionate about sharing it. Where cults are all about control, this path is all about freedom. But whatever helps you find your own path is equally valid! I'm just sharing what I love, and if that helps you in some way, great! If not, I truly hope you find the path that works for you.

....

20. Mat Auryn, *Psychic Witch: A Metaphysical Guide to Meditation, Magick & Manifestation* (Woodbury, MN: Llewellyn Publications, 2020), 21.

Chapter 3
Discovering Magic

It's hard to look back through history without tripping over magic almost everywhere you go. For millennia, it was an accepted part of everyday life. Countless philosophers through the ages discussed this mysterious force, and countless others used it to condemn anything they couldn't understand.

Magic is a part of Witchcraft. There's no escaping that fact. To be a Witch is to understand that there is a power within yourself and within the wider universe you can tap into and use to achieve the results you desire. Therefore, it's best to introduce it in this book early on. However, this chapter is only a taste. There will be no intense spells ahead, merely an exploration of what magic is and how we can use it.

My Definition of Magic

An important part of building my Witchcraft practice was finding a personal definition of magic. There are loads of them out there, and it's something academics occasionally like to argue about, but I needed to find my own. This is probably the step on my journey that took me the longest. If I couldn't define it in a way that worked for me, I knew I wouldn't be able to practice it.

The definition I settled on is rather broad, but narrowing it seemed to exclude too many things. So here goes: Magic is causing change by spiritual means. This is the definition of magic that most resonates with me right now and is the one I will be using throughout this book.

Let me explain a little bit more. Magic doesn't observe a clear physical cause-and-effect model. It also doesn't draw on the physical properties of objects to make spells work. Magic operates in the realm of spirit. That doesn't mean I think magic is necessarily religious. Historically, the difference between magic and religion has been quite thin. Usually, magic was the religion of other people, as opposed to your true worship. To those other people, the thing you were doing looked an awful lot like magic too. It was often used to discredit the religion of the other people, but this is not really what I mean by magic at all.

The definition I have provided means that for magic to have been done, something needs to change. Magic is defined by results. If nothing happens, it wasn't magic. However, we do need to ask what is meant by *change*. If, after a working, I have more self-confidence or have unburdened myself of shame, then something within me has changed. It doesn't have to be big or flashy to be magical. Changing the way we see the world is magic in and of itself.

But what do I mean by *spiritual means*? At the most basic level, these are forces beyond the physical. A magical worldview accepts that reason, logic, and the scientific method are not the only forces in the universe. We are emotional beings with a spirit, surrounded by a world alive with spirits. Therefore, spiritual means can be anything from accessing our own higher selves and inner divinity to utilising magical correspondences and even calling upon the gods.

What I like about this definition is it emphasizes that neither physical nor magical means are the only way of doing things. They are both different paths to the same destination and are best used in tandem. When we really want to change something, we use every means at our disposal. Magic is just one more arrow in that quiver.

Mundane Before Magic

Building on this idea, you will often hear people say you should use mundane means before magical ones. Broadly, I agree, but I think using both in tandem is a good way to go. The main point is that we shouldn't rely on magic to cause change to the exclusion of physical methods. Probably the most important example is healing. There is no harm in using magical healing methods as long as this is in addition to visiting the doctors and receiving the proper medical care.

There may also be times when a magical solution simply isn't required. One of my favourite stories in Welsh folklore tells of a conjuror who was called upon to identify a thief. The victim of the theft was a rich man with a household of staff, and these were the suspects. To catch the culprit, the conjuror placed a cockerel beneath an upturned cauldron in a pantry. He then sent each of the staff in with the instruction to rub the cauldron, and if they were guilty, the cock would crow.

Each of them went in, but the cockerel remained silent. Then the conjuror asked them to line up and present their hands. All but one person's were covered in the grime of the cauldron. The thief was too afraid to touch it, and his clean hands gave him away.

In this instance, magical means were not needed. The reputation of the conjuror was enough. The lesson we learn is that many problems can be solved by purely mundane means, and discernment in when to utilise magic is an important skill to develop.

Magical Correspondences

Another important aspect of magic is correspondences. If you've picked up any other books on Witchcraft, you've likely noticed long lists of items and the magical properties they embody. So, what does it all mean?

Simply put, correspondences are the spiritual properties associated with something. Just like something can have physical effects when you are exposed to it, so too can items have spiritual properties. A great example is lavender. Physically, it is calming. To put some drops of lavender oil on your pillow when you can't sleep isn't necessarily magic; you are using a physical quality of the plant. But to the Witch, there is more than meets the eye. We might use lavender for protection or purification, among other things. We are not drawing on the physical properties, rather the spiritual ones. If magic is causing change by spiritual means, then correspondences are a powerful way of working magic.

Let's go back to the example of lavender with that in mind. To the Witch, placing the lavender oil becomes something *both* magical and mundane. We accept the physical properties that can help us sleep, but also believe in the spiritual properties that can help. If something is both physically and magically potent, that is a bonus for the resourceful Witch.

Correspondences are like the strands of a web connecting seemingly unrelated things in an invisible cosmic order. A certain herb may have spiritual qualities that correspond to a certain planetary energy, or certain stones might be spiritually connected with certain deities.

There are many collections of magical correspondences available, and these can be very helpful. However, if we accept that correspondences draw on the spirit of whatever we are working with magically, then the best thing to do is go straight to the source. If you are working with the spiritual properties of an herb, ask that herb how it would like to be used. The same goes for any other nonhuman persons—a term many Witches use to describe nonhuman life. We believe these living things contain an animating spirit and therefore are as much people as we are.

Will and Intention

If you've dipped your toes into Witchcraft before, you've probably heard people talk about intention. I personally don't find the word *intention* helpful. I have ADHD, and the list of things I intend to do but never get around to is endless. When working magic, I find the word *will* better describes the concept I'm trying to explain. So, what do I mean by *will*?

Let's think about the example of lavender again. Is it enough to grow it in your garden and expect it to help you sleep? No. Something more is needed. You have to harvest the flowers or buy the oil and then purposefully use it on your pillow when you go to sleep. If you have the will to use lavender to help you sleep, then you will follow through and take the steps to benefit from its physical properties. You put your will into action.

This is not some fluffy desire, but an active process where you are completely focused on the thing you want to achieve. It's not making a wish and hoping things will work out, but believing with all that you are that you can achieve your aims. It is calling upon your spiritual self to bring that change into action and doing the work to see it through.

This idea of bringing our desires into reality is sometimes referred to as *manifestation*. But again, it is not simply wishing for something. The feeling and experience of will is intense. It floods through your whole being and is completely unmistakeable.

Funnily enough, this is another concept that being in the cult prepared me to understand. After having a little tantrum and cursing a fig tree, Jesus was questioned by his disciples. As part of his reply, he told them that if they had unshakable faith, they could tell a mountain to throw itself into the sea and it would happen. He also told them that when they pray and ask for something, they should act as if it has already occurred.[21] To me, this unshakable belief in the outcome you desire is what is meant by will. It is not an easy thing to achieve. You must truly believe in your power as a Witch. But once you tap into this potent force, it can cause incredible change.

Magic and the Bible

It might surprise you to learn that the Bible is full of magic. From the very earliest books, we are confronted with "pagan" sorcerers who are clearly able to perform works of magic. In the account of the exodus, Moses and Aaron enter into a magical contest with the magicians of Egypt. As part of the contest, each of them throws down their staff and transforms it into a serpent, certainly a very powerful feat to perform. The magicians of Egypt are also able to turn water into blood, just as Moses and Aaron do.[22] The Bible does not claim the magic of the Egyptians is useless. The point is they do possess magic; they prove that it works. The Bible only makes the claim that God's magic is stronger.

This is far from the only magic in the Bible. There is the account of the now infamous "Witch of Endor." King Saul was about to battle with an enormous Philistine army, and when God wouldn't answer him, he decided to go and see a necromancer. He had banished all the soothsayers in the land but managed to find one remaining in Endor. He consulted her and she summoned the spirit of the prophet Samuel to give him his answer. Samuel prophesied that Saul and his sons would die in the battle the next day, and that is exactly what happened.[23] The "Witch" had successfully raised a spirit from death, an inherently magical feat, which the Bible recounts as fact. Not only that, but the spirit had successfully predicted the future.

There are also multiple instances of divination, especially by the casting of lots. One example is found in the story of Jonah. When Jonah runs away from God, before he is swallowed by the big fish, he gets onto a ship. God summons a big storm to sink the ship and punish him, but all the other people onboard become terrified and, realising this is a supernatural event, try and find out who is causing it. They do this by casting lots. We don't know exactly what this

....
21. Mark 11:12–25.
22. Exodus 7:8–22.
23. 1 Samuel 28:3–19, 31:6.

practice was, only that it was divinatory in nature, like drawing straws, and that it worked. Jonah is correctly identified as the cause and is thrown overboard for the fish to swallow.[24]

In each of these instances, the magic is not doubted. Magic is clearly a part of the landscape for the Bible's writers. They only seek to assert that their god is more powerful.

Regardless of the authenticity of the Bible as a religious text, this gives us a little insight into attitudes at the time it was written, when magic was an everyday occurrence. While magic not of divine origin was condemned, there was no doubt about its reality. But that did not continue in Christian thought into the modern day.

Bit by bit, the magic and ritual of Christianity were suppressed. During the Protestant Reformation of the 1500s, the ritual and ceremony of Catholicism were condemned as blasphemous. Catholicism was specifically compared to Witchcraft, the practice of saint veneration condemned as tantamount to devil worship, and the Pope himself was seen as the Antichrist.[25] Those very aspects of Christianity that appeared magical in nature inspired a civil war amongst its ranks.

While Christianity overall survived the Reformation, its power was greatly diminished and most of the magic drained. But why should you care? Because the very book people use to condemn magic is filled with it! Understanding that the Bible is filled with magic can help those coming to Paganism from Christianity understand and connect to it, and reclaiming the magical ideas in the Bible can be profoundly empowering.

My Story

I've often wondered, given how much magic there is in the Bible, why did the cult choose to ignore it?

I believe it has everything to do with empowerment. The cult didn't just hate magic; they were afraid of it. If you realised your own power, it threatened the control they had over you, and what is magic but the realisation of your own innate power to effect change? If you didn't have to rely on God to change

....

24. Jonah 1:4–17.
25. Stuart Clark, *Thinking with Demons: The Idea of Witchcraft in Early Modern Europe* (Oxford, UK: Oxford University Press, 1999), 533–34.

things for you, what stopped you from leaving the cult? And if you left the cult, you took your money, your time, and your proselytising with you. Magic is an existential threat to high-control groups, because if you realise your own power, you don't let anyone control you.

Magic in the Bible had to be dismissed, explained away. It was demons playing pretend, or it was just symbolic. Magic was merely an illusion of the devil, never something you were capable of. People never had the power: it was not intrinsic. If any of the magic in the Bible did happen, it was demons that caused it, never humans. Only in that way could control be maintained.

The fear of magic was so great that there were social prohibitions against anything that featured it. Watching it as entertainment was banned; it featured demonic things and you may be corrupted. Even Disney didn't escape the social control. You definitely couldn't admit you'd seen the latest film, or you'd face certain judgment.

There was a strange duality between a denial of magic as something only demons could utilise and a fear of any media that featured Wizards or Witches. They preached both that Witchcraft is a fearful danger forbidden in scripture and that Witches have no power—they are merely a vessel for the power of demons who are supposedly weaker than their god. The power was always in the demons or the devil, never inherent to any person.

The cult didn't stop there, however. Even in non-magical ways your power was stripped away. You were encouraged never to make any big decisions without consulting God first. Your heart was treacherous; you weren't capable of it. And consulting God usually meant reading the literature the cult had produced or going to the leaders to make the decision for you. Ultimately, you weren't even in control of your own decisions; the cult was. Any belief in personal power, especially magic, would have been an enormous threat to that.

Even after I left the cult, I felt aimless and weak. I had learned I was incapable of making my own decisions, and as I still hadn't deconstructed properly, continued to believe the lie. Discovering magic was essential to me finding my own power, to realising I could actually effect change in my own life and surroundings.

The Magic of Mythology

To believe in magic is to go against the mainstream view of society. If we dive back into history, all the way to ancient Greece, we find two opposing world-views. There was *mythos*, which valued narrative and folk knowledge, and *logos*, which deferred to logic and rational analysis.[26] Over the centuries, society has drifted away from seeing the world through the eyes of mythos. We have become a little disenchanted and prefer the world of cold, hard facts.

The problem is that we are not exclusively rational beings. We are a mix of reason and emotion, driven by both. The path of magic recognises this, accepting that some things can never be measured or explained by logic. Some things, like art, music, and love, can only be felt and experienced. Mythology challenges us to feel, to live out the lessons it teaches in our own lives. It only lives when we enact it. Too often, people get caught up in the idea that myths are simply old words on crumbling pages, but that is attempting to force mythos to be logos. Myths are not the words; they are the current carried below them that speaks to our soul, challenges us to know ourselves, and teaches us deep truths about the human condition. Rather than explanation, myths cry out for interpretation. They allow us to bring a piece of ourselves into the dialogue, changing to accommodate everyone who approaches them.

My practice and the magic of the coven are strongly influenced by mythology. In all honesty, I think you would struggle to find a magical path that isn't. As a result, this is something I will mention quite often throughout the pages of this book. We gain so much magic from our myths. Welsh Witchcraft is heavily inspired by the four branches of the Mabinogi, mythological tales arising from the Welsh oral tradition and probably recorded in the late Middle Ages, among other traditional lore. We try and incorporate this powerful stream into most of our workings.

The power of living the myths is especially apparent when you get together with a group. I have spoken to many people after ritual who are completely unable to tell me what they experienced. Words fail to capture the transcendence of what occurred. It simply cannot be measured or easily expressed.

....

26. Ivana Marková, *The Dialogical Mind: Common Sense and Ethics* (Cambridge, UK: Cambridge University Press, 2016), 15.

Exercise: Creating a Protection Spell Jar

Just for fun, let's bring this all together to create a piece of magic: a spell jar. Again, this is not a commitment to practicing Witchcraft. Rather, it is just a little taste of how simple it can be. If you've ever strayed into Witchy social media, you've probably seen these all over the place, but it's rarely explained why they're used. We're going to draw on magical correspondences, sympathetic magic, and will to create a change in the world through spiritual means. Our first spell jar is going to be for protection. The world of spirits is a little like the human world; there are all kinds of individuals there, and it's best to keep the less-friendly ones away.

Most of the ingredients we are using for this are things you may already have around the house. The only exception is dried nettle, but as with all spells, the ingredients are optional, and you are free to substitute it for something meaningful to you. Remember, we aren't drawing on the physical properties of our ingredients, but the spiritual ones. Believing in those properties is very important.

Materials:
- A jar, preferably recycled
- A teaspoon of powdered eggshell
- A teaspoon of dried nettle
- A teaspoon of black pepper
- A teaspoon of garlic powder
- A square of white paper and a pen to write with
- A white candle
- *Optional:* Any substitutions you want to make

Directions:
Take your jar and place the ingredients in it one at a time. Each has a correspondence associated with protection, but feel free to make any substitutions that feel right to you. As you place them in, keep the intention of being protected clear in your mind. It can also help to state out loud that you are adding them for protection.

Once the ingredients are in, take the piece of paper and write the following on it. Make sure the letters are lined up in columns and rows:

SATOR

AREPO

TENET

OPERA

ROTAS

This is an ancient charm called the Sator square and reads the same left to right and top to bottom. It has been used protectively in folk magic for centuries. One example was its use to extinguish fires in Germany. The Sator square would be written on a plate and then cast into the fire to put it out. This belief was so widespread that towns would keep a stockpile of these plates for whenever a fire broke out.

In addition, write your will to be protected below the Sator square in whatever words are meaningful to you. Place the paper in the jar, close it, and then seal it by slowly dripping wax from the candle, taking care not to burn yourself. The sealing with wax helps symbolise the spell is done, while also adding to the protective virtues. Keep the jar in your home to benefit from this protective working.

Types of Magic

Finding a group of people to practice magic with led to many enlightening conversations. One of the early discussions we had as a coven was about the different kinds of magic that have existed historically. The analysis of popular beliefs in history is an important part of a modern Craft. After all, magic is all about what works, and if it worked in the past, it may well work now too. Nothing can be dismissed until you try it and see if it fits your practice.

Historically there were two major types of magic. In his book *The Triumph of the Moon*, Professor Ronald Hutton describes them as "high magic" and "low magic."[27] Our coven decided we prefer the terms *ceremonial* and *folk magic*, as

....

27. Hutton, *The Triumph of the Moon*.

they are more descriptive and have less of a judgmental tone. The term *low magic* can make it seem almost inferior when that is certainly not the case.

Ceremonial Magic

Ceremonial magic was historically the magic of the upper classes. As the name implies, it was ornate and ritualistic, relying on pomp and ceremony to get things done. It often involved the summoning of angels or demons and the construction of elaborate sigils. Many steps would be meticulously followed to gain the desired magical result.

Many of the modern occult societies made use of ceremonial magic, with its detailed and specific instructions, often recorded and obtained through the use of grimoires. Those instructions are often incredibly specific, involving specific timings according to planetary days and hours, or sigils cast in specific metals. The famous *Key of Solomon* is a great example of a ceremonial grimoire, involving both specific sigils and timings for its magic to work.

It's interesting to note that ceremonial magic, being the magic of the elite, was seen as more socially acceptable in a time when Witchcraft was actively persecuted. Court astrologers and magicians were active even as the church hunted down the common folk magicians, with John Dee in the court of Elizabeth I of England being a prime example.

It is worth noting that Christian words and imagery were an important part of ceremonial magic, perhaps making it more palatable to the Christian establishment.

Folk Magic

Folk magic is ecstatic. It is the magic of the common people, often downtrodden and oppressed. It is concerned with getting things done rather than elaborate ritual and is unafraid to get down and dirty. Famous examples of folk magic include the evil eye, known throughout many cultures as a means of cursing, and the making of poppets. We also have many records of charms used for healing. These were simple techniques, often written charms or spoken words with minimal ingredients necessary.

Folk magic did not depend on elaborate or expensive tools and did not rely on learning from books. Many folk practitioners were illiterate, being common folk, and learned their trade through their families.

Divination was also a key aspect, with techniques such as dripping wax or lead into water and divining from the shapes used. Interestingly, folk methods of divination were officially persecuted by the witch hunts, whereas more learned forms such as astrology escaped relatively untouched.[28]

Finding My Own Magic

So how did I find my magic? How did I discover that part of myself that held power? The path to revelation started not long after I left the cult, even though I didn't realise it at the time.

An important belief of the cult is a belief in demons. As fundamentalists, they take biblical accounts of possession literally. To them, demons are fallen angels, those who followed Satan in his rebellion in heaven, who helped him when he tried to usurp God.

They came down to the earth before the flood, lusting after the women on the mortal plane. The result of this unholy union was the Nephilim, violent creatures who dwarfed regular men, the literal spawn of beings later described as demons. The cult taught that it was in large part because of the horrors of demons and Nephilim walking the earth that the flood happened.

As part of their belief in demons, members of the cult told horror stories of possessions or things moving of their own accord in people's houses. Though rarely published in official publications, the stories spread like folklore, and most people claimed to have had some experience with demons.

When I left, I wanted to stop believing, but some of the accounts were incredibly vivid or from people I really trusted, including close family. I thought I could look into it a little more closely to deconstruct, but that search only led me down the path of more questions.

I found that most traditions had supernatural beliefs of some kind, even into the modern day, that even reasonable, rational people had experiences they simply couldn't explain. While I claimed to be atheist at the time, I knew there were mysteries no one could give me an explanation for. And so I kept searching and kept an open mind.

....

28. Jason Philip Coy, *The Devil's Art: Divination and Discipline in Early Modern Germany* (Charlottesville, VA: University of Virginia Press, 2020), 33–35.

It was not until I met my partner that I started to find a satisfying path. He was a Witch long before he met me and patiently answered the questions I had. At around the same time, he was escaping an abusive situation and asked me to help him with some magic to protect himself. I was sceptical but loved him and agreed to try.

The magic worked. I could not question it. It was an almost-miraculous, overnight solution. We were offered a house far from the abuse and the finances to make it happen, all on the same day. As I said earlier, magic only exists when it works, and it certainly existed here.

I started to walk the path but wouldn't yet identify myself as a Witch. We started to attend a local moot and worked at refining our own Craft at home. At the moot, we met other practitioners and slowly grew into a working group. Time and again I saw magic work firsthand, and each time what little doubt I had melted away more.

I was shocked and excited. I actually had a power that was intrinsically my own. I could actually change things and claim some control over my life.

The working group slowly evolved, and as I became more settled into my Craft, we became an official coven. The coven helped me deepen my connection and unpack the residual trauma of the cult. A key part of that was revisiting cult experiences with my new knowledge of magic.

The Purpose of Magic Today

Magic is used for many reasons by a wide variety of traditions. Witches don't have a monopoly on it. There are far more uses of magic than I could cover in this book, but I would like to mention a few that I believe are important.

Magic to Gain Knowledge

A major reason some people practice magic is to gain knowledge. Connecting with spirits through ritual or communing with deities can teach you a lot. In addition, there is a wealth of magical material people can study to learn more. Sometimes, people are derogatorily referred to as *armchair magicians*. I don't really understand the problem with this. Gaining knowledge is a valid path of magic, and that doesn't always require elaborate spells and ceremonies.

Magic is also a way of connecting to the deeper mystery of existence. As we have discussed, it taps into ways of knowing and sensing that are often neglected in wider society. It is precisely that quality that allows us to find knowledge within magic that is hidden to the wider world. The very word *occult* can loosely be translated as meaning hidden or secret knowledge. Magic is the key to discovering it.

Magic to Gain Power

Another reason people find magic is the power it gives them. When all else fails, people turn to magic as a refuge. Historically, magic was more widely used among the marginalised and oppressed, as we will discuss later in the book. When society tried to strip all their power away from them, magic was a way of claiming it back.

When I ask people why they found their way to magic, the answer I most often hear is the power it offered. They might stay for the spirit connection or to pick away at the mystery, but it is the promise of power that first brings them here.

Magic for Transformation

For many people, magic is a path of personal transformation. They use it to get to know themselves better and to transform their inner selves. This is closely linked to gaining knowledge and to spirituality, but it is a more personal path. Magic is a powerful way to gain knowledge of self, and few people who walk this path emerge unchanged.

Magic to Forge Spiritual Connection

Spiritual connection is also a powerful reason to practice magic. Many rituals call on spirits and gods, helping us to form sacred relationships with them. Beyond spirits, magic can help us connect to our heritage, our ancestry, our culture, and our community. It can also help us connect with loved ones we may have lost, keeping their memory alive. In a Christian cosmology, these ancestor spirits are trapped in either heaven or hell, but to the Witch, they are all around, and magic can help us reach out to them. We find a cosmology outside the binary of heaven and hell, and a rich and vibrant world of spiritual beings with whom we can connect.

For most people, it is a fusion of these reasons that brings them to magic and keeps them here. What matters is finding your own reason. What is it you most want to gain from magic?

The Role of Ritual

An important concept alongside magic is that of ritual. My favourite definition comes from the book *Pagan Ritual* by Anna Franklin. She describes it like this: "Pagan ritual, whether it is an act of worship or magic, employs a specific series of stages, using symbolism and ceremony, to create a sacred place and state of consciousness whereby the participants are put in touch with forces outside themselves."[29]

By this definition, we probably wouldn't call the spell jar we made earlier a ritual. It is more of a spell, a simple working of magic. We could ritualise the process, add some ceremony, and invite spirits and divinities into the space, but that is not required for the spell to work. Most Witches will use both simple spells and more elaborate rituals in their practice to achieve their ends. This fits quite well with the distinction between ceremonial and folk magic mentioned above. Ceremonial magic is usually ritualistic, whereas folk magic is more practical in nature. However, for the modern Witch, it's not so clear cut. All streams of magic will influence our practice, and rituals and spells may draw inspiration from any source.

Cult Experiences through a Magical Lens

I would like to conclude by briefly mentioning some of the experiences I had in the cult that I now see completely differently after being immersed in the world of magic.

Leaving My Body

The most profound spiritual experience I have ever had occurred when I was fifteen. I had been out preaching with the cult, and we were just getting ready to leave. One of the people we had attempted to preach to approached me after

----

29. Anna Franklin, *Pagan Ritual: The Path of the Priestess and Priest* (Earl Shilton, UK: Lear Books, 2008), 5.

the other people in my group had gotten into the car. He cornered me and tried the ultimate Uno reverse: converting me to his religion.

Since the cult taught that all other religions are demonic, I was really scared. I didn't know what to do; I was completely isolated and couldn't get away. That's when the strangest thing happened: I left my own body.

To this day, I don't know what the man tried to say to me. Maybe if I'd listened I'd have escaped the cult far sooner. Maybe I'd have ended up in a worse one. Who knows? All I remember is looking down at myself, floating outside of my own body, completely detached from the physical experience.

At the time I attributed the experience to God, as I had been taught to do. I believed he had reached inside me and pulled me out of myself to save me from the corruption of another faith. I vividly remember telling everyone I knew about the experience, how strange and profound it was. They dismissed me at the time. It did not fit their beliefs, even as I tried to force it to fit. I gave God all the credit; it was the only way the experience would be remotely acceptable.

I know now how wrong I was. Crossing the hedge is a feature of many streams of modern Witchcraft. That is exactly what I did back then, completely by accident. I left my body, travelled astrally—whatever you want to call it. The key thing is that I did it, not some far-off deity. What started as a very confusing experience became the most significant spiritual experience of my life.

That was far from the only time I left my body over the years, but I learned to keep it to myself. It did not suit the cult narrative, no matter how I tried to explain it away. I became scared and ashamed of this part of my life, a power that is now integral to my practice.

The Magic of Prayer

One thing I'll discuss in more detail later in the book is the concept of prayer. If magic is causing change by spiritual means, then prayer could reasonably fall under that definition. While I was in the cult, I genuinely believed my prayers were being answered. What I asked for would often come true.

A potent way the cult strips your power from you is by attributing that power to God instead. They tell you that you must wait on God, that once you pray it's out of your hands. You must simply wait for God to act, like waiting in some cosmic queue for your request to be fulfilled. It took me a long time to realise there is another possible way of seeing it: we are divine. God can be within us, not the external far-off concept the cult presents. We are capable of achieving our own desires. We do not need to wait powerlessly. We can be the nexus of power, the source of magic.

I now believe I was working magic without even realising it. It doesn't matter who you pray to; what matters is how much you believe in the outcome. You are both the one who asks and the one who answers. We are the higher power, restricted only by our own disbelief. We don't need anyone else to save us; we have all the tools ourselves. I do believe deity may also answer prayers, but the point remains that we are far from helpless.

Pushed to Leave

Perhaps the most magical thing I notice looking back were the nudges I kept getting to leave the cult. From being born in the Harz Mountains and immersed in their magical stories to time and again feeling myself being drawn to ancient and magical sites, my path to becoming a Witch had a feeling of inevitability.

It wasn't just my German upbringing either. As a child, my family moved to Wales, and I went to a Welsh language school and was raised in the culture. I was the product of two magical worlds, all the while trapped in a cult. But the magic would not leave me lost forever.

I remember vividly when I began to doubt the teachings of the cult; I was sat in a pub on holiday in Ireland, and the song "Losing My Religion" by R.E.M. started playing in that moment. It was so profound a synchronicity, it left me in tears. A year or so later, I went on holiday to Scotland and visited the Callanish Standing Stones on the Isles of Lewis and Harris. The feeling of connection there was one I couldn't explain; it was far more spiritual than any religious sermon I had ever heard. I felt a deep connection to something ancient, something I could not yet name. It again left me doubting the teachings of the cult.

When the time came that my doubts became strong enough for me to consider leaving, a close family member was kicked out of the cult and subject to a strict shunning policy. That coincidence led me to formally renounce my membership of the cult.

Time and again at key moments of my story, I was pushed in the direction of leaving. Looking back, I cannot help but be awed at how magical it all was. Even stuck in such an awful belief system, there were forces looking out for me that I was unaware of, and my own power was guiding me before I was even aware I had it.

Witchcraft is a joyful path. It gently called to me and led me to a group of people who would share that joy with me. It led me to my coven, with whom I practice magic to this day.

Chapter 4
Connecting to Culture

Culture is filled with magic. It flows through the land, pulsing in the myths and legends that make us who we are. You don't have to look any further than the flag of Wales to see this: the proud red dragon on a field of white and green pulled straight from our magical lore. This majestic beast is part of the very essence of what it means to be Welsh, and he stretches back centuries into an enchanted past swirling with stories of Merlin, Arthur, and battling serpents. Whether we notice it or not, our very identity is infused with wonder and enchantment. We carry it with us in our blood and bones, in the history and myth that fuel our imagination, and in the very landscape we call home. The magic woven through it all connects us deeply to ourselves and to our culture if only we take a moment to notice.

Culture is an incredibly important part of Witchcraft. It is those beautiful facets of our identity: our language, our history, our rites of passage, our art, our food, our beliefs, and all the other things we value that naturally entwine with the practice of a Witch. Every part of who we are is influenced by these factors, so why would Witchcraft be any different? We bring what makes us who we are into our practice and therefore create something that is unique to us and that works for us. It becomes a beautiful expression of everything we are, honouring ourselves, our community, our land, and our heritage. Most of all, a practice rooted in the culture that makes us brings a deep sense of connection and joy.

Discovering myself and my culture was an essential part of leaving the cult. To find my way to Witchcraft, I had to find who I am as a person and the beautiful cultures that have combined to lead me down this path. Being trapped in the cult left me disconnected from myself and the many strands of my identity, and I will always be grateful that Witchcraft helped me discover that sense of connection. But what is culture?

Culture is an incredibly difficult thing to define, influencing almost everything we do, from the clothes we wear to the films we watch, and even the food we eat. It is all the things that make us who we are and ties us back to everything that came before. It is a living and vibrant expression of self and community, constantly evolving and helping us to understand ourselves. Ultimately, I believe culture is about belonging and connection. In this chapter, I will discuss four aspects of that connection: to community, to land, to heritage, and to self.

Community

Leaving a cult and stepping into Witchcraft was a phenomenal culture shock. Everything was different. Where the cult had a culture of control, Witchcraft had a culture of freedom, and nowhere was this more obvious than in the community. Immersing myself in that culture and community allowed me to tap into a powerful current of practitioners around the world, each walking their own path. It may seem counterintuitive that a decentralised practice that values individuality would create a strong sense of community, but the magical worldview we all share by choice truly brings us together. Whether we're lighting a candle, dancing around a cauldron, or frolicking naked in the woods, we're tapping into the same enchanted mindset and can understand each other. This culture of freedom takes the judgment and shame out of a practice, letting you experiment and give your all to ritual in a safe space. Connecting to this culture of freedom can be a very powerful thing.

However, this is a culture we all have a part in creating. Within fundamentalist Christianity, there is a culture of superiority and judgment. You are taught that only your denomination knows the truth, and everyone else is wrong and inferior. Judgment is not only tolerated but encouraged, and the sense of superiority can be addictive. It was essential for me to get out of that mindset to become a Witch and truly immerse myself in the freedom that comes with it. If someone's practice works for them and isn't harming anyone, then it is valid. You may not do things that way yourself, but it's not your job to tell anyone else how to do it either. Once I learned this vital lesson, I could enjoy all the beauty that the culture of Witchcraft brings.

I have attended and taught at many festivals and events, and the energy that being in a room full of Witches and Pagans brings is unmistakeable. It is intoxicating, vibrant, and alive. People of different paths are gathered for a common purpose, seeking the deeper mysteries of life and having a good time doing it. I have made lifelong friends of Druids, Wiccans, Traditional Witches, and every other path you can think of. The culture of freedom makes Paganism and Witchcraft an incredibly special place, one that we all should treasure and protect.

But community goes beyond the world of Witchcraft. Living in Wales, my culture involves the language, myths, and landscape that I share with all the people around me, regardless of their beliefs. I believe Witchcraft can be particularly powerful in connecting to the culture of where you live, and again this is very evident in Wales, particularly in the stories of the Mabinogion, which are a cornerstone of Welsh culture. These stories are taught from primary school here and are celebrated in every corner of Wales. Witchcraft also has an appreciation for these tales and serves as a powerful conduit for transmitting these cultural treasures. Witches the world over know of the Welsh gods found in these tales, and Rhiannon has even made her way into pop music, loved the world over. We become connected to all those who share in these stories with us. Treasures and traditions that might otherwise be unappreciated are infused with new life by practitioners that truly value them.

However, this does come with a caveat. These cultural treasures exist beyond Witchcraft; they are sacred to the people whose culture is forged around them. While I'm speaking here from a Welsh perspective, this applies more broadly across many mythologies. As Witches, we may value and engage with these myths and characters, but it is not for us to dictate how the culture that originated them interacts with them. Without a level of respect for where they come from, how can we possibly hope for them to connect us to this ancient and powerful cultural stream?

Exercise: What Connects You?

This is a simple journaling prompt exercise. It is designed to open up the question of which strands of culture most call to you.

Materials:
- Your Llyfr Cyfrin
- A pen or pencil to write with

Directions:
Take your Llyfr Cyfrin and think about these questions, writing down the answers that come to you. Let these prompts serve as a starting point and see where they might take you.

- What mythologies are you particularly drawn to?
- Why are you drawn to them?
- Do you have some physical connection to the landscape or people of these tales?
- Are there any other mythologies you would like to explore?
- How can you make sure you treat these cultural treasures with respect?

Be honest in your answers; you don't need to share them with anyone. This is simply an opportunity for you to explore your own thoughts and relationship to an important corner of culture for the everyday Witch.

Land

The land we are on is an important part of our culture, and nowhere so much as in the world of Witchcraft. Magic is rooted in the landscape we inhabit. We seek out the wild places, the ancient shrines and monuments. You don't have to look much further than Stonehenge on the Summer Solstice to appreciate how much Pagans love a good monument. But the connection to the land, and the way the land shapes our culture, runs far deeper.

Again, the culture of freedom in Witchcraft means there is no one way of doing things, and it is easy to turn to your own backyard for inspiration. Where you live is magic. Every inch of this incredible planet we call home is magic. There is no need to travel halfway around the world to feel connected. The stream at the bottom of the garden, the tree you pass on your walk every day, or the park in the middle of your commute are more than just patches of nature. They are invitations to connect. As previously mentioned, an important belief in Witchcraft is animism, or the belief that everything in this world has a spirit of its own. That will be discussed further in later chapters, but simply it means there are spirits everywhere for you to connect with. The land itself is alive, and it wants to know you. Simply by existing in the space that you do means you connect to something. I like to imagine it like a sofa you sit on day after day. The butt indentation slowly forms. It remembers your shape and becomes more and more comfortable. The world around you remembers your shape too.

This is most beautifully illustrated by the Welsh concept of *hiraeth*. The most basic translation of hiraeth is homesickness, but the concept is so much more. Some time ago, I attended a workshop run by Kristoffer Hughes, chief of the Anglesey Druid Order.[30] Kristoffer described hiraeth as the ache you have for Wales, a longing to be there, a craving for the stories and mythologies embedded in the very landscape. But it is not merely the longing you have for the land. What makes this feeling so intense is that the land longs for you right back. You are so much a part of your home, so familiar to the spirit that courses through it, that when you are not there, the land itself pines for you. It is connected to you, calls you home with an urgency you cannot fully express in words. A part of who you are belongs to the place you call home; it is connected in a way that cannot be broken. Wherever you are in the world, there is an invisible strand pulling you back to the land that longs for you. While the word hiraeth is specifically and culturally Welsh, the feeling it describes is universal. The ache the land feels for you is something that anyone connected to place can relate to.

Where you live is part of you. It is part of everything you do, including your Witchcraft. Knowing where you live, what grows there, where the streams and rivers flow, how the cycles of nature manifest—these all tie you into the cycle of life you were always a part of. The food you eat and the air you breathe are also of this landscape; you are literally made of it and one day will return to it. While this connection will naturally be felt most strongly wherever you call home, it is entirely possible to connect to the world around you wherever you are. This is a pure and simple connection to nature, the culture inherent in the natural world. It is not an elaborate connection to the past or any

....
30. Kristoffer Hughes, in-person workshop, Bodorgan, Anglesey, April 16, 2023.

specific community, simply the world around you as it is manifest to you in the moment. It is a powerful and fundamental part of any Witch's practice. If we are to return to nature, then we must return to nature.

Exercise: Introduce Yourself to the Land

This is another simple exercise to grant you a moment of connection wherever you might be. The land already knows you, but you may not yet have properly introduced yourself.

Materials:
• Yourself
• The land wherever you happen to be right now

Directions:
Find a patch of earth nearby. It may simply be a small patch of grass, a local park or woodland, or you may wish to venture a little further to a place that means something to you. If it is safe and comfortable for you to do so, consider taking off your shoes and letting your bare feet touch the soil itself. Feel the pulse of the place through the soles of your feet, its rhythms matching your own.

Once you are comfortable where you are, reach down and touch the earth with your hands. Speak to her as you would an old friend. Tell her your name, what brings you to be there. Take note of the life bursting forth from the soil, all that this planet sustains. Know that you are part of the cycles and rhythms of nature. She already knows you. She always has.

Tell her what it is you appreciate about her, what makes you grateful for being on the surface of this planet. Once you have said all you need to say, sit with her and let her answer. Take note of your feelings or any sudden changes in the environment. Has the breeze suddenly picked up, or have the clouds parted just so? She will answer in her own way if you are alert to hear it. Stay with her as long as is comfortable, then say goodbye and take your leave.

This simple exercise can be carried out wherever you are in the world and is a small gesture of respect and appreciation for the planet that nourishes us all.

Heritage

Culture is also the thread that ties us back through the past, giving us a sense of who we are in the stream of time. Our heritage, all that came before us, makes us who we are in this moment and cannot be ignored. This may include our ancestry, which ties us by blood or adoption to our ancestral roots, but it is also so much more. The people who blazed a trail, in whose footsteps we now follow, are as much a part of our heritage as those in our family tree. These ancestors of the Craft may include famous Witches who helped us have the freedom to practice, or they may be civil rights leaders without whom we would not have the liberty we do today. All these people deserve to be honoured and respected.

Heritage may also include the place we happen to be. As mentioned earlier, every year thousands of people gather at Stonehenge to celebrate their spiritual heritage. DNA and blood do not matter; the place itself calls to our spirit. The place does not care if you can prove a long line of descent; it cares that you are there, keeping spirit and tradition alive. In this way, you tap into the spiritual heritage of place, a potent way to connect. The land loves those who show up, and in this way, you can walk the same path as a long line of spiritual practitioners.

Connecting to heritage can be a little difficult when you live in a different land or on a different continent than your ancestors, but it is far from impossible. I often feel this when it comes to the German side of my identity. I often long for the mountains and forests of my childhood and visit as often as I can, but there are other ways I honour this side of my heritage. As a folk Witch, I am deeply inspired by the charms and practices of magical practitioners of the past, preserved in grimoires and in folklore. I use these to inform my own spells and rituals, drawing on the same magical current my ancestors once did. You don't have to be on the land your ancestors walked to be inspired by the things they did.

In fact, if we look through history, we see that when people moved, they took their practices with them. Folk magic and folk charms went where the people did; they are not static in any particular landscape. German folk magic is a particularly good example of this. When German-speaking people started to emigrate to the US, they took their practices with them, and these survive down to this day in the form of the *Braucherei* tradition of the Pennsylvania Dutch. When you read the charms and customs of this tradition, they carry powerful echoes of German folk magic, influenced and informed by their geographical location in the US. Folk magic adapts itself to wherever the folk are and whatever the folk need, and anyone can tap into this current and draw upon their heritage.

Again, however, this is something to be approached with respect. How can we connect to our heritage if we do not respect it and the living cultures and traditions that embody it today?

Self

Finally, connecting to culture in your Witchcraft is a powerful way to connect to yourself. Being in a cult, I was cut off from many of these cultural streams. Since so much of who we are is informed by our culture, I was left unable to properly connect to myself. There was no satisfying way to connect to mythology; the community I had was designed to police me, the land was not alive but merely an expression of an all-powerful creator, and heritage did not matter since everyone would be resurrected. So why worry? The doctrine was designed to make everyone think and act the same way. It was not designed to help you find yourself, but to bury any part of yourself that didn't conform. It was only by connecting to the many different aspects of culture that I began to reclaim myself.

Being a Witch is hugely empowering, and it celebrates the individual. Every part of you is sacred and important. The cult diminished the self to the point that even birthday celebrations were forbidden, as they put too much emphasis on you and not on God. The culture of Witchcraft, on the other hand, relishes in the sanctity of the self. In many ways, Witchcraft is a lifelong journey of self-discovery. For many, meditation is part of their path, challenging them to look inward and connect with what they find. Certain paths also emphasise our personal divinity or higher self, and this can be a great way of recognising your innate power.

Ultimately, connecting to ourselves and accepting what we find will better help us connect to the many other threads of culture. To weave the beautiful tapestry of our identity begins by discovering who we are. And it is only then that we find how we fit into the world around us. You can picture culture like a great tree, with roots reaching deep into the core of the self and branches reaching out to position that self in the wider world.

Only when we prioritise self-care and self-discovery can we be of service to others. A wheel with a still centre turns smoothly, and all the spokes are in balance. But if the centre wobbles or is unstable, the entire wheel falls apart. We must be a still centre if all the other aspects of culture and community are to turn smoothly around us.

Exercise: A Small Self-Care Ritual

The following working was taught to me by my partner shortly after we met as a simple way of turning the mundane magical. It is deceptively simple but works on multiple levels.

Materials:
- Three drops of lavender oil mixed with three teaspoons of carrier oil
- A small piece of cloth or fabric

Directions:
One of the best forms of self-care is a good night's sleep, but this can be one of the most difficult things in the world to do. This working is designed to enhance the magical qualities of sleep as well as opening you up to the realm of divinatory dreams. The first step is perhaps the most difficult: going to bed.

Once you are comfortable, take the lavender oil and the piece of cloth. Drip exactly three drops onto it, and as you do so, repeat these words: "As the three drops transformed Taliesin, so may they send me to the realm of dreams."

Hold the cloth close to your face and breathe in the scent of the lavender. Let it linger as you gently slow your breathing. Allow yourself a moment of gratitude. You're doing amazing and deserve to take care of yourself. You deserve an incredible and refreshing night's sleep.

As you allow yourself to relax ever more deeply, place the cloth under your pillow and rest your head. Allow yourself to drift to the realm of dreams, open to any messages and symbols that may appear. If sleep does not come easily, don't force it. Simply allow yourself to rest, your body supported by the mattress below and your mind free to drift wherever it may go. To rest is sacred, and your body is sure to thank you for it.

Cultural Christianity

Within the Western world, Christianity has been a dominant force for centuries. This has left an impact on many aspects of culture, from churches and cathedrals dotted across the landscape to the very way we think and talk about divinity. Within the UK, bishops still have a role in government, and the influence trickles down into every area of life. This is not necessarily a bad thing, but it is something for a Witch or a Pagan to be aware of, especially if coming from a Christian background. Some of this influence is so automatic we often don't notice it.

Early in my time with the coven, we would have many conversations about what we describe as this *cultural Christianity*. What was interesting is how even members who weren't raised religious noticed it in themselves. Simple things like the exclamations "Oh my God!" or "Jesus Christ!" are almost automatic, but there were deeper things as well. The idea that God is always watching, judging all your actions, is a difficult one to shake. The default to monotheism is also interesting, as if we are conditioned to accept the idea of one god in charge more easily than a pantheon. The concept of divinity will be explored in a later chapter, but many of the automatic thoughts we have about God are often tinged in Christian doctrine.

This is also true historically. The magical practitioners of the past usually operated in the dominant cultural climate, which happened to be Christianity in most of the Western world. Many of them did not have a choice; religion was violently enforced. This manifests in the magical charms we have recorded; many of them use very Christian imagery and wording. This is true in both Welsh and German folk magic, with narrative charms often telling stories of God and the Trinity in order to achieve some supernatural outcome. A great example is the "Credo Fechan" protection charm of Welsh lore, which invokes both God and the Virgin Mary.[31]

When I first stepped into Witchcraft, I found those Christian elements in folk magic very difficult. Christianity had hurt me very deeply, and I didn't want to be reminded of it in my new spiritual path. My position has softened a little over the years, but I don't think I'll ever be comfortable reciting the Lord's Prayer in any of my charms or rituals. The good thing is, I'll never have to. Since Witchcraft is a culture of freedom, I can do things my own way. A powerful way of honouring that freedom and reclaiming your spiritual path is to strain the Christianity out of the charms of the past.

This may seem controversial, but it is not without precedent. My favourite example is the Merseburg Charms of Germany, recorded in Old High German on the blank page of a Christian service book in the ninth century. They are completely pagan, invoking multiple pagan deities in the form of a narrative to produce a magical effect. There are two charms recorded, but for the sake of this chapter, I will focus on the second Merseburg charm. It goes like this:

Phol and Wodan were riding to the woods,
and the foot of Balder's foal was sprained.
So Sinthgunt, Sunna's sister, conjured it;
and Frija, Volla's sister, conjured it;
and Wodan conjured it, as he well could:
Like bone-sprain, so blood-sprain,
so joint-sprain:
Bone to bone, blood to blood,
joint to joints; so may they be glued.[32]

....

31. Richard Suggett, *A History of Magic and Witchcraft in Wales: Cunningmen, Cursing Wells, Witches and Warlocks in Wales* (Stroud: History Press, 2008), 67.
32. Benjamin W. Fortson IV, *Indo-European Language and Culture: An Introduction* (Oxford, UK: John Wiley & Sons, 2011), 325.

This was a healing charm for a horse's leg, and as you can see, it invokes multiple gods and is thoroughly pagan. So why am I invoking it to talk about straining the Christianity out of folk magic? Well, there are other variations on this charm formula. One of them was noted by Jacob Grimm in his discussion of the Merseburg Charms. It comes from Scotland and was recorded by William Chambers in 1842, going something like this:

The Lord rade,
And the foal slade;
He lighted,
And he righted.
Set joint to joint,
Bone to bone,
And sinew to sinew.
Heal in the Holy Ghost's name! [33]

These charms were recorded hundreds of centuries and miles apart, but do you notice any similarities? Jacob Grimm certainly did, and in his *Teutonic Mythology* wrote: "It is certain that the same or similar words have been superstitiously repeated countless times in all the countries of Teutonic tongue."[34] Notably, these charms, while used in similar ways, called to completely different gods. This seems to suggest that the exact deity called to didn't matter as much, only that they made sense to the magic being worked, for example Wodan having an association with horses.[35] This implies it is perfectly reasonable and precedented to substitute the Christian God for one or more deities that we work with or that make sense to us. After all, the folk magical practitioners of the past had very little choice, often living within an enforced Christian culture. We, however, have far more freedom to adapt and reimagine.

Again, however, this freedom works both ways. Many Witches are perfectly comfortable with the Christian elements within folk magic and find they work

....

33. Robert Chambers, *Popular Rhymes, Fireside Stories, and Amusements of Scotland* (Edinburgh: William and Robert Chambers, 1842), 37.

34. Jacob Grimm, *Teutonic Mythology*, vol. 3, 4th ed, trans. James Steven Stallybrass (London: George Bell and Sons, 1883), 1233.

35. Kenneth Northcott, "An Interpretation of the Second Merseburg Charm," *The Modern Language Review* 54, no. 1 (January 1959): 45–50, https://doi.org/10.2307/3720832.

very well. This is a completely valid way to practice, and having a bad experience of Christianity ourselves is never a reason to attack or dismiss the way someone else practices their Craft.

Cultural Witchcraft

This chapter has been a quick glance at some ways culture influences Witchcraft and serves as a quick introduction rather than an exhaustive guide. The culture of Witchcraft is a beautiful treasure, and woven through all individuals drawn to this magical world. To be a Witch is to draw on our community, our land, our heritage, and ourselves to forge a practice that truly represents who we are. When we do that, we create a spiritual and practical path that respects and reflects who we truly are, and that is where we find true empowerment. We do not need to take practices from halfway around the world that have no meaning to us personally, mindlessly incorporating them into our lives because that's how it has always been done. There are practices in our backyard that do the exact same thing while also connecting us to that stream of culture.

A great example is cleansing. We don't need to use endangered or exotic herbs imported from afar to cleanse. We don't need to rip away practices sacred to other cultures. Within Welsh tradition, rosemary is a powerful herb for cleansing and can be used alone or in incense as a form of smoke cleansing. In German tradition, nine different types of wood are used, known as the *Neunerlei Holz*. The exact types of wood vary from region to region, but a bundle composed of nine different types of wood is a powerful way to smoke cleanse. This is just one simple suggestion to illustrate what cultural Witchcraft can look like.

Our culture exists so that we can find fragments of ourselves in it—the things that set our soul on fire—and so that we can relate to other people like us. It is inherently about connection and common ground. It is a beautiful thing that can help us flourish as individuals and as Witches when it is respected. As we walk this crooked path, we continually add to the tapestry of ourselves and lose the things we no longer engage with or that no longer serve us. This is the natural journey of the Witch, concerned with becoming our best, most empowered selves and leaving behind that which no longer helps us on that path.

I must, however, end this chapter with a warning. Culture must be respected; it is a living thing kept alive by us all. Some cultures are closed and not up for grabs. The culture of a group or ethnicity can be, and often has been, weaponised against them. It is something that has been used to marginalise some groups, to ridicule them and push them down. If we are not raised in or initiated into that culture and way of life, we will never truly understand the cost and suffering it took for those groups to keep their traditions and practices alive. To misrepresent a culture or attempt to force it to be something it isn't for your own ends is to appropriate it. Cultural appropriation is at best ignorant and at worst malicious and exploitative.

This is not an attempt to preach, but to show the subtleties and nuances of culture. When properly respected, it is a beautiful, syncretic thing. But when handled insensitively, it can cause harm to others. To enjoy the beauty and scope of culture, we must be sensitive to the role it plays in the lives of others, especially those who have experienced centuries of oppression. Culture is a lived experience, not a theory. It is important to listen to voices from within a culture if we truly want to learn and connect.

Chapter 5
Coven and Community

Imagine a cave in central Europe forty thousand years ago, in the grip of the Ice Age. A small group of people huddle in this cave, sheltering from the giant creatures stalking the forests all around: mammoths, mastodons, giant bears, woolly rhinoceroses, and even cave lions. They hide deep in the cave huddled around a fire—their only source of warmth and light.

One of the people begins to speak. They describe a being unlike any that exists in the physical world around them. They speak of a person with the head of a lion. As they describe this being, they reach for a statue that represents it. This figure has taken hours to create. Modern estimates suggest upward of four hundred hours of gruelling labour.[36] It is intricately carved from ivory, and as they speak, it is passed around. It moves from hand to hand, and even now it is smoothed from the wear of the many hands that have clutched it.

This scene is not some fantasy but describes the story behind an artifact discovered in 1939: the *Löwenmensch* (Lion Man) of Hohlenstein-Stadel.[37] As of the time of writing, this is the oldest statue ever discovered and represents a being conjured from the imagination. But more than that, it shows evidence of an early community gathering to share stories of something beyond the physical and putting extreme effort into creating this figure.

I find this fact incredible. The earliest evidence we have shows that humans formed community around the spiritual and shared stories and beliefs in the depths of caves. This has never changed. We can look back through history and

....

36. "The Lion Man: An Ice Age Masterpiece," The British Museum, October 10, 2017, https://www.britishmuseum.org/blog/lion-man-ice-age-masterpiece.
37. Neil MacGregor, *Living with the Gods: On Beliefs and Peoples* (New York: Alfred A. Knopf, 2018), 3–13.

easily see how culture and community are organised around spirit, expressed in stories and ritual.

While it may seem like there is less of that magic in the world today, the thriving Pagan community is powerful evidence that it isn't going anywhere. The latest census in the UK, taken in 2021, showed Pagan numbers continuing to grow.[38] In my own experience of presenting at Pagan and Witchcraft events, I have observed the same thing. Not only are more people attending, but the passion and excitement seem to grow each year as more people are drawn to this philosophy and way of life. But how do people find and connect with the community of Witchcraft?

A Solitary Path

It might seem strange that I start this chapter talking about solitary Witchcraft, but for many, this is the preferred way to practice. As we've discussed, Witchcraft is ultimately something you do, and it's perfectly possible to do it on your own. There also isn't a centralised doctrine, so there's no instruction manual. This means there are many valid paths, and for many Witches, their path is as unique as they are. If you are drawn to what you read in this book but prefer to keep yourself to yourself, that is completely fine, and you are in good company (or not, if that's what you prefer).

However, there is a wider community out there that you can engage with as much as you choose. This book only exists because that community does, because there are people I can share my practice with. There are countless other books that also supply this thriving community. The wide variety of people and materials also lead to a variety of ways to get involved to whatever extent you are comfortable with. For me, that means the formal structure of a coven, but it can be as simple as an online forum of like-minded people or following some social media accounts you find inspiring. There are more ways to Witch than I can discuss in this chapter, but hopefully I can offer you a taste of the vibrant world of modern Witchcraft.

....

38. "Religion, England and Wales: Census 2021," Office for National Statistics, November 29, 2022, https://www.ons.gov.uk/peoplepopulationandcommunity/culturalidentity/religion/bulletins/religionenglandandwales/census2021.

Coven

As I have mentioned before, I am part of a coven. My personal definition of a coven is: "A formal group of practitioners who share a magical philosophy." The word might make you think of the opening scene in *Macbeth*, where one witch asks, "When shall we three meet again?" And honestly, if you peel away a bit of the stereotype, it's not a bad place to start.[39] For my coven, we shall meet again on Thursday, as we do every week. Much like the witches in Macbeth, we gather to discuss and work magic. But we also meet to build community, to connect with our spirituality, and to explore any exciting things we may have discovered. We also focus on the wider community, sharing aspects of our philosophy, worldview, and magic online and at in-person events. Since we are rooted in Welsh culture, this is usually focused on the Welsh cultural continuum and streams of magic.

A Philosophy and a Worldview

Within the world of Paganism, there are many ways to work magic. There are Wiccans who cast circles, Traditional Witches who tread the mill, and Druids who meet to mark the solstices, among many others. This wide variety of approaches makes the Pagan community a wonderfully eclectic space. What makes it really special is that all these traditions can work together. I have been part of rituals in all these frameworks, even though they are not the practices of my coven. This freedom means that local working groups are completely valid, where practitioners from any stream may gather together and enact ritual or work magic. What separates a coven from this kind of working group is a shared underlying philosophy and worldview.

Many people seem to think Witchcraft is just playing pretend with no real thought behind it, but there is a deep and rich philosophy behind any tradition. Just because that philosophy may not always be mainstream does not mean it doesn't exist. The theories of magic and ritual within Wicca have been developed over decades, drawing on traditions and ways of working magic that stretch back centuries! As the influential Witch Stewart Farrar puts it in

....

39. William Shakespeare, *Macbeth*, act 1, scene 1, Wordsworth Classics (Ware, England: Wordsworth Editions, 1992).

his book *What Witches Do*, "Tradition is not merely familiarity, it is momentum."[40] Ritual is empowered by the history and previous workings it contains. An incredible amount of thought and research goes into these workings. They are far from random.

A coven may use an existing philosophy and way of doing things, as recorded in many fantastic books over the years, or they may create their own philosophy that reflects the worldview of all the members. The coven I am part of started as a working group, but as we got to know each other better, it became clear our worldviews aligned. We had many long conversations about our beliefs, ranging from the nature of the gods to how magic worked. As I had left a cult and was forming my beliefs, I wanted to find a way to articulate my philosophy. Drawing on these conversations and the research I was doing, along with a great deal of help from my partner, I wrote up a few paragraphs and presented them. We all liked it and found it resonated with us. The thing we all already felt in our bones now had a name: Bardic Witchcraft.

A coven, however, needs more. The philosophy needs to be put into action. Luckily for us all, one of those early members was Mhara Starling, an expert in Welsh streams of practical magic, who quite literally wrote the book on the subject. She agreed to be coven leader and help create a series of rituals and practices built on this new philosophy. The Sarffes Goch Coven was born.

Online Communities

The problems of the modern Witch need modern solutions. While the internet can feel very isolating, perpetuating unreasonable beauty standards and ideals, it can also be a powerful way to bring people together. Online communities were vital for me, both in leaving a cult and in finding my Witchcraft community. When leaving the cult, I felt incredibly alone and only realised other people had been through the same thing when I connected with them in the virtual world. The friends I made helped me feel validated and understood the nuances of an experience few people go through. They are an important part of my support system down to this day. Without the connecting power of the internet, I know the experience would have been far more difficult. Seeing

....

40. Stewart Farrar, *What Witches Do* (Suffolk, UK: Book Club Associates, 1992), 21.

people who had already left lead happy, healthy lives helped me find the courage I needed to leave and build my new life.

To a certain extent, the same thing is true about the world of Witchcraft. Finding my people online helped me root myself in my spiritual practice and refine my philosophy. However, the community of Witchcraft is rather broad, and finding your people can take a little work. Thankfully, many online spaces have subcommunities dedicated to certain paths of Paganism, and joining those groups or forums can streamline the process a little.

The internet is not without its pitfalls, however. Witchcraft is an open and inclusive space, and as wonderful as that is, it does mean that anyone can access the community, particularly online. I have had my fair share of experiences with people who live to stir up drama or build their "brand." The growth of Paganism also means it attracts people wanting to exploit the community. If you are already following witchy accounts online, you may have received messages offering readings by accounts pretending to be someone else. These are almost always scammers trying to take advantage. Though it can be frustrating, curating your online space is a great way to protect yourself and feel safe connecting with your community. The block button is often your best friend.

Despite the pitfalls and unique challenges of the online landscape, it remains an invaluable space to build and connect with community. Many of the events I will go on to discuss are arranged and advertised with the help of online spaces, and it is quite possible to build friendships you will treasure throughout your life. In addition, many conferences and workshops are now held online, allowing people from all over the witchy world to be in community together. Some of my most treasured discussions have been in my living room with people halfway around the world.

These spaces are also particularly valuable if you are not yet out of the broom closet. For whatever reason, you may not want to share your interest in Paganism and Witchcraft, and the anonymity of the internet gives you an opportunity to explore this path without revealing yourself. If you decide it's not for you, then you can step away without consequence. If it does resonate, then you can get as involved as you want to.

Online communities are also a great space for anyone who may have health challenges and struggle to get to in-person events. Ritual sites can be inaccessible, especially if they are ancient monuments littered with stones. In recent years, many groups have started to live stream their rituals so that anyone can participate and feel that sense of connection. A great example of this is the sunrise at Stonehenge on the Summer Solstice, which is live streamed by English Heritage.

In-Person Events

As good as the internet can be, however, it is not the only way to engage with community. In-person events are a great way to meet people locally who share your worldview and immerse yourself deeper in this magical world. Many Witches find that a balance between online and in-person community creates a healthy way to connect with the wider Pagan world.

Moots and Local Groups

Within the UK, the most common form of Pagan meeting is a pub moot. I had never really heard the word *moot* until I became a Witch. Essentially, it's just a very old word for a meeting to discuss things. That suits us Witches and Pagans quite well, since we like old things and love to discuss. But what exactly is a Pagan moot?

This really is a case of it does what it says on the tin. As public events, you sometimes get people attending who are questioning or new to the path, or even drop-ins from people who happen to overhear. This all contributes to vibrant and lively discussion, often helped along with a drink or two. Rather than formal, structured occasions, moots are usually social meetups. There may be a topic for discussion or a speaker, but the social aspect is front and centre. In a way, they are like little Pagan social clubs. As a result, moots are a great, low-commitment way to see if the Pagan community resonates with you.

I have met some of my closest friends at these events. These meets are the lifeblood of local Pagan communities and something I deeply treasure. Whether there are five people or fifty in the room, there is always a buzz, and you always leave with a smile on your face.

If you decide you want to dip your toes in the Witchcraft community, how can you find a moot of your own? The first step is to search online. Type your local area plus "moot" into your favourite search engine and see if anything shows up. You could also try "Pagan event," "Pagan meetup," or "Witchcraft" in the search bar, since a meetup may go by different names depending on the area. If nothing shows up, try visiting a local metaphysical or spiritual shop. Often, even if no social events are held there, they may host workshops or classes, or have information about any local meetups. At the very least, you will meet some like-minded individuals running the shop who you may be able to connect with.

If these suggestions don't turn up any leads, then you may be the person the community has been waiting for. All that is needed is for someone to get the ball rolling and set up an event locally, and everyone who searches for one in the future will have somewhere to go. Pubs will often allow you to use the space free of charge as long as you buy drinks. If you approach some local establishments, you will get an idea of what is available in your area. As an alternative, spiritual or metaphysical shops may also have a space they'll let you use and can be a hub for local Witches and Pagans. If you put yourself out there and get something going, you may be surprised at the results. Reach out to your online community and let them know about the event. Get the word out there and see where it goes. Some of my local moots have attendees who travel over an hour to get there. It is often a case of seeking community, will travel.

If that isn't something you have the space, time, or desire to do, try casting a wider net. See if the next town over has a local group. Often, groups meet on a monthly basis, so having to travel a little once a month is not a huge commitment. Being decentralised, we don't really have churches or houses of worship. The cost of freedom is a little bit of effort to find a community of your own.

Festivals and Conventions

The bigger events of the Pagan calendar are the festivals and conventions. These are the events you are likely to have to travel for, but it is worth the effort. Throughout the year, groups and organisations hold larger events, which draw a diverse crowd of attendees. These events often include talks, workshops, and rituals, as well as a wide variety of shops and stalls with all manner of witchy delights. They are a fantastic opportunity to meet new people and learn from community members, as well as discover what other events may be taking place. I personally make sure to get to every convention and festival I can possibly attend. It is worth mentioning that there is usually an entry charge, but as most events are held annually, this is rarely overwhelming (at least with the good ones).

Camps, retreats, and open rituals also fall within this category of event, being more formal meetings that draw a bigger crowd. All are a great opportunity to enjoy the wider Pagan community and connect with like-minded people. Again, this is something you have to research depending on your area, but Pagan events are hosted regularly in many places.

The Healing Power of Community

Leaving a cult hurts, and the shunning truly leaves you with no one, especially if you didn't have the chance to plan your exit. The cult community is one of the things that is used to control you, but the reason it's effective is that community is something we all crave. Being ostracised can make it difficult to trust again. You have already lost everyone once. Why try again? The truth, however, is that a healthy community will never shun you. When you find that kind of community, it is like a balm for the soul. It is something precious that will support you and help you grow, never stifle you or try and keep you down. Finding that is always worthwhile.

Exercise: Opening Up to Community

This exercise is a gentle affirmation to connect with community that helped me a lot after leaving the cult. My self-worth was shattered. I felt stupid for having been taken in, and even worse for having trusted and loved people who could so quickly turn their back on me. I became convinced I would always be alone and would be safer without ever opening up again. It took time and effort to move beyond that, but it was definitely worth it.

Materials:
- A mirror
- Yourself

Directions:
Look yourself in the eyes in the mirror and repeat these words. Truly feel and believe them as you breathe them out into the world, and repeat as often as you need:

I am worthy of love and respect. I do not need to earn my value;
I exist, and therefore I matter. Though I may have been hurt before,
the community I deserve is out there for me. I can learn to trust
once more and find the people who value me for who I truly am.
I am worthy of love and respect, and I offer it to myself, as I know
others will offer it to me also.

Do not mindlessly repeat these words. Feel the truth within them. Force their reality onto the world and be the empowered Witch you deserve to be. As you become more comfortable with the truth of this affirmation, start to put yourself out there. Connect with witchy groups online. Visit your local Witchcraft shop. Perhaps even attend a local moot. Start small and be gentle with yourself. Love yourself as you deserve to be loved, and the whole world will soon catch up.

Initiation and the Craft

One aspect many spiritual traditions have in common is the idea of initiation. While moots, festivals, and online events don't require them, these are common within covens and even in solitary practice. I was familiar with this idea from the cult, even if I had a different name for it. To me, it was baptism. I was baptised at age seventeen. This involved a private dedication to the god of the cult and a public, full-body immersion in water. Ironically, I appreciate that symbolism more now as a Witch than I ever did as a cult member.

Full-body immersion is a powerful visual symbol of the underlying meaning of initiation: the death of the old life and rebirth into the new. Historians of religions have pointed out that this initiation is an integral part of spiritual systems, it symbolises not merely death and rebirth, but a death of the mundane self and a rebirth into spiritual enlightenment, or the sacred.[41] This is really powerful symbolism and expresses a dedication to something more than the self. It is the setting aside of the self for something higher, invoking ideas of

....
41. Mircea Eliade, *Rites and Symbols of Initiation: The Mysteries of Birth and Rebirth*, trans. Willard R. Trask (London: Harvill Press, 1958).

sacrifice and enlightenment. A great example of this in the Welsh cultural continuum is the story of Taliesin, a figure central to Bardic Witchcraft.

What follows is my retelling of the myth of Taliesin. It is not identical to
the earliest versions but is told to highlight the very spirit of initiation that beats
at the heart of the tale.

*There was once a goddess called Ceridwen, who set out to brew a potion of
inspiration for her son. She was a devoted mother, and her child had been
born so ugly, she knew she needed to take action to enhance his prospects in
life. The brew she set her mind upon would take a year and a day to complete
and must be tended constantly. She did not have the time to tend to it herself
and sought out a local boy to do so on her behalf. His name was Gwion Bach.*

*Gwion stood and dutifully tended the cauldron for a year, applying him-
self to nothing else. He stoked the fire, stirred the bubbling brew, and performed his duties faultlessly. Finally, the fated day arrived. The brew was
ready, but there was a surprise in store. Though intended for Ceridwen's
child, the brew of Awen had other plans. In the form of three droplets, it leapt
forth from the cauldron and onto Gwion's thumb. He promptly stuck it in his
mouth to stop the burning, and in that instant, the spirit of prophecy and
inspiration rushed into him, and he gained the knowledge of all things.*

*Perhaps the spirit of inspiration had grown fond of him throughout
the year of service. Perhaps it was rewarding him for his hard work. What
we can say for certain is that his entire existence was transformed in that
instant. A far more physical transformation was soon to follow.*

*Once Ceridwen learned what had transpired, she was enraged. In her
anger, she transformed herself into a greyhound and rushed at Gwion,
intent on gaining her vengeance. He, of course, knew this would happen,
already filled with the spirit of prophecy. Nonetheless, he knew this is how
things must be. He himself must live the myth for his initiation to be complete. He transformed himself into a hare for her to give chase.*

*As Ceridwen drew nearer to him, Gwion continued his initiatory jour-
ney and assumed the form of a fish, submerging himself in the realm of
water. Ceridwen followed in the form of an otter. As she once again drew
close, Gwion continued his journey by leaping to the realm of sky, assum-
ing the form of a wren. Ceridwen, of course, followed in the form of a*

hawk, her wings hastened by rage. Once again, she outpaced him, and the final part of his journey began as Gwion the boy transformed himself into a grain of wheat.

Sensing her victory, Ceridwen became a speckled hen and devoured the grain. The boy Gwion Bach was dead. But his death had been ritualised by the chase. It was significant. It was a beginning. For within the womb of Ceridwen, life began to stir. A grand rebirth was at hand. Nine months passed, and the grain inside her came back into the world, a newborn babe. Stunned by his beauty, all thoughts of vengeance and rage departed. She named him Taliesin, the radiant brow, and cast him adrift in otherworldly waters. This is not the end of the tale, for no tale ever truly ends, but it is where we must leave it.

Through this tale we see the figure of Gwion Bach going through the process of initiation: dying to his mundane life as the boy who stirs the cauldron and being reborn as Taliesin, the embodiment of inspiration and prophecy. His initiation involves powerful emotions and a chase through all the realms and elements. Clearly, this is no mundane act. There is a far deeper meaning for those who seek it.

Ritual is sometimes described as participation in a myth, and when we go through the process of initiation, we are participating in the story of Taliesin and every other myth that invokes this powerful idea. We are filled with Awen; we become the embodiment of divine inspiration as we act out this drama in our own lives. The momentum of this tradition carries us forward into the next stage of our life. In every moment we may be reborn into a world of wonder and enchantment, filled with wonderous transformations and bubbling cauldrons. We may not be devoured by a goddess in the form of a hen, but we can choose to open ourselves up to the wonder of the universe, to observe the sanctity of existence.

Do you need a coven to go through the process of initiation? Absolutely not. You can and likely do initiate yourself every day. A gym induction, starting a new job, moving house—those are all initiations of a sort, and ones we can all do alone. When we ritualise initiation, however, we transform it into something spiritual. We make it symbolic and choose to act out the myth. This is certainly something a solitary Witch can do, and I encourage any who choose to walk this path to act out some form of initiation ritual for themselves. A key part of Witchcraft is celebration, as we will discuss in a later chapter. Whether solitary or as part of a group, an initiation is a perfect time to celebrate and observe this milestone.

The initiation I provide in this book is not an initiation into Witchcraft as such. Rather, it is an initiation as a seeker, someone exploring this path. If you choose to stay when you have finished this book, you may wish to re-do this exercise, tweaking it as a solitary initiation into the Craft itself. Many covens have their own initiation rituals, but these are usually private and only revealed to individuals when they join.

Exercise: Solitary Initiation

In her wonderful book *The Devil's Dozen*, Gemma Gary makes an important point about solitary initiation. I cannot put it any better than she herself writes: "At a successful rite of witch-initiation, one is never alone for true initiation is a transformative process of death, rebirth and illumination, imparted by numen and spirit presences."[42] This is a beautiful truth to remember, for it illustrates that the Witch is never truly alone. Even when the community of humans may not easily be found, the vibrant world of spirits is always present. This is especially true for the animistic Witch, since being initiated into this path means recognising the spirit inherent in all things.

Materials:
- A bowl
- Water
- Two lengths of cord or twine
- A strand of your hair or something connected to you personally
- Pen and paper to record your thoughts

....

42. Gemma Gary, *The Devil's Dozen: Thirteen Craft Rites of the Old One* (Cornwall, UK: Troy Books, 2015), 29.

Directions:

This rite of solitary initiation incorporates knot magic, which is a powerful way of binding things together. It also draws on the powerful symbolism of water immersion as initiation. It is a rite I performed for myself when I took my first serious steps into this enchanted world and is an initiation into exploring the path of Witchcraft, rather than an initiation into any specific tradition. It is an opening of the doors to seeking, rather than a commitment to do things any specific way.

Before you begin this rite, I encourage you to sit down and think about why it is you want to be a Witch or learn more about Witchcraft. Write down your answers so that you may come back to them, and if you do not have the answers yet, come back to this working when you do.

- What is it that draws you to the path of Witchcraft?
- Why do you want to dedicate yourself to exploring this path?
- What does that dedication mean to you?

When you have found your answers, fill the bowl with water and set it on the ground in front of you. Speak the following words:

I call to the spirits of this place. I call to the spirits of this land. I call to the spirits of the very stream of Witchcraft. Witness my initiation and aid me on my path. May I learn from you; may I discover the way that I should walk. May I be reborn as a seeker, open to the mysteries of existence.

Once you have spoken those words, take the first piece of cord and submerge it in the bowl. As it lies below the surface, repeat these words:

This cord I imbue with the spirits of the Craft. I pour into it my intention to learn, to be open to what I may find. I imbue it with the knowledge that I may find my own path, and that I may choose my own way. I do not blindly commit myself, nor do I blindly restrict myself. All paths are open, and I grant myself the freedom to walk them.

Once the words have been spoken, take the cord from the bowl and place it to one side. Now take the second cord and slowly wrap the strand of your hair around it. As you do so, repeat these words. You may also wish to read aloud the reasons you noted down earlier for wanting to explore this path:

This cord represents my very self. I am on a path of discovery and of learning. I am open to the mystery.

Once you have done this, take both cords together. Take a moment to contemplate what this represents. One cord is imbued with the very spirit of Witchcraft; the other represents you as a seeker. With that knowledge firmly in mind, tie the cords together with whatever knot you choose. Make sure the knot remains visible. As we are about to discuss, even with initiation, you should have the freedom to change your mind. If ever you want to leave this path or close the door to exploring it, simply take a pair of scissors and cut through the knot, and your initiation will be undone. Until that time, keep the cord somewhere safe but in sight, and whenever you see it, remember that you are now a seeker of the mysteries of Witchcraft. That alone makes you part of a wide, welcoming, and diverse community.

The Dark Side of Group Work

There are dangers, however, that you should be aware of. As I mentioned, I was baptised into a cult. I dedicated myself to their version of God. That initiation, though, was used as a part of the control the cult held over me, because once it was done, there was no way to leave without extreme consequences. Putting aside the fact that coercion was used in my dedication to the cult (and coerced consent is not consent), there are times when vows need to be broken. We all grow and change as people, and sometimes information comes to light we didn't know at the time. This is an issue beautifully addressed by author and Witch Laura Tempest Zakroff in her book *Weave the Liminal*. She discusses specific circumstances under which oaths may need to be reconsidered or even broken. How a belief system responds to these changes is really important.[43]

It is important to remember that a cult can grow in any belief system, and Witchcraft is not exempt. If there is no way to leave a group without extreme consequences, then that is a huge red flag. Before committing to any group, make sure you know what their policies are for if you change your mind, and let that information inform your decision. It is worth bearing in mind that individuals can choose who they associate with, and leaving can affect your relationship with remaining members. However, problems arise when social relationships are used as a tool for control and people are instructed to ritualistically shun leavers. No one is forced to be your friend, but no one should be forced to shun you either.

It is also worth looking at how decisions are made in any group you are thinking of joining. Is there any accountability? Is there any way for you to flag concerns that may come up? Accountability and transparency are very important, and usually missing in cults. Having one individual in charge who can dictate without question is a recipe for disaster. Feedback and collaboration are essential. Witchcraft is about spirituality, not pandering to anyone's ego. Yes, formal groups are usually structured in a certain hierarchy, but they will rarely be a dictatorship. Think carefully before you join anyone's ego project.

It is also important to know what you are joining. For many groups, some of their information and practices are oathbound or only available once you have been initiated. This is not necessarily a bad thing *if* you are provided with enough information about the group to make an informed decision before you join and there is a clear way to leave without extreme consequence. Most oathbound information will be the precise way that ritual is carried out or the meaning of symbolism within the group. If there are major philosophical underpinnings that are withheld from you, that is perhaps a little more suspect.

Setting Boundaries and Staying Safe

You can enjoy the community of Witchcraft without subscribing to the other aspects. It doesn't matter if you dance under the stars every full moon or just enjoy reading some mythology once in a while. On the whole, our community

43. Laura Tempest Zakroff, *Weave the Liminal: Living Modern Traditional Witchcraft* (Woodbury, MN: Llewellyn Publications, 2019), 197–200.

is not judgmental, and as long as you are open to the spiritual side of life, it will be open to you. You don't have to work magic or commune with spirits; it can simply be that you enjoy being around spiritual people. All are welcome in this world, no matter how involved they want to be. This openness, however, does come with some challenges to be aware of.

Within any community there is the potential for both good and bad experiences. Anyone can access these community spaces, and Witchcraft can be a magnet for some rather interesting characters. Just because they can access the community does not mean that you owe them your time and attention, however. You have a right to feel safe and respected in any space you are in. If you are ever made to feel otherwise in a community space, then let the organiser know. They should take action to make the community safe for everyone. If they do not, then perhaps this particular community is not a safe space to be in and best left behind.

If you do have a bad experience with a community member, please don't let that put you off us all. The bad apples are not representative of the whole space. I have had more than a handful of run-ins with loud and nasty individuals, and it always leaves a sour taste. However, I also receive support from the community in the wake of those incidents. There is good and bad in everything, but in my experience, the good far outweighs the bad. Just be sure you know your own boundaries and stick firmly to them. You will always find your people.

Community Means Contribution

It can sometimes be easy to take our witchy community for granted. We might believe it will always be there, some resource we can take from whenever we need, but that is not how community works. Throughout this chapter I have mentioned the things you can do to find and connect with community. In order to benefit, you have to make the effort to do them.

When I first met my coven, we would attend moots and classes together. We would travel and make an effort to participate, and relied on everyone else who did the same thing. If no one came, if no one participated, then there would simply be no community. It is something you give to, and in the giving, you create it. Then, once it exists, you benefit from it. Community is a two-way street, and its basic unit is you. Without everyone contributing to the vibrant landscape of modern Witchcraft, we would be far poorer. Without each and every one of you, this chapter would be impossible to write.

Chapter 6
The World of Spirits

My first encounter with demons was a possessed painting under the stairs. I never saw it myself, but it was famous in my church. Everyone was talking about it. A new person had recently accepted a Bible study, and she lived in an old vicarage. As part of the rental agreement, she was obligated to keep a painting in the cupboard under the stairs, or so the story goes. The cupboard was never opened, but the things that happened in that vicarage made it clear something supernatural was going on.

Every week when the Bible study took place, doors would bang, things would move of their own accord, threatening voices would be heard from nowhere, and some people even left with unexplained scratches on their arms and legs. It wasn't a story I paid much attention to until one of my family members went to the Bible study and came home shaking. Everything I'd heard about had happened to them. They swore it was all true.

I don't know what was really happening in that vicarage each week, but it illustrates an important point. Almost every religion has a belief in spirits of some kind. Within the cult, there were angels and demons, active in the world around us, and with not much better to do than attach themselves to a painting. It wasn't just paintings, however. Any object could be possessed, and you had to be extremely careful buying anything secondhand. There was a genuine fear of vintage, dust-covered dolls in the secondhand shop, and not just because of how creepy they look. They might just be the latest home of a dormant demon, waiting on the shelf for an unsuspecting victim to pick them up.

Strangely, despite this belief being doctrine, talking about it was discouraged. We weren't to mention what the demons did so as not to spread the fame of Satan. Besides, we didn't need to be frightened because we had God on our side and our spiritual dad was stronger than theirs and would beat him up. The gossip mill wasn't going to let that stop them, though, and I heard an incredible variety of stories about demons doing anything you can imagine. Basically, anything bad that happened could be sure of having a demon involved somewhere.

To this day, I'm not sure how the powerful Prince of Persia or the legion of demons expelled by Jesus ended up chilling in a cupboard under the stairs. Perhaps he just wanted a peaceful retirement. What I do know is that the world of Witchcraft expanded my view of spirits from the rigid binary of good angels and evil demons to something far more diverse. But let's start this chapter by talking about angels from a magical perspective before we explore more of that variety.

Christian Cosmology

In a side gallery of the British Museum there is a strange little collection of artifacts: a polished obsidian disc on a small stand, a crystal ball, and two big wax discs engraved with all manner of signs and symbols. You may be wondering what these have to do with angels. The answer is everything! These were the magical tools of John Dee, astrologer and conjuror to Queen Elizabeth I. Alongside his associate Edward Kelly, he used them to contact and converse with angels, leaving extensive notes about his interactions. To oversimplify it a little, they used these interactions to devise a system of magic called *Enochian magic*, a complex ceremonial system that called on the power of the beings they claimed to be in contact with.

When I first learned about this centuries-old magical system, it blew my mind. Within the cult, angels were the agents and messengers of God. They were terrifying, impersonal forces, capable of slaughtering 185,000 humans in a single night.[44] But they certainly weren't revealing entirely new systems of magic to Elizabethan conjurors. The fact that people could perceive and interact with angels in this way helped to broaden my own worldview. Regardless of the true nature of these beings, they were contacted by professed Christians operating within a Christian framework. The relationship the cult claimed to give me with spirit beings was not the only possibility. The floodgates were wide open to reassess everything I had been taught.

....
44. 2 Kings 19:35.

As I dug deeper into this, I began to notice supposed Christian spirits popping up in magic everywhere. One interesting example was the conflation of saints and demons in magical treasure hunting. Historian Johannes Dillinger gives the example of the summoning and banishing of St. Corona, which used the same formula that would be applied to summoning demons. To the magicians, saints were not simply benevolent angels; they were fearful and must be banished properly once they had done what you wanted.[45]

Another interesting crossover came in the form of pagan gods mentioned in the Bible. In the cult, rather than being dismissed as fantasy and imagination, they were seen as real and powerful entities. Remember, the gods of Egypt were capable of producing miracles in the Old Testament; they just weren't as good at it as God. Many fundamentalist denominations explain this by claiming the deities worshipped by the nations were in fact demons. The demons of the cult were immensely powerful, even able to resist angels in midheaven. It would certainly be in their power to turn water into blood or wooden staffs into serpents, or so the reasoning goes. The gods of the old world became the demons of the new. It is one of the reasons the cult instilled such fear of Paganism. Whether knowingly or not, within their cosmology every Pagan was a demon worshipper.

This kind of thinking betrays an inherent weakness in a binary cosmology. Every entity that exists must be forced onto a side, either good and pure or evil and corrupt. You are either the angel or the demon; there is no fence to sit on. Every deity that is not God Almighty must be a demon in disguise. But the power of the Witch is that we can see the shades of grey.

I personally no longer believe in spirit life in the form presented in the cult. I believe that the variety of spirit life is far wider, as this chapter will discuss. Angels and demons are simply broad categories slapped onto the many spirits that exist to make them work within the dualist cosmology of Christianity. However, some Witches do still work with both these forms of spirit life and find great results in their practice. In fact, it is rather difficult to practice ceremonial magic without borrowing a little from this worldview, since it's about binding demons to your will to achieve magical effects.

....

45. Johannes Dillinger, *Magical Treasure Hunting in Europe and North America: A History* (Hampshire, UK: Macmillan, 2012), 88–89.

Ultimately, while a Witch may work with spirits they describe as angels or demons, rarely will they be exactly as Christianity presents them. Often, the duality is turned on its head, with angels being rather more antagonistic. Demons understand what it is to be human; after all, their fall from heaven happened when they took human form. They understand our needs and offer us what we want. Angels must remind us not to fear them.

While a Witch today may not always force the spirits to do as they want in the same way the ceremonial magicians do, we do still work with and honour the many varieties of spirit life on their own terms. I offer here only a brief look at some of the forms that may take, an introduction to the thriving world of life beyond the physical

The Spirit World

I started this chapter by discussing the beings in the Christian cosmology to high-light an important point: every spiritual tradition has a belief in some form of spirit life. Unsurprisingly, angels and demons are a common thread in many faiths, given the widespread influence of Christianity over the centuries. Various other forms of spirit life do exist, as this chapter will discuss. Regardless of the type of spirits believed in, however, merely their existence necessitates the existence of a spirit realm. After all, they have to live somewhere.

In the cult, the home of spirits was heaven, a far-off realm inaccessible to humans. That concept doesn't really exist the same way in Witchcraft, and the world of spirits is far more accessible. It goes by many names, often known as the otherworld, but I will share with you the way we describe it within my coven.

Annwfn

Annwfn is the name for the otherworld in Welsh mythology and poetry, and being a member of a Welsh coven, it is the term I am most likely to use. Learning about this concept was a really important part of my spiritual journey. Within the cult, spirit life was distant. They could visit earth and appear to people here, but they had to travel, usually being far removed. Annwfn represents something completely different.

Within the Welsh source texts, we see the otherworld running parallel to our world. Almost any liminal space can become a threshold. Our worlds are so close together, doors can appear anywhere! It is so accessible, people often end up there by accident, and it can even be difficult to tell when someone is in Annwfn within the stories if you don't know the cues to look out for.

Despite this everyday closeness, there were still times of the year when the doors of the otherworld opened just that little easier. The most powerful and magical of these were the *tair ysbrydnos* (three spirit nights): *Nos Galan Haf* (Summer's Eve, April 30), *Gwyl Ifan* (Midsummer), and *Nos Galan Gaeaf* (Winter's Eve, October 31). On these occasions, the otherworld was most easily accessible, and the spirits walked freely among us. To this day, these dates have a sacred significance to Witches of various traditions.

An interesting feature of the otherworld in Welsh lore is that it is closely associated with Awen, or divine inspiration. The medieval Welsh poem "Preiddeu Annwn" reinforces the connection between Taliesin, who was born through Awen, and the otherworld. In fact, it is likely the Welsh poets used these otherworldly connections to emphasize the mystic origins of their art.[46] Inspiration came to them from a place beyond what could be perceived by the senses; they channelled it from the deeper world. It flows from that world into ours, breathing inspiration into the physical plane. The spirit world has a very important physical function, and according to this worldview, every single inspired work is by its nature infused with a spiritual component. Inspired working cannot occur without contact with the world of spirit, whether conscious or not.

Exercise: Bringing Inspiration from the Spirit World

Within the poem "Preiddeu Annwn," Taliesin describes a cauldron within the otherworld "kindled by the breath of nine maidens."[47] The cauldron is also the vessel used to brew the Awen in the tale of Taliesin described in an earlier chapter. Clearly the cauldron is closely associated both with the world of spirit and with inspiration. You will draw on this association to conjure inspiration from that very world in this exercise.

46. Marged Haycock, "'Preiddeu Annwn' and the Figure of Taliesin," *Studia Celtica* 18 (1983): 52–78.
47. Haycock, "'Preiddeu Annwn' and the Figure of Taliesin," 62.

Materials:
- A vessel that can hold water
- Water
- A quiet space
- Your Llyfr Cyfrin
- *Optional:* A piece of poetry that speaks to you in some way

Directions:

Place your vessel in front of you and decant the water into it. This vessel represents your cauldron. If you wish, you could recite some poetry as you do so that speaks to you in some way. Remember that inspiration in Welsh lore is closely associated with the craft of the poets, and poetry carries this powerful current.

Once you have decanted the water, take a moment to calm yourself. Focus on your breathing: the air moving from the world around you into your lungs, then being returned to the world around you subtly changed. Simply your presence changes the world, and your breathing is proof of that. Think about the power of that breath. It can extinguish a flame, can cool hot food. Think how it feels when a warm breath gently touches the back of your neck, or how it feels to find a cool breeze on a scorching hot day. This seemingly mundane act that we do thousands of times a day without thinking carries an innate and primal power.

With that thought in your mind, gently blow across the surface of the water and observe the ripples that form. As you blow, repeat these words in your mind:

> *As the breath of nine maidens stokes the cauldron of the other-world, so does my breath stoke the cauldron before me.*

Repeat this eight more times, until nine breaths have passed over the water. Then, place your hands on either side of the cauldron and close your eyes. Feel the power of the water as it pulses with the energies of Annwfn. Picture the ripples your breath has imprinted upon it. Picture them becoming waves on a distant shore, crashing and then receding, drawing inspiration back to you. See how the water seems to glow with this power. Watch as it begins to bubble and spill over the rim, filling the space with the gift of Awen.

When you are ready, open your eyes. Keep the cauldron in the room with you as you go about any creative endeavours of the day. Be open to the many ways inspiration may strike, whether they are what you wanted or in more subtle, surprising ways. When you feel it has fulfilled its purpose, use the water to nourish any plants you may have around the house, that they too may become carriers of divine inspiration.

Once inspiration has struck, take a moment to record how it feels in your Llyfr Cyfrin. Familiarize yourself with this spiritual force and be alert to it in your everyday life. It may be worth dedicating a portion of your Llyfr Cyfrin to recording your experiences whenever the Awen strikes, whether you have summoned it or not.

Ancestors

Most Witches will honour or work with some form of ancestors. Within an animistic worldview, the spirits of humans are no different than those of the trees, rocks, and animals. We are not above them; we exist alongside them, and when we pass on, our spirits continue to exist in another form. Human life may end, but the spirit lingers. This allows us to commune with different forms of ancestors as we would other spirits. There is a caveat, however. Our ancestors exist in the realm of spirit and communicate as other spirits would. It's not like sitting down for a cup of tea with a long-lost relative, more like smelling their perfume around the house as a gentle reminder they are still present.

Of Family

When you mention ancestors, usually the first thing people think of is their family tree: the people that have come before you in the line of descent, who have taught you and raised you. This does not necessarily mean ancestors of blood and DNA, but the people whose culture you carry forward, who have shaped you as you were raised, as they too were shaped by those who came before them. You carry their very essence within you; a tiny part of them is carried in everything you do. This also means that, to a certain point, you can choose your familial ancestors. Chosen family is completely valid, and the way you integrate them into your life means that you carry the lessons of all who have informed them also. Remember, spirit is not physical, and restricting the spirit to physical ties is unnecessarily limiting. When those closest to you pass on, they are as much your ancestors as if they had given birth to you themselves.

Physical ancestry can be particularly challenging for those who have left a cult, since the living generations of their family may well be shunning them. Other things can also complicate physical ancestry. One of my physical ancestors is the preacher Martin Luther, who was hugely influential in the Protestant Reformation and founded the Lutheran Church. I don't think he'd be best pleased that I turned out to be a Witch.

Those intimate family bonds may well be more present within our close circle of friends, and it is this spirit of connection that I mean when I say *family ancestors*. Those people who gave you a sofa to sleep on when you had nowhere else to turn, who always had a place at the table for you when you needed it, and who were always a shoulder to cry on are as much a part of your family tree as anyone else. A wonderful thing about the metaphor of a tree is that a branch from one tree can be grafted onto the trunk of another, fusing them together so they can grow more healthily.

However, if ancestry by blood or adoption is useful to you and gives you a sense of connection, then by all means, connect with those ancestors within your practice. I connect with my direct ancestors and my chosen family in my practice and honour both in rituals to connect with my ancestral stream.

Of Land

The land you live upon has an ancestry all its own: the people who have lived and died there, who walked the paths you walked, who breathed the air you breathe, and whose bones now lie in the earth itself. The land has memory, and it carries the spirit of all who have passed through the initiation of death. The very molecules that compose our bodies may once have belonged to the physical form of others who existed here long before.

The importance of ancestors of place can be seen in the sacredness attached to burial chambers. It is unlikely our direct familial ancestors are buried in these sites, but the people entombed there rest in the very land and landscape we call home, and so are, in a very real way, our ancestors. The memory of their lives is etched into the terrain and landscape, preserved in stone for all of time.

I love the land that I call home. Wales is a beautiful country, and I feel a deep connection to the lore, the legends, and the landscape. Why should that connection be broken when my physical existence ends? Why should that connection have been broken for all those who came before me? The people who were loved by this land still are loved by this land, and simply by being here, I am connected to them.

Of Spirit

These are the ancestors I most often work with in my own practice and who the coven is most likely to honour within ritual. The bards, the cunning folk, the Witches and magical practitioners of the past all paved the way for us to be able to practice in the way we do today. Throughout this book I have referenced historical charms and practices, recorded for us by people long ago. Without their work and efforts, the Craft of a Witch would look very different than it does today. They deserve our gratitude and respect.

This goes beyond those who have walked the magical path before us. One of the most important groups I honour as a queer man is all those who fought hard for the freedom I have to be myself today. I will go into this a little more in the next chapter, but our ancestors of spirit may be any who have influenced and informed our lives today, or who gave so much to pave the way for the rights we now have. These ancestors should never be taken for granted, for without them the world would be a much darker place.

Exercise: A Ritual to Honour the Ancestors

This ritual is about remembering and honouring all those people who have passed on to the spirit realm who matter to us. This includes all those who in some small way have shaped the person we are today, without whose presence on this earth we would not be quite the same. To be a Witch is to be connected, and death does not sever that connection. It may make it more challenging, but the bonds still remain. This ritual honours those bonds and helps maintain that connection. As well as being part of Witchcraft, this exercise can be beneficial to anyone seeking a sense of spiritual connection. It is best carried out at night and is particularly powerful around any of the tair ysbrydnos.

Materials:
- A dark and quiet space
- Some soil from your home or surroundings
- A fireproof surface that you can easily clean
- A candle
- Any objects that remind you of your ancestors (especially those who have recently become ancestors)
- An offering of a drink of your choice
- A bowl into which to pour the offering
- Matches

Directions:
Take a moment to calm your breathing, sitting in a position that is comfortable for you. Allow yourself to simply exist and reflect on the mystery that you are alive. You are here in this moment and in this space. Think of the enormous coincidences that had to occur for you to be exactly who you are right now. Think of the millions of strands of fate that have woven together to culminate in your existence. Tonight, you honour those strands. Tonight, you honour everyone who came before and show them they are remembered.

When you are ready and in a calm and sombre mindset, place the soil you have gathered on the fireproof surface. Place the candle upon the soil and arrange the objects you have gathered nearby in a way that makes sense to you. Strike a match and light the candle, repeating these words as you do so:

> *I light this candle to honour all those who are my ancestors. I offer my gratitude for all who have come before me and who have shaped me. I invite you into this space with me, to be with me and share any wisdom you may wish to pass on. I give you this offering of*

fine drink as a token of my appreciation and ask that you remain
as long as the candle is lit.

Pour the drink into the bowl and place it near the candle. Now allow yourself to be in the space, knowing that the ancestral spirits are present with you. Feel them around you and be alert to any signs or messages they may wish to impart. These may come through any of your senses: a faint voice, visible patterns dancing in the heat of the candle, a familiar scent, the taste of home cooking, or even the sensation of a touch only you could recognise. Sit with the spirits for as long as you wish, allowing yourself to feel whatever it is that you feel, free of any judgment.

When you are ready to conclude the ritual, thank the ancestral spirits in whatever way feels right to you and blow out the candle. Notice that although the flame is gone, the impression it has made on the wax is still there, much as the impression the ancestors have made on you will always be with you. Know that just as you can light the candle whenever you want, so too can you call on those ancestral spirits whenever you need. They are as far away from you as the flame and as easy to call to you as striking a match.

Familiar Spirits

Everyone knows that Witches love black cats. It's one part of the Witch lore that's firmly cemented in popular culture. From Cosmic Creepers in the 1971 movie *Bedknobs and Broomsticks* to Salem in the many adaptations of *Sabrina*, if there's a Witch around, their feline familiar isn't far behind. But familiars are not merely works of fiction. Their origin is in the Witch lore of the past, which has eagerly been taken up by the pop culture of today.

Given the examples discussed, it may surprise you to learn that familiars were not always cats. In fact, they were not truly physical at all, but spirits that accompanied a Witch in a variety of forms and helped them in their workings. The familiar was very important in practising magic, especially in Britain. In fact, the academic Emma Wilby argues that the idea of a familiar appearing to help a magical practitioner was so widespread, we can all recognise it today, not only in Witch lore but in fairy tales. She argues that the supernatural appearances of creatures offering help, such as Rumpelstiltskin or Puss-in-Boots, are drawn from the same lore that informed the familiar encounters historic "Witches" and cunning folk described.[48] When we look at these stories and the folk beliefs, we see a pattern of a spontaneous appearance of a helper in a time of need. These encounters were not subtle; the records we have show a very vivid recollection of the moment the familiar appeared.[49] The spirit would then offer to make a pact with the individual and help them in their magical workings or provide what it was they needed.[50]

The familiar spirit belief could be very regional. For example, in my home area of Germany, one way the familiar spirit appeared was in the form of a being called a *Drak* or *Drache*, meaning dragon.[51] This version of the familiar spirit most often manifested in the form of a ball of fire flying through the night sky, which would enter and leave the house through the chimney. Like other kinds of familiars, the Drak was given offerings to keep it happy, and it would often reside within a kettle. Its main function was to bring food and money to the family that kept it, and it was so notorious that if someone suddenly became rich, people would say they must have a *Drache*. However, the way this spirit operated was a little questionable. It did not generate the treasures it granted to its hosts but left the home at night to take them from the neighbours. It was essentially a spirit thief, stealing from the community for the sake of the individuals that kept it. I draw heavily on this belief in my own practice as a way of connecting to my German culture.

Fairies as Familiar Spirits

Fairies turn up surprisingly often in traditional Witch lore, but defining what, exactly, they are is an incredibly difficult task. If you asked most people today, they would likely describe fairies as dainty little creatures with insect wings, but that is a rather new idea. If you look back further, they appear quite similar to other spirits. The sheer variety of beings that fall under the umbrella of *fairy*

----

48. Emma Wilby, *Cunning Folk and Familiar Spirits: Shamanistic Visionary Traditions in Early Modern British Witchcraft and Magic* (Eastbourne, UK: Sussex Academic Press, 2005), 59.
49. Wilby, *Cunning Folk and Familiar Spirits*, 60.
50. Wilby, *Cunning Folk and Familiar Spirits*, 66.
51. Dillinger, *Magical Treasure Hunting*, 71–72.

also makes describing them rather difficult, and entire books have been written on the subject. However, one form in which fairies seem to pop up rather often is as familiars to magical practitioners of all sorts.

In Welsh lore, the soothsayer Harry Lloyd met with the fairies and received gold from them, much as familiars would enrich their patrons.[52] The accused Scottish Witch Isobel Gowdie confessed to feasting with the fairy king and fairy queen, as well as having a fairy familiar.[53] A cunning man named John Gothray claimed to have been granted powers of healing and knowledge of herbs from the fairies, and that they periodically visited to renew those powers.[54] There are countless other examples, far more than I can discuss here, but the point is that magical practitioners of all sorts have long forged relationships with fairies. These strange creatures are a great example of the shades of grey that Witches may work with. They are not easily described as good or as evil, but are somewhere in between—as likely to help you work magic as to blight you with illness.

As you dig deeper into historic and folkloric Witchcraft, you are likely to encounter many other types of spirit that you can connect with in your practice. Be open to what you find and open to what may appear to you. You may just end up with a familiar of your very own, although fairies may best be avoided.

Elemental Spirits

Most traditions of Witchcraft acknowledge the four classical elements of earth, air, fire, and water. These are the building blocks of all creation, and as such are intimately connected with nature. Anything you can imagine partakes in the elements. They appear across most magical and esoteric traditions, having been developed across millennia. They bridge the gap between physical and spiritual and are a nexus of correspondences waiting to be discovered.

An incredibly potent and important form of spirit life is embodied within these four classical elements. Many traditions of Witchcraft call on these four elemental powers every time they engage in ritual. If you're ever part of an open ritual, you will notice it usually begins by calling the quarters, or the elemental

....

52. Diane Purkiss, *Troublesome Things: A History of Fairies and Fairy Stories* (London: Allen Lane, 2000), 125.
53. Emma Wilby, *The Visions of Isobel Gowdie: Magic, Witchcraft and Dark Shamanism in Seventeenth-Century Scotland* (Eastbourne, UK: Sussex Academic Press, 2010), 77–79.
54. Wilby, *The Visions of Isobel Gowdie*, 244.

spirits associated with each cardinal point. If you've seen the 1996 film *The Craft*, this is portrayed as calling in the watchtowers. Thankfully, these are different watchtowers than the ones I grew up with.

These elemental spirits have an incredibly long history in the practice of magic. The influential alchemist Paracelsus, alive in the sixteenth century, represented the elements as elementals: earth as gnomes, air as sylphs, fire as salamanders, and water as undines. The elements were not merely physical things but embodied by spiritual entities.

The Witch today sees elements in a similar way. Inviting them into a ritual space is calling to a spiritual force, not merely something physical. Though we may represent the elements with physical objects, these are merely symbols of the elements we call to. If you journey deeper into the world of Witchcraft, you will discover just how important the elemental spirits are to the Craft. Virtually every tradition and practice involve them in some way.

Exercise: Experiencing the Elements

The elements of Witchcraft are neither entirely physical nor spiritual. This means that they can be understood a little through the way they manifest physically in the world; we do not need to rely on purely spiritual means. Stop for a moment and think of the image each element conjures up. What springs to mind when you think of fire? How about water? Or air? Or earth? This exercise builds on the fact we all have some basic concept of these elements and invites you to explore it just a little further.

Materials:
- A hot drink of your choice
- A mug made of ceramic or clay

Directions:
Prepare your hot drink in the cup you have selected, taking care not to burn yourself. Allow it to cool until it is comfortable to hold, then sit

comfortably with it. Now take a moment to contemplate the cup and the way a fragment of each element may be embodied in it.

First, notice the heat that comes from the cup. This heat partakes in the element of fire. Notice how it warms your hands and spreads into the surroundings. Focus on that feeling and allow any thoughts that it conjures to surface. Now, start to think a little beyond the physical. When you think of heat and fire, what emotions spring to mind? Perhaps passion? Perhaps anger? Give yourself a moment to explore them. Once you have done so, take a final moment to consider how fire may manifest in other situations. Is there fire in your relationships? How about within you? Sit with whatever comes to mind and experience the element of fire.

Now, turn your attention to the steam of the cup and your breath as you blow on it to cool it. Again, notice how the steam swirls in the air or how the breath flows from your lungs. Allow any thoughts these physical manifestations bring to surface. Now, as you contemplate the element of air, what emotions spring to mind? Perhaps reason and logic are among them. Give yourself a moment to explore. Once you have done so, again take a final moment to consider how air may manifest in other situations. Do your relationships partake in the element of air? Is it present within you? Sit with whatever comes to mind and experience the element of air.

Next, shift your focus to the liquid in the cup. See how it moves and ripples, reacting to every slight movement of your hands and body. Focus on that feeling and allow any thoughts that it conjures to surface. Now, start to think a little beyond the physical. When you think of water, what emotions spring to mind? Perhaps they are all there in a great flood. Give yourself some time to explore this; water is known to be especially emotional. Once you have done so, again take some time to consider where else in life you may partake in the element of water. Take as long as you need and experience the element of water.

Finally, turn your attention to the cup—the grounding receptacle that holds it all together. Notice how without the cup to contain the drink, you would struggle to have a drink at all. Allow yourself to explore the idea of earth as a stable, grounding receptacle. Focus on whatever feeling this may bring to the surface. What emotions may partake in the element of earth? Perhaps reliability? Perhaps being grounded? Give yourself a moment to explore these. Once you are ready, take a moment to consider what other areas of your life may partake in the element of earth. Sit quietly as you conclude and allow yourself to experience the element of earth.

Once you have devoted sufficient time to each of the elements, now comes the most important step: enjoy the drink you have prepared. Anytime you have a hot drink in the future, you can devote a few moments to experiencing the elements if you so wish.

The Spirit of Narrative

In the Sarffes Goch tradition of Witchcraft, we recognise another form of spirit: that which is inherent in narrative. Mythologies, fables, parables, poetry, art, and music all have an animating spirit that carries them into the world. This is apparent in the way many people describe themselves as mere conduits of their art, channelling it into our physical world from the otherworld, or the world of spirit. This idea is firmly rooted in Welsh tradition, embodied in the concept of Awen but also in the idea of the archetypal wizard, Merlin.

Merlin did not begin life as a wizard. His legend is inspired by a Welsh poet and prophet by the name of Myrddin.[55] Poets in Welsh history often served the kings and nobles of the land, singing their praises, recording their genealogy, and creating their legend. The historical Taliesin, for example, recorded praise poetry to king Urien Rheged.[56] Interestingly, the legends of Merlin and Taliesin are intertwined in Welsh lore, with a popular belief being that the spirit of Merlin was reincarnated in the form of Taliesin.[57] Kristoffer Hughes points out that this implies a prophetic spirit incarnating in human form, and

....

55. John K. Bollard, "The Earliest Myrddin Poems," in *Arthur in the Celtic Languages: The Arthurian Legend in Celtic Literatures and Traditions*, eds. Ceridwen Lloyd-Morgan and Erich Poppe (Cardiff: University of Wales Press, 2019), 35–50.

56. Ifor Williams, ed., *Canu Taliesin* (Gwasg Prifysgol Cymru, 1960), xi.

57. Patrick K. Ford, "The Death of Merlin in the Chronicle of Elis Gruffydd," *Viator* 7 (1976): 379–90, https://doi.org/10.1525/9780520331952-014.

it is noteworthy that this spirit manifests in the form of poets.[58] The spoken word carried immense power, able to weave narratives that could strengthen or destroy entire kingdoms. The academic Patrick Ford draws attention to this power, stating that poets wielded "immense and seemingly magical power."[59] He also points out that the power of words spoken in a certain way is demonstrated in the phrase *hocus pocus*. One theory holds that these words originated in the Catholic religious ritual of transubstantiation, when the priest says the words "This is the body," transforming the bread into the literal body of Christ. In Latin, this phrase is "hoc est corpus," and it is not much of a leap to get to hocus pocus from there.[60] The right words spoken at the right time have long been believed to have the power to change the world.

It is no surprise, with this in mind, that the archetypal spirit of inspiration embodied in the Welsh poets was transformed into the archetypal wizard, Merlin. This spirit represents more than just inspiration. Words themselves are magic; they always have been. Reading can be seen as a magical act: strange marks on a page being translated into words in our mind. The ink and paper are literally talking to us in a similar way that animistic cultures might see the natural world speaking to them.[61] Words have the power to change the way we think and to change the very world. But this power relies on the order they are woven into, the narrative that they carry. Or, to put it another way, the spirit that flows through them. It isn't necessarily the words themselves that contain the power. It is something deeper, beyond the marks on a piece of paper.

As you walk the witchy path, you may well hear Pagans of all sorts talking about participating in the myths—that the stories that underpin our practices are lived out in our lives. In a previous chapter, we discussed the story of Taliesin and the way that we can act out that myth when we go through initiation ourselves. It is this deeper component of stories that the coven calls the Narrative Spirit, a living entity we interact with when we connect with our lore. We must allow it to move through us and change us, and then we breathe it out into the world. When we read the Mabinogion, we are not reading dead words on

....
58. Hughes, *From the Cauldron Born*, 210.
59. Ford, *The Celtic Poets*, xxii.
60. Ford, *The Celtic Poets*, xx.
61. David Abram, *The Spell of the Sensuous: Perception and Language in a More-Than-Human World* (New York: Vintage, 2012), 131.

a page, but connecting to the narrative spirit beyond words that bubbles just below the surface.

This is reflected in our practice in that we act out the mythology in ritual, speaking it into being. To truly move us, a narrative spirit must leap off the page and into our very soul. Its spirit must speak to our spirit, which cannot occur in the physical world. One example is that in our elemental invocations in ritual, we represent the four elements in the form of the transformations Ceridwen undertakes as she chases Taliesin. In this way, we connect not just to the elements, inviting them into our ritual space, but also to the very spirit of the tale of Taliesin.

A powerful narrative spirit can also be observed in the history of modern Witchcraft, specifically in the birth of Wicca. One hugely influential figure in the birth of this new religion was Gerald Gardner, and he wanted to teach it to as many people as possible. The only problem was that in the 1940s, Witchcraft was still illegal. The Witchcraft Act was not repealed until 1951. To get around this, Gardner wrote a novel, and in this fiction, he hid the rituals of his Witch religion.[62] Another hugely influential figure in early Wicca was Doreen Valiente, and she records that this book would be handed to prospective initiates as a form of test.[63] The way they responded to the depictions of ritual would reveal if they were suitable for initiation. It wasn't the words themselves that were the test, nor the story. It was the spirit carried in the tale that revealed something deeper and spoke to those who were open to it. Doreen herself received a copy directly from Gardner, and by all accounts, she passed the test.

This power can also be incorporated into a daily practice. A powerful way to interact with this narrative spirit is by immersing ourselves in mythology and allowing it to move through us. But there are subtler ways as well. One of these is creating our own art and allowing the narrative to be expressed through our creativity.

....

62. Hutton, *The Triumph of the Moon*, 224.
63. Valiente, *The Rebirth of Witchcraft*, 39.

Exercise: Channelling the Narrative Spirit

This is a simple exercise to tap into a narrative spirit and draw it into the world, and pairs well with the inspiration exercise presented earlier. It is difficult for facts and figures to convey that spirit because it is present below the surface and thrives on interpretation. Therefore, art of any kind is a great medium to tap into and express it. For me, this usually takes the form of poetry, since I am deeply inspired by the Welsh bardic tradition. However, the exact medium doesn't matter, only that you are comfortable and don't force it.

Materials:
- Whatever you use to create art. For me this is pen and paper.
- Your Llyfr Cyfrin to record the experience

Directions:
Find somewhere comfortable to work and clear your head. This exercise works best if you don't think about it too much. Just allow whatever comes to you to come. Once you are comfortable, repeat these words:

The Awen I sing—from the deep I bring it.[64]

This is a phrase from the middle Welsh poem "Angar Kyfundawt," translated by Kristoffer Hughes. It is an invocation to the very source of inspiration found in Welsh lore. Let it flow through you, and without thinking, begin to create. Allow those less-conscious parts of yourself free rein onto the page or the canvas. There is no way of doing this wrong.

Keep going until the force of inspiration leaves you, then take a moment to look at what you have made. On a surface level, it is nothing more than marks or colours on paper, but is there more to it? Is there something deeper? Can you sense a spirit running through it, something that has flowed through you to birth this piece into being?

---

64. Kristoffer Hughes, *The Book of Celtic Magic: Transformative Teachings from the Cauldron of Awen* (Woodbury, MN: Llewellyn Publications, 2014), 48.

If you feel moved to, record in your Llyfr Cyfrin what it felt like to channel this piece into being while the feelings are still fresh. You may wish to store your creation in the book alongside it as well.

If inspiration does not strike when you first sit to perform this exercise, do not be disheartened. The spirit of narrative is not ours to command; we can only invite it. Come back to this exercise another time, and you may find it visits more easily.

Communing with the Spirit World

After this quick tour through the world of spirits, one question remains: How can we interact with these complex beings? Spirits are not physical, even though they may be able to incarnate physically depending on who you ask. Going out with them for a coffee and a catch-up seems unlikely.

Within the cult, spirit communication was one sided. You could pray to God, but he didn't talk back. Spiritual revelation had already happened, and you could look to the Bible for any answers you needed. The spirits of the Witch are thankfully a little chattier, just as long as you learn their language.

Spirits are subtle beings who speak in symbols and synchronicity. There may be times you get a vivid and obvious message, but most often they are a gentle presence at the edge of consciousness, appearing in dream and symbol. We discussed one way of communing with them in the ancestor ritual presented earlier. Being alert to the subtle ways they interact and open to the meaningfulness of ritual is essential. If you believe an experience is mundane, you will make it mundane. The spirits cannot communicate with someone who is not open to it. Anything they say will be dismissed, like a ringing phone that is never answered.

Since symbols are the natural language of spirit, divination is a powerful way to communicate with them. It is also a great way to learn to trust your intuition, making you more open to spirit communication in the future. I will end this chapter with an easy exercise to begin opening up to spirit communication.

Exercise: A Daily Tarot Card

· ·

One of the most well-known divinatory methods today are tarot cards. Reading tarot is a complex process that can take a long time to learn, with multiple levels of meaning present in any reading. The purpose of this exercise is not to learn the ins and outs of reading the cards but tapping into their use as a communication tool loaded with symbolism, as well as training our intuition to be alert to the subtle ways spirits may choose to converse. As such, I will not be describing the traditional meanings of the cards. In fact, being glued to those meanings can actually be detrimental to this exercise.

Before looking for messages for others, it can be helpful to practice by reading for yourself, seeing what messages the cards have for you and how they may manifest in your day.

Materials:

• Any deck of tarot cards
• A table
• *Optional:* Your Llyfr Cyfrin to record your pull

Directions:

This exercise is best performed in the morning so that you can be alert to the symbolism throughout the day; however, it can be performed at any time.

Shuffle your deck of cards until you feel they have been shuffled enough. Place them on the table and connect with your intuition to decide if you should cut the deck. If you feel drawn to, then do it and pull the top card of the deck; if not, pull the top card of the shuffled deck. Place it face down in front of you. Take a moment to go within and see if you can intuit which card you have pulled. This is unlikely, but simply taking a moment to be in that mindset can help with the rest of the working. We are going beyond logic and reason into the realm of symbol and spirit. Anything is possible here.

Once you are ready, turn the card over. First, see what feeling the card evokes. Does the card speak to you in some way or trigger a strong emotion? Does it remind you of anything going on in your life right now?

Once you have allowed the emotion of the card to inform your reading, take in the art and symbols. Is there anything that speaks to you? Anything that immediately catches your eye? Do the colours have any resonance, or even the shapes?

Now, look at any words or numbers on the card. Do they have an immediately apparent meaning? Is there something in your life right now that corresponds to what you see?

Finally, the most difficult step: putting it all together. Take the card as a whole. Search for the meaning in it. Feel free to bring any knowledge you have of tarot to this step, or look up the meanings of the cards in the accompanying booklet if you wish. Does anything jump out as relating to anything you are experiencing right now? Is there a story being told that fits your life? It's okay if not; it may not be referring to something that has already happened. Find a meaning in the symbols that makes sense to you, and if you wish, record it in your Llyfr Cyfrin. Return to it at a later point and see whether it makes more sense to you then.

This may be a little difficult at first. Society tries to drag us away from symbol, spirit, and interpretation. As with learning any skill we have not used before, it can take time to warm up to it. Repeat this exercise as often as you wish (perhaps daily), and with time, you will feel more confident and comfortable with your skills and interpretation. It is likely you will experience some rather profound "coincidences." Remember them; they are particularly worth noting down.

Getting Comfortable with Spirit

As you become more comfortable with the art of interpretation, you will also become more comfortable with spirit communication. You will learn what the cards mean to you and how they answer your questions. Use this knowledge. When you feel the presence of a spirit, ask it questions. Pull a tarot card (or spread if that feels right) to glean the answer. Pay particularly close attention to your emotions and how they might help inform your reading. Interpret the answers and have confidence that spirits will speak to you in the language of symbol. You just need to be open to it.

Chapter 7
A Nature-Based Faith

Autumn is my favourite time of year. It's the season when I feel most connected to the world around me. That's not to say the other seasons aren't great, but to me, autumn is really special. You might think it's because the leaves look so beautiful or everything suddenly tastes of pumpkin spice, and that certainly helps. But the main reason I love this season is because every autumn I go out foraging with my dad.

We have our little hidden spots that few people know about and keep a close eye on the weather to pick the optimal times to venture out. Once the stars align, we get up early and set off. We clamber through the forest, the dense pines snatching at our clothes, and hunt for the treasures hidden deep within. The wicker basket always comes home filled with mushrooms: porcinis, oyster mushrooms, and all manner of boletes, in addition to the blackberries, bilberries, and raspberries. For weeks after, we use the dried mushrooms in cooking, and the wild bilberry muffins are to die for.

To me, this is a great time bonding with my dad and being out in nature, but for him it was a necessity. He was raised in East Germany, behind the Iron Curtain. Food was not easy to come by, and a varied diet almost impossible. If you wanted anything extra, you had to learn what nature had to offer. When society failed to provide, nature never stopped.

Every year it makes me stop and think how much we take for granted. What craving can't be fixed with a quick trip to the shops? The convenience is great, but it comes at the cost of a separation from nature. Many of us don't even know where our food comes from. Life has become incredibly urbanised, to the point that we don't need to negotiate with nature; the supermarkets are there to do that for us.

The problem is that we *need* the natural world. Beyond the practical necessities of growing food and oxygenating the air, it fills a spiritual need. For millennia we lived in harmony with the green, in the caves and forests. We cannot close ourselves off from it now, retreating into a world of bricks and steel. Scientists have shown that contact with nature is incredibly beneficial for our mental health, even if they don't fully know why yet.[65] Our very bodies know we still need it, much as our ancestors did. Some deep-seated part of us craves being in the wild green yonder.

Witchcraft exists, in part, because of this need. A defining part of the Craft is a focus on nature. In fact, modern Paganism is sometimes called "the Green religion."[66] Witchcraft emphasizes a reciprocal relationship with the world around us. If we take care of Mother Earth, then she will take care of us. Our planet is not simply a resource to consume, but a living, breathing entity with whom we are in a symbiotic relationship. I would go as far as to argue that this is the single most important part of Paganism and Witchcraft. Connection to nature is a matter of survival, and a spiritual system that emphasizes this is essential. Magic is great and performing ritual is fun, but a return to nature is about the very survival of our home. This may be the most important thing Paganism and Witchcraft can offer the world.

But how, exactly, does Witchcraft focus on nature? How do we work with Mother Earth and protect her? And how does this differ to life in fundamentalist Christianity?

From Death Cult to Living Faith

In the cult, nature was only an expression of God. We could learn about his qualities from it, but nature was not alive itself. It was a work of art, but nothing beyond that. We can see how little it truly mattered to the Christian God in the story of the flood.[67] If animals had spirits and agency, then it would have

65. Rachel M. Nejade, Daniel Grace, and Leigh R. Bowman. "What Is the Impact of Nature on Human Health? A Scoping Review of the Literature." *Journal of Global Health* 12 (2022): https://www.doi.org/10.7189/jogh.12.04099.
66. Vivianne Crowley, *Phoenix from the Flame: Pagan Spirituality in the Western World* (London: Thorsons, 1995), 32.
67. Genesis 6–9.

been a genocide. But in this cosmology, the creator was the only thing that mattered, and he could do whatever he wanted with his creation.

The flood was not to be the only genocide, however. The cult also taught that the world as we know it today was soon going to end. The events around us proved we were in the "last days." They had been teaching this since the start of the twentieth century, and yet still everyone believed it. I really thought I wouldn't make it through primary school, that the world would end long before high school was even on the horizon. Then I believed that I would never graduate. Every single year, the end was coming next year. It was imminent, and you best hope you were righteous enough to survive it. Of course, righteousness meant giving enough time and money to the cult. You had to earn your salvation every day. They were very clear that it wasn't a case of "once saved, always saved." You had to make sure you were doing enough today, because whatever you did yesterday was already irrelevant. This was used as a massive source of fear to keep people from leaving. The stakes were your life; being wrong meant imminent destruction.

They really pushed this genocidal, apocalyptic fantasy. Every single person who wasn't in the cult was going to be killed by God. We had to preach so everyone got the chance to join, but if they didn't listen, then that was reason enough for them to be sentenced to death. It didn't matter how good a person you were; if you weren't in the cult, you deserved the death sentence. I remember people picking out houses they wanted to live in after Armageddon once the current occupants had been destroyed.

Even worse if you happened to be a dreaded "apostate," someone who actively spoke out against cult doctrine. Someone like me. They had whole talks relishing the day apostates would get what was coming to them and the birds would pick the flesh off their corpses. The members are taught to anticipate and celebrate the day God will step in and kill me. As far as they are concerned, all I deserve is destruction.

It saddens me to my core that I used to believe that. Now, I live each day to the fullest that I can. Some days that means simply admiring the dandelion that has pushed its way through the cracks in the tarmac, other days it is a long walk in the forest, and still others it is going out to work ritual with my coven.

Finding Witchcraft was discovering a path that actually values life. Worth is not earned; beings have value simply because they are alive, and *all* life has value. The practice of Witchcraft is embodied spirituality; spiritual and physical experience are not separate. We do not need to wait until death to experience the Divine.

If we value nature as Witches, then we also have to value ourselves. We are part of the universal whole and recognise that all life is sacred. Ours matters just as much as any other. And *this* life matters, not some afterlife we may never even reach. Right now, we are having a physical experience and enjoying the physical world, and that is worth appreciating. Exploring and appreciating nature is not just a spiritual pursuit. Walking in the shade of a tree or feeling the sun's warmth on your skin, smelling the first roses of the year as they bloom, or hearing the crunch of snow under your boots—each and every one of these is an experience to treasure.

However, I've learned that the most difficult part of appreciating life is that if you need help, you have to reach out. If life is sacred, then self-care is also sacred. I have needed the people around me more times than I can count. There is great strength in asking for help; it's the opposite of giving up. Don't guilt yourself into feeling okay or shame yourself into keeping quiet. Sometimes appreciating nature means taking care of you.

Pan: The Green Jesus

One way that the nature-based part of Witchcraft is embodied is in the figure of the ancient Greek god Pan. I'll discuss the gods in a little more depth in a future chapter. For now, it is enough to know that many traditions of Witchcraft honour divinity in the form of a goddess and a god, who both go by many names. For the god, one of the most popular is Pan. He is not *the* Horned God, but often associated with him.

Pan is often seen as the guardian of wild, untamed nature. He is the god that lives in the heart of the forest, making the wild places grow and protecting the many beings that call it home. Professor Ronald Hutton describes the reclaiming of Pan by Paganism as turning him into the "Green Jesus."[68] Where Christianity was focused on civilization and building empires, Pan was the keeper of the natural world. In the eyes of the church, this made him the devil.

....
68. Hutton, *The Triumph of the Moon*, 45.

My own journey into Witchcraft helped me see just how different the attitude to nature is in the Craft than in Christianity. While my initial interest was because of the freedom I found here, the focus on harmony with the world around me was a huge factor in making me stay. Within the doctrine of the cult, it was good to observe the animals and plants for what they could teach us about him, but they were not alive or ensouled themselves. In fact, creation was there for us to use. We were above the natural world, privileged and chosen by God and not equal to it. We were told not to worry about environmental concerns because God would soon step in and fix everything. I even knew people who wouldn't recycle because they didn't have the time to waste when they could be preaching. Since God would fix it anyway, why bother?

The idea of nature being divine was an entirely alien concept to me, but one I eagerly explored. It just makes sense. If there wasn't a holy book to tell you so, why would you believe yourself more important than any other life on this planet? After all, you rely on every other piece of the cycle to sustain your very life. Everything is in perfect balance, and we are a part of that balance. Except we are the ones threatening that balance. If anything, we are the only part of nature that isn't doing its job properly and thereby threatening the survival of everything. Humans are the ones that need to change, and a return to nature is the change that is needed. We need to go green, spirituality and all.

Turning to the Green Jesus is not a matter of worshipping Pan. It is simply an acknowledgment of the divinity inherent in nature, and a more mindful approach to our interactions with the world around us.

Animism

What we believe has an enormous impact on the way we coexist with the world around us. If we believe we have dominion over nature, then nothing will stop us from ripping apart the earth for any resources that might benefit us. If we believe nonhuman life is sacred, or even that it is equal to us, we are far more likely to approach the world with reverence and respect.

Animism is simply a way of seeing the world. It is about distinguishing between persons and objects. Are humans the only people in the world and everything else simply an object to use? Or are there nonhuman persons who we can communicate with? An animist sees the world as filled with human and nonhuman persons. What complicates it a little further is that to see something as a person does not necessarily have to be a spiritual thing. In fact, in describing "new animism," Professor Graham Harvey states that in recognising personhood "neither material form nor spiritual or mental faculties are definitive."[69] Even completely non-spiritual people can have an animistic worldview. The defining traits of animism are respect and reciprocity.[70] We approach the world around us as alive and capable of initiating or reciprocating communication.

The majority of modern Witches identify as animists. However, to most of us, this animistic belief is spiritual. We believe we are one part of a community of spirit beings—that the whole world is alive and we can interact with it. In fact, this belief is integral to the way many of us practice magic. We draw on the spiritual qualities of nonhuman persons to aid us (with their consent of course). But how does a nonhuman person give that consent?

It is this spirit within all things that allows us to communicate with them. Everything on this planet and beyond it has a spirit, and that includes humans. When we communicate with nature, it is not like having a conversation around the dinner table. Words have no meaning. Our spirit connects directly with the spirit of whomever we are in contact with. As we have previously touched upon, much of this communication will happen through symbols and visions, or through synchronicity. These are the languages through which the spirit makes itself heard. However, when introducing ourselves to a being, there is no harm in saying hello. We are used to using words to communicate, and so it puts us into the frame of mind that we are engaged in meaningful conversation. Just don't expect them to necessarily say the words back.

In *The Spell of the Sensuous*, author David Abram takes this one step further. In discussing the power of the spoken word, of language and of writing, he says, "As nonhuman animals, plants, and even 'inanimate' rivers once spoke to our tribal ancestors, so the 'inert' letters on the page now speak to us! *This is a form of animism that we take for granted, but it is animism nonetheless—as mysterious as a talking stone.*"[71]

I think this is a really interesting way to think about the spirit innate in all things and the way that spirit can teach us. We all believe in communication

....
69. Graham Harvey, *Animism: Respecting the Living World* (New York: Columbia University Press, 2005), xxiii, xvii.
70. Harvey, *Animism*, 46
71. Abram, *The Spell of the Sensuous*, 131.

beyond the verbal—that these scrawls and symbols on the page right now can transmit information to you. But you have to learn how to read and translate those symbols before they make any sense. So too with spirit communication do we have to learn to interpret and translate. It is a skill many of us have lost, since it is not often used. But opening yourself up to communing with the spirits is simply learning a new way to communicate with beings that have much to teach.

Exercise: Listening to the Trees

Communing with the nonhuman persons can be as simple as meditating under a tree and opening ourselves up to the spirit inherent in it. Some of the major aspects of my practice have come from simply sitting in a country park near my home. There is an old oak tree that I regularly visit, and I have spent many wonderful hours under their branches. There are also some redwoods standing proud and tall. They aren't as chatty, but they still have a moment for me here and there. This exercise encourages you to do the same thing.

Materials:
• Yourself

Directions

Go out into the local area and find a tree that calls to you. That itself will give you an idea of the personhood of the trees—you can feel the different energy they exude. Once you have found a friendly one, just sit with them. Place your hand on their trunk if you want to. Introduce yourself; tell them you are their neighbour. Then just sit and listen. Be alert to anything they may wish to share. Return as often as you can, and feel the relationship grow. Just as with any other friendship or acquaintance, it takes time to build, but you will certainly feel it building. I find it good practice to introduce myself to as many of the trees in my local area as I can. They have much wisdom to share.

The Genius Loci

Do you have a place that is special to you? Is there somewhere you can go when you are feeling down, and simply being there is enough to soothe you somehow? Or perhaps you have a place you cannot stand to be. If you are there too long, your skin starts to itch and your whole body craves escape. It is not necessarily the physical characteristics that make you feel that way, more the feel of the space. Everywhere seems to have an energy all its own: Deep, dark forests that beckon with a promise of untold mysteries. Beaches of golden sand that seem to stretch to infinity and drain the stress out through the bottom of your feet. An ancient bookshop that demands silence, even when you are stood in it completely alone. Every place seems to have its own spirit.

The ancient Romans called this spirit of place the *genius loci*, and they certainly believed it was very real. They believed every person had a genius, or a spirit, that resided within them. Interestingly, this belief was sometimes fused with the idea of a guardian angel.[72] The belief in a genius loci remains decidedly more Pagan; however, you can imagine it as the guardian angel of a space if that helps. Rather than the spirit attached to a person, it is the spirit attached to a place and is intrinsically animistic. The previous examples demonstrate the distinct personalities a place may have, and it is interesting to note that people may have a different response to the same space. The energy we feel is the relationship we have with the genius loci, and this is something we can build and cultivate.

When interacting with the genius loci, it is always best to be respectful. Remember, you are entering their space as a guest. Good manners will take you a long way. If you are patient and forge a good working relationship with this spirit, you will learn a great deal. They have resided in the land far longer than you have experienced physical existence and have many secrets to share. Above all else, a relationship with the genius loci will grant you a strong sense of connection and spiritual community with the land. This, in turn, will motivate you to continue in your Craft and make you likely to try and protect these natural spaces as much as you can.

....

72. Brian Copenhaver, *The Book of Magic: From Antiquity to the Enlightenment* (Bungay, England: Penguin UK, 2015), 366.

A simple offering you can make to the genius loci is birdseed. This nourishes the local wildlife without doing any harm. Another way to honour the space and offer something is by removing any litter others may have left. Remember, you are a physical being in their space, and performing a physical service like litter picking offers something they cannot do for themselves. However, it is best to wear gloves if you do this, and don't pick up anything that may cause you harm, such as broken glass or jagged metal. Use your discernment so that you don't harm yourself. This helps build a strong relationship with the local spirits.

Bioregionalism

While a focus on nature is an important part of Witchcraft, there is also the question of which nature to focus on. In his book *The Crooked Path*, author Kelden discusses the concept of bioregionalism in Witchcraft. Rather than looking far afield and importing materials, we look to our local landscape to connect.[73] It involves learning the rhythm of your bioregion—the climate, the flora, the fauna, the water, and even the soul. This means becoming familiar with the natural world around us. It gives us a strong sense of community with the place we call home and allows us to deeply connect with the genius loci. Bioregionalism as a philosophy is not unique to Witchcraft. It is about seeing the world not as constrained by imaginary lines and borders, but naturally divided by the landscape itself. A bioregional approach to Witchcraft emphasises the plants, animals, and climate of your home region as the most important sources of magic, offering a deeper sense of connection than importing tools and ingredients from afar that are not rooted in your land.

An example of this that the coven utilises is resin. Rather than relying on frankincense or other imported resins, we will often go to the local forests and gather what the pine trees naturally produce. Not only does the pine resin smell amazing, but it brings the energy and magic of our home region directly into our practice. This approach naturally combines with the focus on culture in Witchcraft to create a practice that gives you a deep sense of connection to where you are.

....

73. Kelden, *The Crooked Path: An Introduction to Traditional Witchcraft* (Woodbury, MN: Llewellyn Publications, 2020), 141.

Eco-Spirituality and Ethics

As much as a return to nature is joyous and celebratory, there is also far more to it. Being conscious of the environment and doing as little harm as possible is an essential part of Witchcraft. We cannot claim to work with the spirits of nature on the one hand while contributing to their destruction on the other. This is especially true when it comes to spellwork or practicing ritual. Without preaching too much, there are basic things we can all do to make our spirituality more environmentally friendly. This is far from an exhaustive list, but if you choose to practice Witchcraft, I encourage you to be mindful of them from the start.

Offerings

First, all offerings must be biodegradable and not harm the environment. Offering anything made of plastic that won't degrade for millennia and may harm the local wildlife is a big no. One thing I've seen mentioned in many spaces is people tying ribbons around trees as part of their workings. This isn't usually a problem if they are made of biodegradable materials and tied loosely so as not to choke the tree. However, often nylon ribbons are used. These do not degrade and will stay on the tree forever, especially if tied tightly. As the tree grows, the nylon will cut into the bark and can cause injury. Think about the materials you use when leaving anything as an offering. Also consider if any food offerings could be dangerous to the local wildlife. We don't want to accidentally poison the very creatures we are trying to connect with.

Crystals

Crystals can be a bit of a buzzword in Witchcraft. However, it's important to think about how crystals are sourced. Are your crystals coming from ethical, sustainable sources? Or are they coming from mines ripped deep into the earth that exploit the cheapest labour possible? One way of ensuring that your crystals are ethically sourced and not harming the environment is to gather them yourself. Quartz is an extremely abundant mineral and can be found in most places. One added bonus is the sense of connection you will feel with tools you gather for yourself.

Litter

An extremely simple thing is to not leave litter when going to ritual sites or visiting nature. Take anything you use home with you and recycle anything you can. Dropping litter is extremely bad manners and a surefire way to ruin any relationship you may be trying to build with the genius loci. Imagine if someone walked into your home with mud-covered boots and refused to clean up after themselves. How likely would you be to welcome them into your space again? When we are out in nature, we are guests of the spirits present and should act accordingly.

Eco-spirituality doesn't mean you have to be an intense activist, but it does ask you to be mindful of the impact your practice may be having on the landscape and environment. If we value our connection to nature, we will want to do the least harm possible.

Celebrating Nature

One of my favourite witchy experiences each year is visiting the Clun Green Man Festival. My partner is a folk Witch whose practice is rooted in the Welsh Marches, and he introduced me to this wonderful festival soon after we met.

At the festival, the story of the Green Man is reenacted as a personification of the changing seasons. It showcases the battle between the light and dark halves of the year. This is a beautiful way of connecting to nature and introducing that connection to an ever-growing group of people. It also shows that the desire to connect with nature and honour the turning of the seasons isn't unique to Witchcraft. The Green Man festival attracts hundreds of people from all walks of life and is only one of many like it. When we participate in these kinds of events, harvest festivals, May Day parades, and the many other customs that recognise the changing of the seasons, we connect with our culture and the natural world in a profound way.

The Wheel of the Year

One significant part of Witchcraft that connects us to the world around us and the cycle of nature is the Wheel of the Year. Even people who know very little about Witchcraft have often heard of it.

There is much debate about where these celebrations started or how ancient they are, but I believe that misses the point. Honouring the changing seasons means a lot to Witches today. It works for us, grants us that feeling of connection regardless of which festivals we acknowledge. More importantly, it helps us find community with our fellow practitioners and with nature.

The cult was obsessed with the Pagan origins of celebrations in order to condemn them as evil, but again they missed the point. It doesn't matter how Christmas started if *today* it brings people together to celebrate and be joyous. If it is relevant today and works for you personally, then it is completely valid. That knowledge makes these festivals all the more important to me.

It can also be very powerful to incorporate the festivals and celebrations that mean something to you personally. If something from a previous faith made sense to you or made you joyful, that's not something you have to abandon. The Wheel of the Year you celebrate represents *you*. If it makes you feel connected and joyful, then it's perfect. Reclaiming what matters to you is perfectly valid.

If you choose to continue practicing Witchcraft, it's helpful to remember that you are not a Witch because of the festivals you observe. Remember, these are celebrations, not obligations, and nothing bad will happen if you miss one.

The eight major sabbats many Witches recognise are as follows:

Imbolc: February 1–2, beginning of spring. Also known as Saint Brigid's Day.

Ostara: The Spring Equinox, usually falling between March 19–21. This one can be a little controversial. Some believe it is the origin of Easter, but there is no real evidence for that.

Beltane: May 1, also known as May Day. Beltane is an incredibly important celebration to me, fusing many streams of my path. In German lore, this is also known as *Walpurgisnacht*.

Litha: Traditionally observed June 20–21, and also known as Midsummer. Litha falls on the Summer Solstice, the longest day of the year.

Lughnasadh/Lammas: August 1. This sabbat celebrates the beginning of harvest season.

Mabon: September 22–23. This sabbat celebrates the Autumn Equinox.

Samhain: October 31–November 1. This is an observation of the end of harvest season and the transition into the dark half of the year.

Yule: December 21–22. This sabbat celebrates the Winter Solstice.

As you may have noticed, these festivals all have to do with what the seasons are up to. They recognise solar events, like the longest day, or harvest celebrations. They are commonly observed outdoors.

These apply mainly in the Northern Hemisphere, and even then, they vary from place to place. The point of the Wheel of the Year is to connect you with the seasons and the nature wherever you are. This is where bioregionalism is important again; all these festivals can be adapted to work for your corner of the world.

There are also cultural differences and other celebrations you may want to observe. Saints' days may be popular in your area, or more emphasis placed on one festival than another. For example, in Germany it is the twelve days of Christmas, known as *die zwölften*, that are particularly magical. They span the period between December 25 and January 6 and have all manner of legends and folklore surrounding them, including being the time when Frau Holle would be most active. As a result, this time of the year takes on a special significance to me, as it ties me back to my culture and heritage.

Magic with the Natural World

A fun way of incorporating nature into a Witchcraft practice is to directly include it in your magic. There are a few simple ways this can be done, which I will discuss here. Again, these are simply a little taste of how a practice can look, and I encourage you to try them.

Weather Magic

In this increasingly urban world, it can be difficult to get into nature. However, there is one part of nature that we can all connect with wherever we are. No matter how high or how wide we build, we will never escape the weather. I know, I'm doing the cliché thing of a British person discussing the weather. But weather magic is a powerful way of connecting to the world around you and bringing your awareness to nature. Collecting storm water, imbuing your working with sunlight, or simply appreciating the sensation of a gentle breeze—all are wonderful ways to engage with the natural world a little more fully.

Exercise: Knotting the Wind

In the past, Witches who lived in coastal regions would sometimes make a living by selling the wind to sailors. They would capture the wind in knots and instruct them to undo said knots if their ship was stuck at sea. A mighty wind would then be conjured, steering them to safe harbour.

Materials:
• A length of twine or string

Directions:
Wait for a windy day. Once it appears, go outside into the wind or sit near a window. (Obviously only do this if it is safe; very strong winds should be avoided.) Now, take a moment to ground and connect to the element of air. Feel the breeze pass over your skin. Feel the way it moves into your lungs, filling your blood with oxygen. Notice how you breathe out, giving carbon dioxide back to the air. There is no barrier between you and the wind—you are as one, locked in a symbiotic exchange.

Focus on this thought, and channel the power you find into the twine in your hands. Feel it pulse with the energy of the air—the same energy that flows through your veins. When you are confident you can feel this power, speak the following words and knot the rope (using whatever knot you prefer):

By my knot the wind's restrained,
Until I wish it be unchained.
With each knot its power stored,
Until I loose this magic cord.

Repeat this twice more for a total of three knots. Then, if ever you have need of the wind, undo the knots in the sequence you created them. The wind will be stronger depending on how many you undo, so best to undo them one at a time.

A Witch may work magic with all manner of weather, and it can be fun to explore if you continue on this path.

The Moon

In addition to the weather, connecting with the moon can be a powerful way to bring nature into your practice, even if you struggle to get into green space. Witches have long been associated with the moon. An awareness of the moon phases tunes you in to one of the cycles of nature. Many of the festivals of the Wheel of the Year are about what the moon is up to. This also gives you a way to use the power of nature in the form of moon water.

Exercise: Creating Moon Water

I'll admit, when I first heard about the concept of moon water, I was a little sceptical. However, I now believe this is an incredibly powerful way of tuning in to nature and using those energies to consecrate. Making something sacred essentially means setting it apart for a holy purpose, and if we can imbue it with spiritual properties, then even better.

Materials:

- A transparent container (preferably glass)
- Water
- *Optional:* Herbs, ethically sourced crystals, or anything else you may wish to add (however, do not place crystals in the water)

Directions:

Making moon water couldn't be easier. Simply fill a transparent container with water. A glass bottle or jar works really well. Then, on the night of the full moon, leave it outside in the moonlight. You may want to add some form of written charm or some herbs or other ingredients, but that isn't necessary. The value of moon water is that it makes you think about what the moon is up to. How many people actually know when the full moon is, or what properties it brings? It also draws on the powerful spiritual properties of the moon to set your water apart. We know the physical effects the moon has on the tides, and the spiritual effects are equally potent. You can use this water in whatever way you see fit in your magical practice. It is also great to use alongside any of the other exercises in this book that use water as a material.

Stones and Spirits

Another fun way to work magic in an animistic worldview is allowing the spirits of nature to carry your worries for you. If you've had a bad day and desperately need to off-load, then living in an inspirited world leaves many options.

Exercise: A Worry Stone

This exercise connects with the spirit inherent in a simple pebble. It allows you to leave your cares and concerns with the stone, trusting it to carry them for you.

Materials:
- A pebble
- An open body of water

Directions:
I find this simple working is best carried out on the beach or the shore of a large lake. Find a pebble that you feel a connection with. Pick it up and recognise the spirit within it. Take a moment to really connect in whatever way feels best to you. Once you have done so, lift the pebble to your face and whisper your cares and concerns to it. Trust it to hold them and to ground you. Now, offer the same courtesy to the spirit. Leave space to hear whatever it may wish to say to you.

Once this exchange is complete, ask permission from the stone to cast it into the water, along with the worries that were burdening you. If permission is not given, simply return it to the ground where you found it. Either way, this simple interaction is sure to make you feel at least a little better.

Be Here Now

Since salvation is not an important concept in Witchcraft, the present moment becomes the most important thing. We aren't rushing to some far-off future or stuck in some long-lost past. The present moment is the most essential thing. Presence is an important part of ritual in the tradition of the coven, and this is reinforced by the expression "Be here now." Those simple words are part of every ritual we undertake and are profoundly meaningful. Whatever is going on in life, the moment of ritual peels it all away. When you immerse yourself fully, you gain the full benefit that ritual can bring.

In addition to the request to "be here now," ritual will often contain a guided meditation. This serves a twofold purpose. It helps connect you to your own higher self and opens you up to any spiritual messages that may be coming through, while also rooting you in the moment and the experience of ritual.

Keep in mind that meditation is not just for Witches. This is a practice we share with many spiritual systems, as well as the secular medical world. The benefits of meditation are widely recognised, and making it a part of your regular practice can help you tune in to your body and tune in to being present.

Strangely, meditation was strictly condemned in the cult I left, being seen as a way of connecting with the demons. I had to work on overcoming that fear before I could start my own daily practice. Be kind to yourself, and sit with any difficult feelings you might have. Stressing yourself out over meditation will have the opposite effect. Be gentle and curious, approaching it in a way that feels right to you.

If you begin a regular practice, never feel guilty if you miss a session or don't meditate as often as you want. The practice will be here whenever you are ready. Guilt will just make it more difficult to be present when you do have the time and energy. I believe the cult condemned meditation because they didn't want people to be present, but to be so busy and so anxious about the future that they never stopped to be in the moment. That risked them noticing the lies of the doctrine. If they stopped worrying about the future, they were more difficult to control. Cults have a vested interest in keeping you anxious.

Exercise: A Basic Meditation

Meditation plays an important role in Witchcraft because it helps you get into the state of presence. It's not about emptying the mind or being intensely aware of some thought or feeling. It is simply about bringing your awareness into the current moment, about being here and allowing yourself to simply be. You can imagine it like an adjustable torch. If the torch of your awareness is usually set to a wide beam, illuminating all your surroundings, meditation is like focusing it to a spotlight. We focus the spotlight of our consciousness on the here and now rather than being distracted by the past and future.

One of the easiest ways to approach meditation is simply through breathing. We all do it every second of every day, but it happens on autopilot. Something rather profound happens when we draw our attention to it.

Materials:
• Your body and your breath

Directions:
To begin this exercise, find somewhere comfortable to sit. However you feel most comfortable is ideal, but try and keep your back straight without tensing up. Let your hands fall comfortably by your sides, and let yourself relax. Pay attention to your body: how it touches the floor, how the breeze in the room might feel passing over your skin. Tune in to the feeling of sitting and being embodied.

When you are feeling relaxed and ready, turn your attention to your breathing. It's something you do thousands of times a day without noticing, but really draw your attention to it. Don't change anything; just make yourself aware. Notice how the air moves into your lungs, passing through your nose on the way. Notice how it feels filling your chest as it rests there for just a moment. Notice how it leaves your body ready for the next breath in. Focus on that rhythm and just observe it for a moment. Keep your attention on the cycle of your breath.

You may feel your thoughts start to wander. That's completely fine. Do not judge yourself for them. Just gently bring yourself back to your breathing like you might lead a child by the hand. It's natural for the mind to wander, and you're not doing anything wrong. As you meditate more often, you may notice your mind wander less as you become accustomed to the feeling of presence.

Stay in this state of awareness for a few minutes, gently bringing yourself back to your breathing whenever you wander. Once you feel deeply relaxed, bring yourself back to the room.

This is an exercise you can repeat as often as you wish to. I encourage you to try it at least once, as it helps understand the feeling of presence I refer to in other parts of this book.

Once you are comfortable with this basic meditation, then you can incorporate the energy of the natural world into it. Rather than focusing on your breathing, go outside and focus on the feeling of the breeze on your skin or the sound as it rustles through the trees. You can incorporate this basic form of meditation into most aspects of life, and a meditative nature walk can be a great way to connect with your surroundings.

The Benefits of Nature

There is so much we gain from the natural world. Being more immersed in nature gives us a better perspective on life. We realise how small we are compared to the great forest, how nature takes care of her own with the natural cycles. Our problems don't disappear when we reconnect with nature, but they seem smaller and more manageable somehow.

This is something I recognised long before I became a Witch. Whenever I would feel overwhelmed or anxious, or if I was just having a particularly bad day, I would go to my local park and sit among the trees. I would often go in the middle of the night when I was struggling to sleep. I have vivid memories of moonlit nights so bright that the moon cast a shadow, and nights spent among the oak trees and healing my soul. After I left the cult and was struggling to transition into life on the outside, I would spend entire days there just being among the stillness of nature. To this day, I visit the same park to work magic. I feel an incredibly strong connection with the spirits that offered me healing when I needed it most.

There are many other ways that Witchcraft connects an individual practitioner to the world around them. Nature is the green and beating heart of the Craft, and that is expressed in countless ways. If you continue your journey into Witchcraft, you are likely to find your own ways to connect. Record them in your Llyfr Cyfrin. If you want to, share them with others. Learn what methods work for them. Continue immersing yourself in this wide, green world, and your Craft will be richer for it.

Chapter 8
The Queerness of Witchcraft

I was twelve years old when someone first asked me if I was gay. I'd been allowed unsupervised internet time, and my browsing history had raised some eyebrows. Of course, like any self-respecting twelve-year-old, I tried to blame my brother, but when that didn't work, the question came: "Do you think you might be gay?" I was horrified. Of course I wasn't gay. I couldn't be. God hated gay people; I knew that much at least. I just liked how naked men looked; there wasn't anything gay about that. I lived in this pit of repression and denial for six more years, adamant I couldn't be. It simply wasn't an option.

As I got older, I heard more and more about LGBTQIA+ people from the cult: How they could just choose not to be. How obviously they had a weak faith or just weren't praying enough. How the world would be a much better place when God destroyed them in the imminent Armageddon and the birds feasted on their flesh. I internalised it all and learned to hate myself. I learned to believe that I deserved to die for who I was attracted to—that a God of love would kill me for not loving the right people.

I threw myself deeper into my faith. The shame I had been taught became a weapon for further indoctrination. Fortunately, it didn't work. After years of trying, my mind finally broke under the weight of being turned against itself. My mental health declined significantly. I knew I would never be fully accepted in the cult, but I could never leave either. I was trapped, at war with myself with no clear way forward. Rejecting a part of myself even manifested in physical symptoms.

Shame destroys you. It is toxic and eats away at you from the inside. As demonstrated in a 2022 paper published in the journal *Religions*, shame is a large factor in causing religious trauma.[74] Shame is so powerful it can leave scars that you carry your whole life.

It was only after I left and started to heal that I realised how much I had been affected. I still have pain, but nowhere near the level I used to. I still have bad mental health days, but I can leave the house. Self-acceptance and hope have given me a new lease on life. The world of Witchcraft gave me a brand-new start.

Witchcraft does not ask you to be ashamed and hide pieces of yourself away. It does not ask you to conform to the one acceptable identity. Identity and diversity are celebrated, not repressed. They become a source of power, not of shame. Since becoming a Witch, I have been able to fully accept my queer identity and find pride in it. There are still remnants of repression, fossils buried deep that I occasionally stumble into, but life is far better. Witchcraft is an inherently queer space and offered me a newfound sense of freedom. What, though, do I mean by the word *queer*?

Who Are the Queer?

When discussing queerness, we immediately find our first similarity to Witchcraft: both are difficult to define. They mean different things to different people, and every individual will take power from them in a different way. *Queer* is a broad term loosely encompassing anyone outside of the "socially acceptable" heteronormative identity. It most commonly refers to LGBTQIA+ individuals or groups, giving us a sense of community and togetherness.

I started this chapter talking about my experiences as a gay man. But sexuality is only one aspect of the queer experience. Queerness is so much more than sexual orientation or gender; it is the common thread that binds those on the outside of heteronormative society. The kind of sex you prefer is a part of your identity—gay, straight, or otherwise—but it is far from the whole thing. "Why is it always about sex with gay people?" was a question I heard far too often in the cult. It made me want to scream, "It's not."

I wasn't having sex, didn't care about having sex, and still I was tearing myself apart inside because I couldn't be my authentic self. When the boys were talking

....

74. Alison Downie, "Christian Shame and Religious Trauma," *Religions* 13, no. 10 (2022): 925, https://doi.org/10.3390/rel13100925.

about the girls they found attractive, I couldn't join in. They were never told it was just about sex. My sexuality is about who I am, who I love, how I express myself, and how I present myself in the world. Having to hide it puts a degree of separation between me and everyone around me. Every thought and every sentence has to be carefully screened and analysed so I don't give myself away. I cannot simply exist; I have to perform. Queerness is a rejection of that performance. It is being outside of heteronormative standards and choosing to exist authentically nonetheless. It is about pride, about dignity, and about rejecting shame.

The word *queer* implies an otherness. In fact, the original meaning of queer was precisely that: odd, unusual, or strange. You are queer because you are different. But when you find other queer people, you become a community of otherness. We understand how it feels to be on the margins, to be ridiculed and ostracised. When we come together, we are informed by that experience and support each other. Instead of having to define our identity within increasingly narrow labels, we are queer and free to explore whatever that means without being boxed in.

If anything, it is the purity culture of fundamentalism that forces sex to be such an important part of sexuality. People don't date to get to know each other or have fun. They date to get married so they can have sex. It literally defines the path of their life.

The word *queer* does have a history of use as a slur used to attack gay people. That is a fact we need to recognise. However, it is worth noting that almost all words to describe queer people were also once used to attack them. Nevertheless, I would never insist someone has to use the word. It is simply one I find particularly useful. Like *Witch*, it is an umbrella term that can make it easier to find and relate to our community. But let's discuss that a little further and consider why we even use the word *Witch*.

Why the Word *Witch*?

To understand why Witchcraft is such a queer space, it helps to consider why we use the word *Witch*. For centuries, being accused of Witchcraft was about the worst thing that could happen to you. It was a tool of oppression. Anyone on the outskirts of society, anyone marginalised, could face this accusation and lose their life. The vast majority of these individuals were not magical practitioners of any kind; they were caught up in hysteria and accusation without any way of defending themselves. Most would not have called themselves Witches. To do so could be a death sentence.

Today, this word, like the word *queer*, has been reclaimed. Rather than an accusation against the powerless, it is a badge of empowerment. It is most often assumed by those of us who feel we are on the edges of "acceptable" society. We delight in stories of fairies, of gods, and of monsters. We search for spiritual truth in places most people ignore. We go out into the forest at night to commune with the spirits. We reject dogma and doctrine. Simply calling yourself a Witch is an act of rebellion. To find a space where this is the norm, where the standards society ruthlessly seeks to reinforce are rejected, is like finding a safe harbour in a raging storm. Our differences are celebrated, contributing to the rich diversity of our community. Our identity is not a sin; rather, it is something we can channel into our practice and take pride in.

I like to compare this to the idea of queer coding villains.[75] For decades there was very little queer representation in movies. What little "representation" there was amounted to making villains seem stereotypically camp without outright saying it. This particularly happened in children's films. The evil characters were also those with the most stereotypically LGBTQIA+ traits. We were painted as evil by association. But what happened? We fell in love with the villains. If they were going to be queer coded, then they were ours. Ursula the sea witch from Disney's 1989 animated movie *The Little Mermaid* is a queer icon, seen at Pride events across the world. She was inspired by the famous drag queen Divine. Captain Hook from Peter Pan has also been suggested as a good example of queer coding.[76] Other examples include Scar from *The Lion King* and even one of the very first Disney villains, Maleficent in *Sleeping Beauty*. We took what little representation there was and made it our own, taking power in our marginalisation and celebrating it as a community. Something similar happened with the reclaiming of the word *Witch*.

While Witchcraft on the whole is more tolerant and accepting, it is far from perfect. Anyone can be a Witch, and that means sometimes hateful people

....

75. Adelia Brown, "Hook, Ursula, and Elsa: Disney and Queer-Coding from the 1950s to the 2010s," *The Macksey Journal*, 2, no. 43 (2021): 1–14, https://mackseyjournal.scholasticahq.com/article/27887-hook-ursula-and-elsa-disney-and-queer-coding-from-the-1950s-to-the-2010s.

76. Brown, "Hook, Ursula, and Elsa."

will enter these spaces. I like to think they don't last very long, however. Hate doesn't remain where it can't spread. This puts an obligation on each of us to uphold what Witchcraft stands for, to keep it a haven for the marginalised and oppressed. Don't ever give hate room to grow.

If after reading this book you remember nothing else, please remember this: Witchcraft was the thing others accused you of. The historic Witch lived at the end of a pointed finger.[77] To perpetuate hate, fearmongering, or exclusionary ideologies is not Witchcraft, but quite the opposite. It is this very mindset that got so many innocent people killed centuries ago. To call yourself a Witch and attack someone else's identity is to drastically misunderstand what Witchcraft is.

Queer people belong to the same spiritual lineage as Witches: the people on the outskirts of society, those who seek refuge in community. Magical practitioners of all varieties are also part of this current, though not to the extreme that the idea of the "burning times" suggests.

Aradia: Scourge of the Oppressors

The first Wiccan covens in the UK practiced their Witchcraft naked. One of the most famous spells they may have done was called Operation Cone of Power, and it involved a coven dancing naked in the woods to stop Hitler from invading the UK during World War II. The folklore that preceded these covens tells us of goddesses who help Witches smite their oppressors and protect the marginalised, of Witches dancing in orgiastic revelry on mountaintops, and of beasts and Babylon. Witchcraft is inherently queer, and as part of that queerness, it is political.

Much of modern Witchcraft is built on folklore and mythical history, and an important piece of that is *Aradia*. This book was published in 1899 by Charles Godfrey Leland and claims to be the religious text of a group of Italian Witches. In all likelihood, it is folklore rather than a true account of a Witch religion, but myth and folklore are powerful to a Witch, and *Aradia* is a part of many modern Witchcraft traditions.

----

77. Peter Grey, *Apocalyptic Witchcraft* (London: Scarlet Imprint, 2013), 6.

Within this text, Aradia is the daughter of the goddess Diana and Lucifer, and acts as goddess of the Witches. She is the voice that passes the rites and rituals to their coven. In the very first chapter, she has this to say:

And as the sign that ye are truly free,
Ye shall be naked in your rites, both men
And women also: this shall last until
The last of your oppressors shall be dead.[78]

Again, Witchcraft was the path of the oppressed, but it was also their way to claim power and fight back against their enemies. I often hear people arguing that politics should be kept out of Witchcraft, but bluntly: that is impossible. Queerness is built into the foundation of the Craft. As queer people, our identity is political. Living authentically is a political statement. Many of us come to Witchcraft to gain power and to fight back against our oppressors. It doesn't get much more political than that.

Queer Ancestors

Another important way of celebrating the queerness of Witchcraft is by honouring our queer ancestors. Those people who paved the way for us to have the freedom we now have are very much our cultural ancestors. This includes the many people who helped secure the freedoms we have today, who suffered simply for being their authentic self. These amazing, talented, intelligent individuals were often persecuted for their identity, including people like renowned mathematician Alan Turing, who helped end World War II and was pivotal in developing computer technology. Turing was eventually chemically castrated for being a gay man. We can also look to doctor and activist Alan L. Hart, who was born in 1890, and was one of the first trans men to undergo gender-affirming surgery.

There are countless more incredible queer ancestors, including such people as Sylvia Rivera, Marsha P. Johnson, Rachel Pollack, Harvey Milk, James Baldwin, Michel Foucault, and Barbara Gittings, among many others. I encourage you to dig a little deeper into queer history and learn about the many amazing individuals who have blazed a trail for us today.

....

78. Charles Godfrey Leland, *Aradia, Or, The Gospel of the Witches* (London: David Nutt, 1899), 6–7.

Queer ancestors don't have to be exceptional, however. Simply existing as a queer person is exceptional. Authenticity is an act of courage, and being yourself in the face of a society that doesn't accept you is activism. All those who walked this path before us are our queer ancestors. I encourage you to go back to A Ritual to Honor the Ancestors exercise in the spirits chapter and perform it with queer ancestors in mind. It is something that I personally find very powerful.

Beyond the Binary

Duality is an important concept within some Witchcraft traditions. This involves the idea of a god and a goddess, a balance of energies that need to work together for magic to work. The concept of duality is not inherently a bad thing, but it can lead to some exclusionary ideas that are best avoided. The main way this seems to manifest is gender essentialism, or an excessive attachment to the concept of biological gender. This has always seemed quite strange to me, considering Witchcraft today is a spiritual path that emphasizes the spirit inherent in all things being more important than the way they physically appear. A Witch won't think twice about asking an herb how it wants to be used rather than going off a list of predetermined correspondences, or acknowledging a rock as a living thing with a spirit despite its physical properties. Yet somehow, they can get caught up in ideas of physical gender. Thankfully, exclusionary ideologies are by far the minority in Pagan spaces.

Within the Sarffes Goch tradition of Witchcraft, we don't find it helpful to think in terms of male and female energies. That's not to say these aren't helpful concepts in some traditions; however, we find the forces of *inspiration* and *creation* better describe the way we work magic. Neither inspiration nor creation are inherently gendered. These are simply processes we view as essential in bardic magic.

For anything to be magical, it requires a fusion of inspiration and creation. As I've discussed a few times in the book, the divine force of Awen in Welsh culture is pure inspiration. It is breathed into you and sparks the creative process. This is an integral part of magic in the Welsh continuum. There is a little more than inspiration required though. You then have to act on it. If you don't bring the inspiration to birth in the world by creating something, it will fizzle away inside you. Only when it is manifest in the world through creation can it inspire others. That can take many different forms, of course, but something must be birthed for the process to continue.

Exercise: Inspired Creation
. . . .

Uninspired creation is a dull and dead thing, while inspiration without creation goes nowhere. To illustrate, try the following exercise:

Materials
- Your Llyfr Cyfrin
- Something to write with

Directions:
This exercise is very simple. All I want you to do is draw a square: four lines meeting at four right angles, all equal length. Once you've done it, think about the following questions:

Did you feel anything? Was there a crackle? Does the square mean anything, or does it just exist because I told you to draw it?

You have simply followed my instructions. The square doesn't mean anything. You have created it. It didn't exist before. But there is no special meaning to it, and it is unlikely to inspire anyone else.

Now, we're going to try something a little different. If you have time, go back and perform the Channelling the Narrative Spirit exercise to channel Awen in chapter 6. Once you have done it, sit until you feel the inspiration flow through you, then draw or write whatever you are moved to in your book. Notice the difference?

Consider the same questions again:

Did you feel anything? Was there a crackle? Does the thing you have created mean anything, or does it just exist because I told you to make it?

Likely your answers are very different this time. Inspired creation feels entirely different than uninspired creation. It is in this union of forces that powerful magic resides. It is the driving force of magic within my practice and can be very powerful indeed. I encourage you to think about the union of these forces and how they may already be playing out in any magic you practice.

Sex Magic (No Space for Shame)

Within the cult, sex was the ultimate source of shame, strictly policed and only to be done in the context of a committed heterosexual relationship, and never before marriage. But that wasn't the end of it. Even within marriage it was policed, with multiple sermons and publications emphasizing that married couples owed each other sex, and that (usually) the wife must render the husband their "marital due." Every part came with shame built in. It was something secret and private, never spoken about. It emphasized how "sinful" and out of control humans were. Within the cult, simply being alone with a member of the opposite sex overnight was enough grounds to be cast out and shunned. The default assumption was that every human would immediately succumb to lust and sin. No couple were allowed to date unchaperoned, or they also would be subject to discipline.

When I left, I was incredibly traumatised around sex. I had never even kissed anyone, didn't know how any of it worked. Even outside the belief system, I experienced an intense amount of sexual shame. I was hardwired to believe that ever being intimate with a man meant I deserved to die. That was something very difficult to break through, and there are moments to this day when I struggle with it. The difference now is that I can talk about it. I have a loving partner who hears me and never makes me feel ashamed and a community that I can turn to and discuss these things with when needed.

Witchcraft was also a major part in recovering from this shame. Instead of being something hidden and repressed, sex is seen as a natural part of the human experience. Why would the gods want us to be ashamed of love and pleasure? In fact, a piece of poetry called "The Charge of the Goddess," which is recited during ritual by some Witchcraft traditions, contains the line "Let my worship be with the heart that rejoiceth, for behold: all acts of love and pleasure are my rituals."[79] This gives a beautiful insight into the way Witches might worship. There is no concept of sin. There is no need for shame. Witchcraft is celebratory and joyous. We take power in our otherness; why would we shame ourselves for it? Consensual sex is an expression of love and/or pleasure, no matter what

....

79. Doreen Valiente, *The Charge of the Goddess: The Poetry of Doreen Valiente*, expanded ed. (The Doreen Valiente Foundation, 2014), 13.

kind of sex it is. The strange obsessive purity culture some people cling to has no place in the Craft.

One expression this celebratory attitude toward sexuality takes is sex magic. I'm not going to go into any depth about it here, merely mention that it exists to showcase how different the attitude in Witchcraft is. I also want to be clear that, as with all aspects of magic, this is not a necessity nor an obligation, simply an option that some Witches and magical practitioners choose to explore further along their path.

Sex is incredibly powerful, and various cultures have recognised that throughout history, with tantric sex being a great example. It holds an allure that is difficult to describe, some magical quality that calls to us on a primal level. The electricity of flirting, the crackling power of seduction, the call of sex appeal that none of us can deny—we recognise them each and every day, and know instinctively they hold power. Sex can be and has been used in magical workings for centuries. The passion and energy of two (or more) individuals entwined in carnal pleasure can be channelled into workings. You can even do it on your own.

Warnings and Pitfalls

There are dangers to sex magic, however. As with anything powerful, it can be abused. It should always be your uncoerced and enthusiastic choice to engage in sex of any kind, whether in a magical setting or not. *Consent is absolutely vital, and coerced consent is not consent at all.* Cults will attempt to control your behaviour, and in Christian fundamentalism, this most often takes the form of severely restricting the kind of sex you are allowed to have. It can work the other way, however. A controlling group or individual may attempt to coerce you into things you're not comfortable with. Immediately leave any group that puts that kind of pressure on you. It is absolutely unacceptable!

Sex magic relies on consent. The quality of the interaction and strength of the connection is where the magic comes from. If anyone tries to force you to participate, it's not magic they are interested in. If they don't take no for an answer, get the authorities involved straight away. Coercion has absolutely no place in a healthy spirituality. Though Witchcraft celebrates love and passion, this is *always* with enthusiastic consent, and you should never be pushed to participate in something you are not comfortable with.

If you continue down the witchy path, you will notice that this is no space for shame, sexual or otherwise. That alone makes it somewhere incredibly healing to be. For me personally, exploring sex magic was incredibly liberating. To find power in something that once brought me so much shame was an intense act of reclamation. And in accepting the magic inherent in sex, I was able to enjoy it more freely without the voice in the back of my head telling me how disgusting I am. To quote a famous Witch, "Witchcraft does not need to apologize for involving sex magic. It is other religions which need to apologize for the miseries of puritanical repression they have inflicted on humanity."[80]

Rite of Passage

Exploring our sexuality and gender identity, however, happens long before we ever actually have sex: the first crush your friends tease you about, that first awkward dance, touching fingertips as you walk down the hallway, your first kiss. All these milestones are an important part of figuring out who you are and growing into your identity. Unfortunately, many queer people don't get to experience them as others might. Instead of being encouraged in this exploration, we are often met with anger and shame. For many, it can seem better to hide who you are and go along with what other people want you to be. Sadly, this can mean many milestones are missed or experienced far later in life. The love we have to give is ignored and shamed. While other people celebrate their first relationships or suffer through their first breakups, we are pushing our feelings down in order to fit in. Just think about the concept of "coming out." We have to let the people in our lives know our identity once we are ready to stop hiding it.

Celebration is a hugely important part of Witchcraft. We celebrate the turning cycle of nature, we gather together at festivals, we find any excuse to be joyous. A big part of that is acknowledging rites of passage. These are the events in our life that transition us from one place to another—celebrations like weddings or coming-of-age ceremonies, which are often governed by religion. For queer people, many of these rites of passage are simply ignored or glossed over; however, Witchcraft gives us the perfect opportunity to acknowledge and celebrate them all.

....
80. Doreen Valiente, *Witchcraft for Tomorrow* (London: R. Hale, 1978), 134.

Things like your first kiss; the first time you hold someone's hand; coming out to yourself, to a friend, to your family; and the first time you go to a gay bar or attend a Pride parade are all important. All these deserve to be honoured as the milestones they are. Everything deserves to be celebrated, especially when it comes to rites of passage that take courage to experience and often cannot be shared.

Exercise: Celebrating Your Identity

The rites of passage you may have missed also deserve to be noted. If you never got the chance to have an awkward prom dance with anyone or never got to celebrate your first kiss, it's not too late to acknowledge that now. I like to observe all these rites of passage rolled into one in a little rite of celebration. It's something I do whenever I need a boost, but also something I do every year on the day I left the cult and started living authentically.

Materials:
- A cupcake
- A small birthday-style candle
- A lighter or matches

Directions:
For this exercise we're going to draw on the strong cultural imagery of the birthday cake. Every year, the candles on a birthday cake are blown out to celebrate growing one year older. I like to use this same technique to celebrate embracing my identity more fully and living ever more authentically. Plus, it means I get to have cake, which is always a bonus.

Set the cupcake on the table in front of you and place the candle in it. Take a few moments to sit quietly and be present. Think about all the milestones in your life that have brought you to where you are now. Think about any you may have missed. You are exactly where you need to be and deserve to celebrate yourself. Feel the pride of living authentically swell in your chest. Despite all the hurdles you have had to overcome, you are living your truth. No matter what rites you may have missed, you are living as your authentic self today. That takes incredible courage. Being who you are is itself a milestone worthy of observation.

Hold onto this feeling, and as you do so, light the candle. Watch the glow of the flame, and in it, picture all the shame that people have tried to put onto you. You have overcome it all. You have won. Let all the milestones that brought you here, all the times you chose authenticity over shame, flood into you. Take a moment to offer yourself unconditional acceptance, but also extend it outward to anyone else performing this exercise, whenever and wherever they may be. Once you feel ready, say these words:

I banish all shame and choose to live as my authentic self. I celebrate my courage and honour the many hurdles that have brought me to this point. I celebrate myself and my authenticity.

As you speak the last word, blow out the candle, and feel any remaining shame leave the room with it. Now eat the cupcake if you want to and know that I celebrate your authentic self with you, as does every single other person who performs this exercise.

Celebrating Diversity

Queer people around the world are seeking spiritual connection, just like any other group of people. That connection has been denied by many mainstream religions for centuries. The only way to be spiritual was to bury any part of yourself that didn't conform. Things have gotten a little better, and today most religions will accept queer members. However, this is often a conditional acceptance. We are accepted if certain passages of the holy book are ignored. One denomination accepts us only for another to attack, othering us all over again. We can be gay; we just can't act on it. Terms and conditions always seem to apply for any queer person seeking spirituality.

I experienced this myself in the cult. When I couldn't live with hiding my identity any longer, I came out to a few close friends. I told them I was bi, as that was safer and what I wanted to believe myself. There was still hope for me;

I could still have a straight relationship. Admitting I was gay would shut that door and make it even more difficult for them to accept me. Not that there was much acceptance there to begin with, but I clung to what little was offered.

This is a major reason why I was drawn to Witchcraft. There is no hint of conditional acceptance here. You are celebrated as you are. Our identity should be celebrated. It is not something to ignore, avoid, or suppress. Witchcraft accepts us as we are; we don't have to leave any pieces of ourselves at the door. The diversity of Witchcraft and Paganism is one of their greatest strengths. It means we have an incredibly rich and inclusive community.

When I left the cult, I left as a gay man. I had to be. My identity was in retaliation to their doctrine of hate and control. If I was gay, I could never fit into their belief system. However, since leaving I have realised that identity is far more fluid and changing. It is something you should be free to explore without terms and conditions imposed. My identity is something I explore daily. I am happily engaged to a wonderful man, and while I still identify as gay, I feel more drawn to the term *queer*, as it leaves room for exploration and growth.

Why People Find Witchcraft

Witchcraft draws people from all walks of life, but what is it that draws people to this path in the first place? Witchcraft is a minority; we are the weirdos, the misfits, the outcasts. Do people come here to be othered? In my experience, no. People who are already othered find their way to this space and a community that warmly accepts them—people who are queer, those who care about the environment in the face of societal apathy, those who feel powerless in the world. Individuals on the margins find this path and find community. The things that once set us apart and made us feel alone end up being the very things that pull us to this wonderful community space.

People aren't necessarily drawn to Witchcraft because they want a relationship with the gods or because they're searching for a spiritual path. It can be the need for community or a search for something to empower them in the world. These are valid reasons to find the Craft and again highlight the queerness of this space. Whatever draws you to this path is valid, and you can find acceptance and community here if you wish to continue walking it.

Representation Matters

I'll conclude this section with a personal story. As I was building up the courage to leave, I started to make friends outside the cult. I met people who were living happy lives as their authentic selves. I saw LGBTQIA+ people represented across society, with happy families, fulfilling careers, and overall great lives. Seeing the representation helped me realise it was possible. Othered people simply living their lives was activism. Without it, I don't know if I could have ever left or seen through the lies that all queer people were unhappy.

This is one of the main reasons I find Pride so necessary. There are still people stuck in awful situations, being lied to about what it means to live as your authentic self. It's why I'm so open about my identity. I want people to be able to look at me and see that I am a gay man and that I am happy. The cult lied, and I am living proof of that!

Breaking Free from Repression

Becoming a founding member of a majority-queer coven has been an incredibly liberating experience. Finding community among people who can understand and relate to me has helped me begin the process of unpacking my repression. This is a journey that will likely last a very long time, but having queer community certainly helps the process.

Early in my journey, I remember talking with my coven mates about the frustration I feel—that because I am being shunned, the people I left behind can imagine all sorts of things about my life. I knew they would. When someone leaves, you are taught their life will fall apart. They cannot possibly have a happy and fulfilling life without "God's blessing." I got really upset at the fact my fictional story would be used to indoctrinate other people and that they would never see me thriving. To this day, I struggle to post any negative experiences I am having on social media just in case one of the old cult members sees it. I have to live a perfect, happy life to justify leaving and prove them wrong, or so I convinced myself.

My coven helped me begin to realise I was still giving those people power over me. It didn't matter how they saw me or what they thought of my life. The only thing that mattered was how I saw myself. Together, we came up with an exercise to help me reclaim a little of my story and to get rid of a little of the repression. There is no quick and easy solution, but the small things along the way all help.

Exercise: A Letter for Those Who Othered You

This exercise is magical in the sense that it can be healing and change how you feel, but it is also a deeply practical exercise that can help you relieve the feelings of frustration and abandonment a little. It can be carried out for any experience in life, or simply to remind yourself of the good things you have going on.

Materials:

• A pen and paper, or a digital device you can write on

Directions:

To put it simply, this exercise is writing a letter to anyone who may have made you feel othered or less than. The purpose is not to attack them, nor is it to curse them (though there's nothing wrong with that if it's what you want to do.) Rather, this letter is to tell them all the good things you have going on in your life. List everything that has improved since you last saw them.

For example, if I were to write a letter today, I would include the fact I am in a happy and thriving relationship with a loving man. I would talk about having this book published and how amazing a journey that has been. The many friends I have made who love and accept me would all be mentioned. The fact I am healing every day and in better shape than I ever was in the cult would certainly be in there. The list goes on, but even small things are worthy of note. Did you see a really beautiful sunset that made you appreciate the world, or just have a particularly tasty breakfast? Put it in the letter. Anything that makes you feel good and appreciate your life should go in.

It's up to you what you do with this letter once it's written. It is not meant to be sent; this is just for you. Personally, I like to (safely) burn it during a small ritual while also saying a little incantation along the lines of "May I continue to thrive as my detractors wither."

Chapter 9
Reclaiming the Devil

The big bad wolf. The wicked stepmother. The troll under the bridge. Every story needs its villain. And often, if there is no immediately apparent villain, one will be provided for you. The point of the villain is to make you afraid, show you everything that is corrupt and could go wrong. There are no stakes if the villain couldn't win, and victory for the bad guy is the worst possible outcome.

One of the original and most enduring villains of all time is the figure known as the devil. He has an expansive history in theology and folklore, with generations of writers building upon his extensive mythos. Witches have been woven into his legend across the centuries, and anything that seems different or dangerous was absorbed into the diabolical. He is the ultimate evil, the villain beyond all villains. He can steal your soul away and drag you straight to hell.

Being raised in the cult, I was taught to fear Satan as a roaring lion and an angel of light. He was devious and deadly, constantly on the lookout to devour those who stray from the path, but also a master of disguise who hid his evil behind a veil of beauty and charm (or crystals and incense).

It was only when I left the cult that I realised that's not really who he is at all. But this chapter is not meant as an unpicking of the many ways the devil has been associated with Witchcraft, or a thorough examination of this character. It is a glimpse into the way the figure of the devil can be used to vilify and distort, and a reclaiming of the many things fundamentalism chooses to label as Satanic.

The very fact we need to reassure people we have nothing to do with the devil shows how pervasive cultural Christianity is. We need to prove our Craft is safe and nonthreatening, make it acceptable to an intolerant majority. It is easier to say we have nothing to do with the devil than attempt to explain the complicated reality. By forcing anything outside a Christian belief into the mould of Satan, Christianity condemned Witchcraft as mere devil worship, and in so doing, they placed the costume of the devil onto entities and practices that matter to us.

The Serpent in the Garden

I begin with some light heresy. A little heresy every now and then is good for you. So here goes. I offer you a retelling of the biblical story of the serpent in the garden.

In the beginning there was a tyrant, and he created a walled-off garden as a prison. He kept his prisoners in ignorance, deprived of the ability to think for themselves. One of the creatures that worked for this monster noticed the plight of his victims and determined he should help them. He snuck into the garden disguised as a serpent and whispered in their ear the truth of their predicament. If they would only take a bite from the fruit of the tree of knowledge, then they would be free. Their mind would be their own; they could decide for themselves, chart their own path. Their existence would mean something beyond offering worship to soothe the inflated ego of their captor.

The captives listened, and immediately they were freed from their mental prison. But the tyrant would let his spite and rage rule him once more, and he cursed his captives and cursed the very earth, casting them out to suffer as much as possible. If he could not hold them in his mental control, then he would punish them as much as he possibly could. The tyrant, however, still had an ego to soothe. He still craved worship. The problem was how he could compel the very beings he was torturing to offer it to him. A villain was needed. In a final act of treachery, he placed the blame on the serpent and told all the generations that followed that only through worship could they escape the very suffering he had inflicted upon them. He even wrote a book about it, to make sure everyone was convinced.

This is not how the Bible tells it, but that makes it no less powerful. The story was actually one of my early thought experiments as I was leaving the cult. Fundamentalism leaves no room for alternatives, but when you stop to think, you realise reality is far too complex for one simple answer. I began to see the devil not as some binary agent of evil. His role was far more nuanced than that. The role of the devil in Witchcraft is testament to that fact.

The Horned God of the Witches

In the early twentieth century, something extraordinary happened. An Egyptologist called Margaret Murray turned her attention toward the history of Witchcraft. She published a book in 1921 that took the world by storm. Titled *The Witch-Cult in Western Europe*, this book claimed to prove that the victims of the witch trials were actually followers of an ancient religion and that the God of the Witches had been misappropriated as the devil by those who sought to oppress them. This theory has now been widely discredited, and we know most of the victims were ordinary people caught up in a horrific situation. However, we have discussed the power and magic of mythology in a previous chapter, and this theory became an important part of the mythological history of modern Witchcraft.

There are small grains of truth to be found in it if we squint a little. Academics have discovered regional beliefs in goddess figures and other entities that got caught up in and distorted by the witch trials, for example the *"donas de fuera"* discussed by Gustav Henningsen.[81] There is no real evidence for a large-scale pagan religion though. At the time when Witchcraft was reborn into the world as a spiritual tradition, people did believe this theory, to the point that the first book published on a modern Witchcraft tradition contained a preface by Margaret Murray.[82] Despite its historical inaccuracy, the idea of a witch cult became part of the modern mythology of Witchcraft. As part of that, the concept of the devil also took a prominent place in ideas of Witchcraft. A full discussion of the links between the devil and the Craft would take an entire book by itself, and this brief look at one strand shows how complex a picture it can be.

What is really interesting is that the portrayal of the devil having goat hooves and horns is quite a modern concept. Before the nineteenth century, he

....
81. Gustav Henningsen, "'The Ladies from Outside': An Archaic Pattern of the Witches' Sabbath," in *Early Modern European Witchcraft: Centres and Peripheries*, edited by Bengt Ankarloo and Gustav Henningsen (Oxford: Clarendon Press, 2001), 195.
82. Gerald Brosseau Gardner, *Witchcraft Today* (Secaucus, NJ: Citadel Press, 1954), 13–14.

was usually portrayed with bull horns and clawed feet. The change seems to have been when Pan became popular as a symbol for nature. The church once again tried to turn the God of the Witches into the devil, using their imagination to merge him with Pan.[83] They couldn't have a pagan god running around unchecked and unvilified.

Reclaiming the devil can mean taking back the Horned God. While he may not have been historically worshipped by a cult of Witches, he is nonetheless a part of our mythos. Stripping him of the costume Christianity forced onto him can be very powerful. That's not to say we cannot refer to him as the devil or take joy in the imagery he has partaken in. It just means acknowledging he is not *simply* the Christian devil.

Today, the Horned God is perceived in a multitude of ways. To many, he is an archetype that represents many other gods, like Pan discussed earlier. He is the wild and bestial entity that resides within the fertile fields and forests, intimately connected with the natural world. He presides over the cycles of life and death and is a central figure many Witches venerate equally alongside the goddess.

Exercise: An Offering to the Horned God

This exercise was particularly powerful when I first left the cult. It felt like a liberating act of heresy and reclamation, allowing me to interact with and take back power in all that had been othered. By making an offering to the God of the Forest, I learned to separate him from the cult concept of Satan and respect him as the powerful entity he is. I find that this exercise is best performed in a woodland or at least near a tree. The Horned God has long been associated with the green wilds and forests.

Materials:
• An offering

---

83. Hutton, *The Triumph of the Moon*, 46.

Directions:

To decide what to offer, spend some time thinking about what the Horned God means to you. What does he represent? What kind of offerings would he appreciate? In my practice, I like to bake some seeded bread so that the animals and birds of the forest can be fed by the offering. Whatever you decide to give, make sure it is biodegradable and environmentally friendly. Leaving an offering that harms the forest is more likely to anger any deity that resides there than help you to connect with them.

Once you have chosen your offering and made your way to where you want to give it, take a moment and say the following words:

> *Horned God of the Witches, Lord of the Forest, the one sometimes called devil. I leave this offering for you with a request to know you. Show yourself to me and help me understand you.*

Once you have said the words, place the offering at the base of a tree. Stay there as long as you want, and let yourself feel anything that comes. As always, be alert to any ways the forest may communicate with you.

If you are uncomfortable with the idea of making an offering to a deity, or the concept and energy of the Horned God are not right for your practice, then you can change this exercise to be an offering to the forest itself and any spirits that might dwell there. If you prefer to build your relationship with the genius loci, then substitute the previous words for these:

> *Spirit of the forest, spirits of the trees, all the living beings in this place. I leave this offering for you. I thank you for allowing me to share this space with you and ask that you share your wisdom with me. I walk this land alongside you and offer you my deep respect.*

Of course, you are free to say anything you wish in place of either of these invocations. Ecstatic ritual is extremely powerful, and you may well sense a spirit or presence in the space with you that completely changes what you set out to do. That is completely fine. The point of this exercise is simply to leave an offering and feel a sense of connection to something ancient but certainly not evil. The rest is up to you.

A Convenient Scapegoat

There is a lot of debate about what caused the historic witch trials in Europe. It's a really complex subject and far more than this book can discuss. However, many academics agree that there was a folkloric belief in magical practitioners in certain areas of Europe that became entangled with the witch hunts.[84] These regional beliefs were distorted, and magical practitioners were instead accused of working with the devil. He became a convenient scapegoat for the things people couldn't understand.

Night Phantoms

One example of this I often turn to is the horse herdsman Chonrad Stoeckhlin.[85] He lived in southern Germany during the sixteenth century and, like most people of the time, was a Christian. Through a strange sequence of events, Chonrad found himself travelling in vision with a group of spirits he called the night phantoms, initiated into this procession by a guardian angel. Through these flights, he learned the arts of healing and divination, and brought those back with him to benefit his society. Sadly, Chonrad eventually found himself tried as a Witch, brutally tortured into changing his story. The night phantoms became demons, his spiritual journeys illicit liaisons with sex devils.

Another figure who met a similar fate was Diell Breull, who lived about fifty years after Chonrad. Diell claimed to travel out with the night phantoms four times a year, and his nocturnal flights ensured a good harvest. His first journey with this spirit procession occurred while he was in a deep depression following the death of his wife and child. He was carried away to the Venusberg, the fairy realm and home of the goddess Venus in German lore. There he met with Frau Holle, a goddess who is very important to me personally, as my practice is heavily inspired by my German heritage. She showed him many things, including visions of those who were soon to die and knowledge of herbs. Again, however,

---

84. Emma Wilby, *Cunning Folk and Familiar Spirits*.
85. For a full discussion of the story of Chonrad Stoeckhlin, see: Wolfgang Behringer, *Shaman of Oberstdorf: Chonrad Stoeckhlin and the Phantoms of the Night* (Charlottesville, VA: University of Virginia Press, 1998).

these wholesome spiritual travels were distorted under torture and turned into meetings with the devil. Diell was executed in 1632.[86]

These are only two examples, but already a picture begins to emerge. Anything that wasn't Christian, that didn't fit the dominant worldview, could become the devil. People were tortured to near the point of death to extract the confession the inquisitors wanted. In one session, Chonrad Stoeckhlin had the skin burned off his body from his genitals to his head and was brought to the brink of death.[87] The inquisitors would not be satisfied until any spiritual being that could grant supernatural power became the devil. Naturally, a fear and distrust of any non-Christian spirits would arise from this.

Part of reclaiming the devil is recognising this fact. We can learn much from the lore of the witch trials. As we have discussed previously, myth and folklore are powerful sources of magic. But we do not need to accept the diabolical aspects of the lore unquestioningly. When we peel back the layers, we may find far more benevolent beings whose identity has been twisted through doctrine and fear. It is often better to allow a spirit to tell you who they are than to immediately assume they must be demonic or evil. This is exactly the culture of fear that Christianity once used drastic means to instil.

Not-So-Familiar Spirits

Reclaiming the devil also means opening up to spirit communication, not as some demonic pact or bargain but simply as an interaction with a living and vibrant world. This was a completely alien concept to me when I left the cult. Any spirit that tried to communicate with you was automatically a demon. Reclaiming the devil meant forging relationships with spirits I would have once immediately dismissed as evil. It is breaking free from a binary cosmology that judges all spirits by whether they serve an all-knowing god or not. We allow the spirits to be complex persons, not serving some cosmic role as the force of evil. Yes, there may be spirits who are less friendly, but this isn't the default assumption a Witch makes. And rarely is a spirit purely bad or simply out to cause harm.

....

86. Carlo Ginzburg, *The Night Battles: Witchcraft and Agrarian Cults in the Sixteenth and Seventeenth Centuries*, trans. John Tedeschi and Anne C. Tedeschi (Baltimore, MA: The Johns Hopkins University Press, 2013), 52.

87. Behringer, *Shaman of Oberstdorf*, 103.

The gods of the old faith often become the demons of the new. For example, within the demons mentioned in *The Lesser Key of Solomon*, there are several who take their names from older gods. For example, Bael was likely derived from the Canaanite Baal, and Bifrons was an epithet of the Roman god Janus.

Reclaiming the devil can mean stripping away the evil costume forced onto all spirits outside the Christian cosmology. It means opening ourselves up to the fact shades of grey exist in the spirit world, as they do in all spaces. The following exercise is recorded to highlight how this bias can even be found in historic folk magical practices.

Exercise: Creating a Magic Mirror

This exercise is taken directly from a nineteenth-century collection of German folk magic. In it, there is a working for creating a mirror in which one can see everything. I will record it as it was written, according to my own translation. It is included here as a historic example of folk magic and the way that Christian bias can be found in these charms. However, with a little adaptation, this can be used to create a magical mirror for divination if you choose to continue walking this path.

Materials:
- A mirror bought without haggling
- A shovel or other digging implement

Directions:
"Buy a mirror for the price it is offered, without haggling. Write the following characters upon it:"

"*S. Solam   S. Tattler   S. Echogartner   Gematar.*"

"Bury it at a crossroads in an odd hour; the glass of the mirror must be facing downward. Thereafter, return on the third day at the same hour and dig it up. However, you must not be the first person to look into the mirror, but a dog or a cat must look into it first."[88]

It's pretty clear to see the darker associations in this piece of folk magic. An animal is made to look into the mirror first, as the soul of the first creature to gaze into it was thought to be forfeit. This is a Christian overhang in folk magic, but I really don't see any problem in de-Christianising magic if that makes you feel more comfortable, especially if you are not drawing on those Christian aspects to make it work.

Feel free to adjust this charm in whatever way you see fit, and you will have a lovely magic mirror to use in your practice.

From Fear to Freedom

For most of my life, I lived in fear. I remember breaking down as a young child, certain God would destroy me because I was playing Pokémon, and we'd just had a talk about how demonic it was. That day, I threw all my games in the bin, a decision that still haunts me to this day. Every decision I made was influenced by the fear of being corrupted by Satan and therefore being sentenced to death.

The consequences of falling prey to the devil were extreme. In the short term, I would lose all my family and friends. They would treat me as if I was dead until the day God stepped in to finish the job for them. Realising I was gay only made it that much harder. Now I was literally embodying the devil and had to be afraid of myself as well.

A huge part of reclaiming the devil is taking back all those things that you were told made you other. It is about taking power in the things you were told were weakness. It is unashamedly embodying all the things they tried to tell you were wrong and refusing to let them make you feel guilt or shame.

Cults want you to unquestioningly obey. They are founded on control and need your obedience. One of the songs I used to sing with my congregation was called "Listen, Obey and Be Blessed," and it was particularly targeted toward children. They made animated versions of it with a choir of children singing to really help indoctrinate them. They need this obedience so that they can keep you in fear.

....
88. Jahn, *Hexenwesen und Zauberei in Pommern*, 151.

The Witch does not unquestioningly follow anyone. We chart our own path and question everything. This is our greatest strength, celebrating our diversity and personal sovereignty. In Christian cosmology, the devil in the garden prompted the first humans to question. It's easy to see how a reinterpretation and reclaiming of this figure could be appealing to Witches.

Exercise: A Charm to Overcome Fear

When I first left the cult, it was ingrained in me that Witchcraft was the devil. All magic came from him and the demons. All other religions were evil too, especially anything associated with Paganism. Calling yourself a Pagan was essentially the same as selling your soul straight to Satan. Even after leaving, the fear of magic and spirituality was very difficult to shake. It took time for me to unlearn the fear that had been deeply embedded into me, but turning to magic really helped me.

Written charms have been extremely popular and powerful in magic throughout history. One form of written charm that has survived for many centuries is the abracadabra triangle. In short, this charm begins with the word *abracadabra*, then removes one letter each line until you are left with only the A in a triangle shape. This can point either upward or downward. This was used either to increase or decrease something. For example, a decreasing triangle might be used to reduce and carry away illness. We are going to draw on the same imagery to reduce and carry away fear.

Materials:
• A pen and paper

Directions:
Begin by writing the following words on your paper:

As the letters on this page decrease, so too does my fear. The fear that has been given to me by an intolerant world has no hold on me. May it be gone, carried forth by this charm. So be it.

Then draw the following symbols:

ABRACADABRA

ABRACADABR

ABRACADAB

ABRACADA

ABRACAD

ABRACA

ABRAC

ABRA

ABR

AB

A

Say: "As the charm is done, so my fear is gone."

Once you have written this charm out, carry it on your person for as long as you need. It is particularly helpful to carry it when you are feeling a little anxious. When I first left the cult, I found it helpful to carry this kind of charm on me whenever I visited a metaphysical shop to help me banish the ingrained fear that was not my own.

The Devil of Land and Lore

The name of the Sarffes Goch tradition itself is an act of reclaiming. It translates to Red Serpent, which honours the important role serpents have played as representations of magic throughout history. But it also invokes the imagery of the devil in the garden, tempting humanity with the fruit of the tree. That is not to say we worship the devil. We honour the Welsh pantheon of deities, and perhaps the closest figure amongst them is Gwyn ap Nudd. However, we draw upon the powerful imagery and symbolism of the serpent that has accumulated over centuries, and this includes the devilish associations.

I cannot say much more about the inner mysteries of the tradition here in case I stray too far toward oathbound knowledge. But finding joy and meaning in "devilish" symbols is a powerful act of reclamation. This is also not restricted to our tradition. Many Witches incorporate serpentine imagery or reclaim the devilish associations of the Horned God. These things are not really Satanic but incorporate the idea of a land-based spirit that sometimes wears a devilish costume.

This idea can also include the Wheel of the Year. In the cult, almost all celebrations were forbidden. There was an obsession with the Satanic and Pagan origins of almost every major holiday. Even the traditionally Christian celebrations like Easter and Christmas were banned. The joy was sucked out of every aspect of life. Not participating was rebranded as "standing out as different," and that by being different we were preaching. Our non-participation could lead others to salvation. Even birthdays were forbidden because they celebrated the self too much and didn't give honour to God. In fact, I was often told that birthdays were the most important celebration in Satanism and were inherently selfish. Witches are not bound by puritanical repression. We celebrate life in all its beauty.

Reclaiming the devil meant reclaiming the act of celebration. Now, I take every opportunity to celebrate and be happy, completely rejecting the puritanical values that were once enforced on me. The devil in Witchcraft is joyous and celebratory.

The Class Divide

When we look at the magic of the past, we notice a class divide begin to open. Funnily enough, the devil seems more interested in the lower classes, while the magic and divination of the upper classes is somehow immune to his Satanic influence. The aristocrats were permitted to do as they wanted, while the magic of the everyday people was vilified and attacked. This is especially apparent in the art of astrology, especially in Lutheran countries. While the common people were persecuted and killed for practicing unsanctioned forms of magic, the learned magic of the elite often seemed to be given a pass.

Heinrich Cornelius Agrippa von Nettesheim is a great example of this. Famous among magicians down to this day, Agrippa published works on magic titled the *Three Books of Occult Philosophy* in 1533. While he was persecuted for his reputation as a magician, he also lectured at universities and even held the patronage of archbishops and emperors.[89] At the same time that everyday people were being burned as Witches, he held positions of power and influence.

....
89. Coy, *The Devil's Art*, 35.

Of course, his work is important and influential to this day, and I'm in no way trying to diminish that. But it does highlight the differing views held toward the learned magic of the privileged in society.

Witchcraft was the magic of the devil. The down-to-earth, simple magic of the unlearned was the thing that was truly feared. It was overwhelmingly the poor and marginalised that were persecuted on the mere suspicion of magic, while self-confessed sorcerers operated openly. This elitism can still sometimes be found among magicians today. If you're not casting a circle or engaging in elaborate ritual, your magic is seen as inferior somehow. If you're not drawing sigils and pentacles, are you even working magic? In my opinion, reclaiming the devil means accepting the power of everyday, practical magic. Not everything has to be elaborate or learned. Profane magic is as powerful as any other. To reclaim the devil is not to judge the practice of another, but to allow yourself the freedom to explore and indulge in any magic you desire. You don't need to buy fancy tools and trinkets; the things around you are more than enough.

One of the most famous witch trials in England was that of the Pendle Witches. In the trial records, one of the Witches, Demdike, is accused of being instructed by her familiar spirit Tibb to create a likeness of clay of someone in order to kill them, slowly crumbling it over a period of days.[90] This was not elaborate, ritualistic magic. It was a simple working. Some clay from the local riverbank was all that was needed. Through the trial records, this became a diabolical working under the guidance of a demonic familiar. But how might we reclaim this for our own Craft?

Exercise: Creating Clay Poppets

Poppets work on the principle of sympathetic magic. What you do to them happens to the person they represent. But that doesn't have to be used for harm. You can create a poppet of yourself and imbue it with correspondences for confidence or use poppets for distance healing. Of course, they are still used in cursing when that's necessary. Reclaiming

90. Edgar Peel and Pat Southern, *The Trials of the Lancashire Witches: A Study of Seventeenth -Century Witchcraft* (Nelson, UK: Hendon Publishing, 1985), 45.

the devil doesn't mean stripping away any negative use of magic but acknowledging that it is a tool that can be used for any purpose.

Materials:
- Clay that dries, or a basic salt dough
- Something to tie the poppet to its target
- *Optional:* Herbs you can work into the clay

Directions:
Get the clay you are using ready and work it until it is malleable. Alternatively, you can use a basic salt dough. Combine one cup of plain flour with half a cup of salt. Slowly add half a cup of water until you have a workable dough.

Once you have your clay or dough, simply shape it into a representation of the person you're working magic on. This doesn't have to be hyperrealistic; it just has to be recognisable to you. Once you have created something vaguely humanoid, you can work in any herbs or ingredients you wish to achieve your magical means. At this stage it is important to incorporate something from the target of the working into the poppet, be that hair, a photo, or something else.

Once you've made your poppet, you can leave it to dry or speed up the process by drying it in an oven set to the lowest setting for around three hours. While the herbal correspondences incorporated in the clay are great for benevolent magic, if you're feeling a little more baneful, you could follow the pattern of the Pendle Witches and crumble it slowly over several weeks to enact a curse.

There is no need for elaborate ceremony or ritual; this is a simple way of working sympathetic magic that anyone can use.

The Ethics of a Witch

While the devil can be used to highlight perceived human flaws and weaknesses, his existence can also allow us to absolve ourselves of responsibility. We aren't to blame when we do something wrong. The devil made us do it. He's the source of all sin. However, since we don't believe in sin, a Witch must take responsibility for their own path.

This leads us into the idea of magical ethics. One of the strangest beliefs I regularly encounter is that if you don't have a god to tell you what to do, then you'll immediately regress into someone evil, self-centred, and unethical—that the commandments in the Bible are the only thing keeping humanity from regressing into monsters. That is an incredibly pessimistic view of human nature, in my opinion. Regardless of faith, humans are capable of great good but also of acting in ways that harm others. Some of the greatest atrocities in history were perpetrated by people claiming to adhere to the divine moral code, while some of the best people I've ever met were atheists. Faith rarely dictates morality, and if you need a god to tell you not to murder, you're probably not that great a person to begin with.

In fact, part of what led me to leaving the cult was the realisation that their doctrine celebrated an upcoming genocide. When God ended the world, he would kill everyone who didn't believe in him. This was the epitome of good in their belief but strikes me as an incredible act of evil.

An interesting question soon surfaces, however. If we don't get our morality from a holy book, where does it come from?

You're probably bored of me saying this by now, but there are, once again, no easy answers. The price of freedom is that there are no easy boxes to fit into. "Knowing good and bad" means holding ourselves to a higher standard. We don't receive our ethics through a list of rules and regulations. We have to think for ourselves, weigh situations on a case-by-case basis. Accepting that reality is complicated means right and wrong are often context dependent, and that shades of grey often exist.

It also means we aren't judgmental. Of course, that doesn't mean we have to tolerate any kind of behaviour. The skills of shrewd judgment and wisdom are important. We must use our discernment and not blindly trust. When people do abhorrent things to harm other people, we shouldn't tolerate that. Freedom is not anarchy. But when it comes to everyday decisions with no clear answer, we give everyone the space and respect to reach their own conclusions.

Magical ethics are important. We have to know our own moral code if we are to work magic. There is a great chapter on magical ethics in *The Witch at the Forest's Edge* by Christine Grace that I would really recommend. Taking the time to question your own ethics will make it much easier to develop a magical practice if you decide to continue on this path. Reclaiming the devil means giving this some thought and figuring out for yourself the knowledge of good and bad. Go ahead, bite the apple.

The Clergy of the Craft

In Christian theology, the serpent in the Garden of Eden is seen as the devil. As shown through my retelling, he was merely trying to encourage humanity to claim the knowledge of good and bad, giving them the ability to self-govern. We no longer needed someone to dictate right and wrong or mediate our morality. We became our own guides.

Clergy today are often seen as the mediators of relationship with God and keepers of doctrine. They exist to remind you your morality is flawed and to tell you what God wants you to do. They fill the role of telling you right and wrong. Reclaiming the devil means accepting we don't need that. We can trust ourselves and guide ourselves. We don't need anyone to mediate our relationship with the Divine, because we are divine.

The existence of an evil devil wishing you harm necessitates someone to protect you—to provide doctrine and safeguards. You need someone who can warn you of the dangers of your fickle heart, keep you safe from your wicked self. The role of clergy in some faiths is exactly that: dictating doctrine, saving you from yourself, and becoming a middle point between you and the Divine.

Witchcraft has priests and priestesses, but they serve as teachers, not custodians of doctrine. They don't tell you what to think; they simply hand you tools. They also serve to lead ritual. However, they don't hear confession. There is no sin in Witchcraft, so there is no need for this role to be filled.

Priests and priestesses in Witchcraft don't mediate your relationship with the Divine. We don't need a middleman to talk to our gods; we have free access to them whenever we need. The priesthood in Witchcraft are teachers and guides, but they do not claim to walk the path for us. They may facilitate and teach you how to talk to your gods, but their most important roles are facilitation and teaching.

I Am the Devil

To the people still in the cult, I am the devil. As a gay Witch, I am everything wrong with the world. I have fallen to Satan; he has got his claws into me and corrupted me. (I must get around to thanking him someday.) This book is the devil. The fact I wrote it makes me irredeemable. I have committed the ultimate sin for which there can be no forgiveness: speaking out against their doctrine. They describe this as a "sin against the holy spirit," and it means I am condemned to death according to their teachings.

The list of what isn't the devil is far shorter than what is. Anything fun, anything empowering, anything remotely interesting is probably Satanic. It makes me wonder why I tried to serve God for so long in the first place.

Simply being your authentic self, without being constrained by fear or doctrine, is the single most powerful way to reclaim the devil. I know I am a good person, and if being who I am means I'm on the side of Satan, then he must not be that bad of a guy either. The inner divinity of a Witch might realistically be called the devil, because to the intolerant, everything we are is Satanic. According to puritanical doctrine, the fact we recognise ourselves as divine automatically puts us in league with him.

When you lay it all out, only one conclusion can reasonably be reached: The God of the cult is the truly evil one. He condemns everything he doesn't like, kills indiscriminately, and demands constant praise and worship to soothe his fragile ego. The devil encourages us to know ourselves, make our own decisions, and engage ourselves in the mystery. I'd rather be on his side any day.

Chapter 10
Contemplating the Divine

Have you got a moment to talk about our lord and saviour, Gwyn ap Nudd? No, don't worry; I'm only joking. This isn't a chapter preaching about the gods. I've done enough of that to last a lifetime. Besides, there is no one-size-fits-all approach to divinity in Witchcraft. Anything I say is my opinion, and many Pagans and Witches may disagree with me. I may well end up disagreeing with myself in a few years' time, and that's okay. Again, there is no doctrine or Bible to turn to. In many ways, to be a Witch is to be a theologian. You have to figure out what makes sense to you.

Before we go any further, it is important to once again emphasize that belief in any gods is not an essential component of being a Witch, much less incorporating them into your practice. I know many Witches who completely reject the idea of divinity, instead forging relationships with the spirits of the land or their higher selves. I would argue a belief in some form of spiritual dimension of life is an important part of the Craft, but that does not have to take the form of gods and goddesses. However, taking some time to contemplate the nature of spirit, in whatever form you believe it takes, can be helpful at any point along your path.

Dialogue with the Divine

Contemplating the nature of God was an enormously important part of my deconstruction from the cult. I had been given a very specific picture of who God was—one I was not allowed to question. He was the ultimate expression of love, of justice, of peace, while also being an agent of war, the being that had condemned humanity to suffering and death, and a harsh and unflinching judge who required the sacrificial death of his own son to show mercy and forgiveness. These paradoxes made it incredibly difficult to develop a personal relationship with the Divine within fundamentalist Christianity. It was like trying to form a relationship with an abstract concept rather than a living deity. I had to take time to form my own thoughts about divinity and find new ways to connect.

This is where I may get a little too philosophical. My belief is that whenever we contemplate divinity, we enter a dialogue with the gods. If I sit down to think about Ceridwen, then I believe Ceridwen is there. We cannot engage with the gods without them being present. I don't mean that they are always around, always watching. Rather, when we maintain the intention to perceive them, then they will be there. Simply thinking deeply about divinity is a spiritual act. We set ourselves apart from the mundane world and enter a sacred space in our mind. We become a little divine since we invite them into this inner world. In this liminality, we may gain knowledge of them if they choose to share it with us.

In *Plato's Phaedo*, Plato describes thinking of the soul as being in conversation with itself.[91] The part of us that reasons and can think is not physical; it exists in the realm of the mind. In my opinion, reasoning about the gods invites them into this space with us. Rather than simply a dialogue with ourselves, our thoughts become a dialogue with the Divine. We become a fusion of human and god, capable of comprehending both. We can enhance this dialogue through ritual or invite divinity into our inner temple, but all that is truly required is an act of contemplation.

How, though, do we know what to contemplate? This question reveals a secondary facet of the gods, showing that a personal relationship doesn't have to be the starting point. The gods have revealed themselves by embedding their stories in narrative. They've shown us a glimpse of who they are. In my opinion, this communal cultural knowledge often serves as a foundation and beginning for experience of the Divine.

This also means that when we contemplate our own innate divinity, we invite the god within to enter that space with us. We enter dialogue with the divine aspect of the self; we learn from our own sanctity. Our mind becomes a temple when we visit there to commune with the gods, but the temple is not where they live.

------

91. Plato, *Plato's Phaedo*, ed. John Burnet (Oxford: Clarendon Press, 1911).

However, we must be careful not to mistake the dialogue for truth about the Divine. The gods are only one half of the conversation; we bring just as much of ourselves to it. We see only half the picture; the rest is obscured by our human viewpoint. Therefore, two people may contemplate the same divinity and come away with drastically different opinions. It is in the moments of shared gnosis that we discover deeper truths. That does not mean we need our beliefs validated by other people. Any truths we glean, whether stemming from the distant gods or our personal divinity, are valid. We simply cannot insist on them as objective truth and force them onto others. Taking this reasoning further, it also means that any divinity I can conceive of is real, even if only in the dialogue of my perception, but that they can be real only to me. Divinity can be entirely personal.

When I first left the cult, long before I stepped into the world of Witchcraft, I tried to understand the Bible. I still felt like it was a sacred text. It had spoken to people for centuries. I thought about it like this: The Bible writers were contemplating the Divine and therefore becoming divine. But they were still half human. All truth found there was channelled through them and their biases. Getting caught up in the line and letter of a verse was foolish, because there was no way of unpicking the biases the writers brought to it. There was benefit to Christianity if a broad view was taken: the idea of a loving and tolerant divinity. I am not anti-Christian. But I am anti-controlling religion of any sort. Christianity has been used to exercise this control, but it is far from the only method out there.

The Doctrine of the Gods

To be human is to deal in narrative. Everything we do and everything we are is a story. From our youngest years, we learn from the tales we are told. We don't stray into the deep, dark woods because the big, bad wolf may be hiding there. We are no stranger to finding the lesson in the tale, and this is a skill any Witch will become very familiar with. We narrate our lives, turning everything we do into a story. We often tell it in the most entertaining way we can. The truth is less important than the tale. If we are in any way made in the image of the gods, I think it is this.

The gods reveal themselves in narrative. They always have. Even the Bible is presented as a narrative that must be combed through to discover the deeper truths. Myth and poetry are the languages of the gods, and we must learn to speak them if we are to discover our deities. The epic poetry in which is hidden the Greek pantheon, the Icelandic sagas that reveal the Norse pantheon, even the medieval prose of the Mabinogion that reveals the Welsh. The gods love narrative and are experts at weaving themselves into it. But the gods do not reveal themselves in words on a page; rather, it is in the narrative spirit below those words that they are found. If angels are the messengers of God, then surely our mythology is the archetypal angel.

If the gods love myth and legend enough that they allow themselves to be discovered through them, then surely they will also accept them as gifts and offerings. We can praise our gods with stories, poems, songs, and all the joys of creativity we know they adore. This is also a wonderful way to make eco-friendly offerings.

Exercise: Telling the Story of the Gods

This is a very simple exercise but can be a rather profound experience. It will allow you to briefly explore the idea of discovering divinity within the narrative.

Materials:
• A myth of your choosing

Directions:
Choose the story of a deity you feel particularly drawn to. For me, this would either be a branch of the Mabinogi or the story of Taliesin. Now, rather than reading silently, read the words out loud. Embody the characters, change your voice, let the story come to life through you. Feel the story. Let it resonate in the deepest parts of your being, flooding through your entire body. See how different the experience is? As you become more comfortable, try reciting it from memory. See how it shifts and shimmers in the telling, as if it's alive and taking its own shape.

Progressive Revelation

When it comes to divinity, and honestly spirituality in general, I am a firm believer in progressive revelation. That was a completely new idea to me when I left the cult. Fundamentalist Christianity is very much a revealed religion, meaning that their doctrine has already been provided in a one-and-done revelation. The door to further spiritual truth is closed, the mystery already solved. I now find the idea of a one-time revelation very difficult to swallow. It leads to a rigid belief system that refuses to adapt.

Each generation receives their own piece of the mystery; the river never stops flowing. This means that the Witchcraft of today will look different than even a generation ago. It also means that the Witchcraft of tomorrow will look different again. That knowledge helps you not to be too precious about your beliefs. Your spirituality answers the questions you ask, informed by the moment you live in. However, even those questions will change, never mind the answers. Change is the only constant.

Even the animism of today is different than the animism of the ancient past. Everything changes and adapts to answer the questions of today, much as life evolves to meet the challenges of the environment. What refuses to change will die out.

The Path of True Freedom

Doctrine is like a coat of paint over the truth of divinity. It does nothing to reveal it; the extra layer merely obscures. What can we learn from a static list of dos and don'ts? What personal relationship can we have with a being defined by the rules they make? What freedom can there be when every decision has a predetermined correct choice? Doctrine chokes the life out of spirituality and leaves it merely as religion. Doctrine is the shell left behind when the gods die.

This knowledge hands us the power to make our own decisions, but that power comes with responsibility. We must figure out our own ethics and values and decide on our own path each and every day. The way we treat each other is not policed by some rules in a book; it comes from our own innate goodness. That, in my opinion, is far more worthy of celebration than mere obedience out of fear. If you need the fear of punishment to simply act as a decent human being, then you are not one. True freedom is a revealer. When we choose kindness and choose to treat each other well, despite that not being commanded by some higher power, we reveal something about ourselves. We choose this path because it is the right thing to do and show that humans have the capacity for great good.

Doubt Is Divine

In the cult, I was taught that doubt was the worst sin I could possibly commit. A weak faith was vulnerability to the Satanic force all around. I needed a blind and blazing faith. Questions were simply to be repressed. Possibly the only thing worse than having personal doubts was sharing those doubts. If you caused someone else to "stumble," then you were truly damned.

Becoming a Witch taught me just how wrong this opinion was. Blind faith is the true weakness. Yes, belief is powerful and can be used to great magical effect, but blind faith just leaves you stumbling in the dark. Just think about it. The very concept of magic necessitates doubting that what we can immediately perceive is all there is to the world. We must make contact with the otherworld, which is felt and experienced beyond the senses. We must literally be able to doubt apparent reality itself.

In his book *Consorting with Spirits*, Jason Miller stresses how important it is to allow a spiritual experience to occur and for us to exist within it without questioning—to simply be present and allow yourself to be in the flow of experience. However, once the experience has occurred, it is important to be able to critically analyse it. To quote him: "Engage the experience without doubt while it is happening. Analyze it critically after it is over."[92]

The job of the Witch is not to constantly doubt everything, nor is it to accept everything unquestioningly. It is to find the middle ground between doubt and acceptance, between mundane and magic, between physical and spiritual. We walk the crooked path between myth and logic. Paradox and liminality are essential parts of a magical worldview. How can you hold an iron, unshakable faith when the gods and spirits could be multiple contradictory things at once? Flexibility of belief is required, being able to shift with whatever is revealed to you. Besides, it is only through doubt that we can refine our beliefs. In Paganism the possibilities are endless, and all doors are open. Why would we lock

....

92. Jason Miller, *Consorting with Spirits: Your Guide to Working with Invisible Allies* (Newburyport, MA: Weiser Books, 2022), 53.

ourselves into a cupboard? To quote Sir Terry Pratchett, "The presence of those seeking the truth is infinitely to be preferred to the presence of those who think they've found it."[93] To be a Witch is to be the perpetual seeker, in love with the mystery and all the doubt that comes with it.

Making Space for Faith

Doubt doesn't mean becoming cynical, however. As a Witch, you will occasionally be confronted by paradox. Two seemingly opposing things can both be true, especially on a path with this much freedom. One of those paradoxes is about to hit us head on. Having just discussed the divinity of doubt, I'm now going to talk about the power of belief.

In the chapter on magic, we discussed the power of magical will. When we work magic, this state of mind can be incredibly powerful. By immersing ourselves in belief, we turn it into a powerful tool of creating change. This is a very important component of any spellwork. Belief can also be powerful in overcoming shame. When my belief system changed from cult to coven, much of the shame I experienced began to melt away. Allowing yourself to believe in your path without judgment and making space for your faith can be powerful ways of healing. This doesn't mean to accept everything uncritically, but it does mean allowing there to be questions we cannot answer. The mystery does not invalidate your personal beliefs.

Contemplating the Divine

I was deep in conversation with my partner one day. We were discussing the nature of divinity and what it means to be a devotional Witch. He asked me to describe my concept of divinity, and without thinking, I grabbed a glass from the counter and launched into a speech. This physical illustration of how I perceive the gods came to me suddenly in a flash of inspiration.

To demonstrate this for yourself, take a glass and fill it with some juice. What shape does the juice take? It takes on the shape of whatever holds it. Now take a glass of a different shape and pour the juice into it. Has it changed? It's still the same amount of liquid; it still takes up the same amount of space, but the way you perceive it is different because of the container it is in. Now imagine what the

....
93. Terry Pratchett, *Monstrous Regiment* (London: Corgi Books, 2014), 195.

juice would look like if the glass vanished. It would be little more than a puddle on the ground, completely formless. It would be difficult to see it at all.

In my opinion, divinity is very similar to the juice, while a specific culture is the glass. We cannot perceive divinity in a vacuum, only in the way the gods present themselves to a certain culture at a certain time. The culture is the vessel that holds them. If the same divinity presented themselves to different cultures at different times, they would still look drastically different because the vessel is different. A culture reveals something about themselves in the way they perceive their gods.

Trying to rip a god completely out of their context is like shattering the glass. The liquid probably won't get too upset; it is the container you have harmed.

Cultural Deities

While I believe direct personal experience is incredibly important in forming a relationship with the gods, once again this comes with a disclaimer. The deities that appear to us through specific mythologies are culturally relevant. They do not exist simply for Witches, but have appeared to specific peoples at specific times. The dialogue of their existence is not with any individual, but with an entire culture. Take an example from Wales.

The goddess Ceridwen is revered by Witches and Pagans in all corners of the globe. There are temples and shrines dedicated to her all over the world. However, her life begins firmly within Welsh culture. She serves as the initiatrix in the tale of Taliesin, the archetypal bard famous throughout Wales to this day. In an extremely Christian society, the bards would argue about the source of inspiration, with some saying that it flowed from the cauldron of Ceridwen. She is not only a goddess, but also a treasure of Welsh culture. These aspects of her identity are not easily separated. She has been loved and revered in Wales for centuries, and that history and cultural relevance are important. If we believe the gods have power and agency, then we must believe they revealed themselves to a certain culture for a reason. To rip them completely from that context does them a great disservice. Witches do not own the gods, nor do we get to dictate what they are.

Apotheosis

An important concept within Witchcraft is the idea of apotheosis. A god or goddess doesn't need to start as a divine being. Many don't. The point is that a being can be elevated to divine status. You don't need to be born divine; you can become divine.

My partner is from the Welsh Marches, the liminal border region between Wales and England. His practice is built around the lore, legends, and land in this region, caught between two cultures and shaped by both. In fact, his practice is shaped so much by it that he goes by Witch of Salopia online, Salopia being an older name for Shropshire. It was a workshop he taught on his patron deity that really helped me understand apotheosis, and I'm grateful to share a little of it here.

The River Severn flows through the land of the Marches, travelling down from Wales and ending in the Bristol Channel. She breathes life into many towns and cities along her flow. What many don't realise is she is also home to a goddess, Sabrina, also known as Hafren in Welsh. However, this goddess did not start out that way. Her origin myths show her as a playful nymph or a drowned maiden. She is certainly a river spirit when she first appears, but not quite yet divine. Over the centuries, the towns and cities on her banks grew, and people became ever more dependent on her. As her status grew, she took on greater importance in writing, in legend, and in the stories people told. Her playful nature became sharpened by her ability to flood and drown, and she was given offerings to appease her temperament. Eventually, she was immortalised in verse as a saviour goddess in *Comus* by Milton, famously the author of *Paradise Lost*. Today, she is worshipped all over the world, her journey from nymph to goddess firmly established.

The deities of the Welsh pantheon also follow a similar journey. While some of them may hint at older gods or goddesses, the process of apotheosis means we don't need to look at whether they were divine; we need only ask are they divine today. And clearly, the deities of the Welsh pantheon are revered across the globe.

Worship as a Witch

"Do you worship your gods, or do you work with them?" This is a question that often comes up in Witchcraft spaces, and there is no definitive answer. I do believe, however, that the question is at least a little influenced by the Christian culture of the West. Within the cult, to worship God meant total submission. It was to obey completely and without question, follow every commandment, bow, and scrape. Essentially, worship was spiritual servitude. However, that is not the dictionary definition of the term. According to the Cambridge online dictionary, it simply means "to have or show a strong feeling of respect and admiration for God or a god."[94]

Of course, dictionaries don't arbitrate meaning, and to many people, worship will include the Christian idea of submission. In addition, worship in the cult was the only way for me to earn value. I could only be a good person if I was worshipping hard enough. It's very hard for me to shake those connotations from the word, and it's one I'm uncomfortable using to describe my practice. However, that doesn't mean other people shouldn't use it. The term that best describes your relationship with your deities is the one you should use. The problems only surface when we insist our way of approaching the Divine is the only acceptable way, or that everyone has to use the same words we use.

I personally know many Witches who proudly worship their gods. I love that they do. I love the variety of Witchcraft. But never has one of them told me I must use the word *worship* or invalidated the trauma that makes me uncomfortable with it. Whatever term works best for you, use that. At the end of the day, if you continue this journey, it is *your* practice and spiritual path, and only you can dictate where it goes.

I personally prefer to describe myself as "working with" the divinities I acknowledge in my Craft. To me, this implies a reciprocal relationship with them rather than one based in submission. I have heard arguments that this diminishes the status of divinity, that the gods are above us and we should acknowledge that. I don't personally agree; however, even if that is the case, you can work with your manager even if they hold a higher rank. Working alongside someone doesn't necessarily make them your equal.

Finally, even if you believe in gods, you don't have to worship or work with them. To worship is an active process, distinct from passive belief. Worship requires more than simply an acknowledgment of existence. I like to think of it like rocket science. I am not a rocket scientist. I know this field exists and am

94. "Worship," Cambridge Dictionary, accessed June 28, 2023, https://dictionary.cambridge .org/dictionary/english/worship.

awed when I hear news of space exploration. However, it is not a part of my daily life, and I rarely devote much thought to it. If you choose to practice and don't want to include deities but are comfortable believing in them, that is a completely valid path.

Pagan Prayer

Prayer has been used by magicians for millennia. In fact, one of the early theories of magic we have comes from the philosopher Plotinus, born in 205 CE. He claims there is no real difference between the effect of magic and the effect of prayer: both get results.[95] What's really fascinating is that prayers were used in ancient magic in the form of cursing tablets as a plea for justice. These tablets were in widespread use in the ancient world, used for all manner of magic (including erotic magic). Their use was so widespread it's likely they influenced the tradition of cursing wells in Wales.

A plea for justice tablet was often used when something had been stolen from an individual. They would write their petition on a lead tablet, twist it up, and deposit it in a well or elsewhere underground. Often, the prayer would include giving the stolen item to the deity invoked, in effect making them the victim of the theft and punishing the thief their problem.[96] Personally, I think this is an ingenious solution. No one wants to end up on the wrong side of an angry god. It's something I have incorporated into my own practice.

Exercise: A Prayer to Bind

The ancient plea for justice prayers were written, not spoken aloud. This was something alien to me coming from the cult. All prayer was spoken, addressed directly to God. However, the idea of written prayers is very powerful, acting almost as a letter to the gods.

95. Bernd-Christian Otto and Michael Stausberg, eds., "Plotinus," in *Defining Magic: A Reader*, Critical Categories in the Study of Religion (Milton Park, UK: Acumen Publishing, 2013), 28.
96. Daniel Ogden, "Part 1: Binding Spells: Curse Tablets and Voodoo Dolls in the Greek and Roman Worlds," in *Witchcraft and Magic in Europe: Ancient Greece and Rome*, by Valerie Flint, Richard Gordon, Georg Luck, and Daniel Ogden (London: Athlone Press, 2000), 41.

Materials:

• Pen and paper

Directions:

Presented here is an example of the ending of a prayer for justice from one of the recovered cursing tablets. It gives an example of the kind of language used and may be helpful in writing your own.

> *Lady Demeter, I beseech you as the victim of injustices. Help me, goddess, and make a just choice, so as to bring the most terrible things and even harsher terrible things upon those who contrived such things and laughed at us and inflicted griefs upon both myself and my wife Epictesis. Queen, heed us in our plight and punish those who are glad to see us in such a condition.[97]*

Obviously, this example is for quite a specific purpose, but there is nothing stopping you from writing prayers for other petitions. The only limit is your own imagination.

Take a moment to think about what you need and which deity you might petition. Once you have the thought clearly in mind, begin to write. Let it flow; it doesn't need to be elegant or wordy—this is purely between you and the Divine. You might use the example as a guide, but you don't have to. Do whatever feels right and helps you experience the power of written prayer.

Who Answers?

We briefly touched on prayer in our chapter on magic. Within the cult, prayer was essentially one-way communication. You asked God for something, then stayed alert to notice the answer. And as I said in that chapter, I often did notice an answer. However, leaving the cult changed my perspective on where that came from.

....
97. Ogden, "Part 1: Binding Spells," 44.

Many Witches believe in the concept of a divine self—that there is a spiritual part of you that is itself of the gods. It's an incredibly empowering belief and one I can certainly subscribe to. One way of understanding prayer is through this belief. My divine self is now the being I believe answered my prayers, even if I didn't know I was calling on him at the time. I was asking, and I was answering.

The cult used prayer as a tool of control. If you were having doubts or had difficult questions, you were encouraged to pray and wait on God. It became a powerful thought-stopping technique to crush any dissent. It also made you feel powerless. If you needed anything, you had to rely on God to answer. You weren't capable of creating any change for yourself. Prayer became a way to reinforce your own insignificance and deepen the indoctrination.

Again, Witchcraft was incredibly empowering. In changing my perspective on who answers, I took back my own innate power. That's not to say divinities cannot answer our prayers. I'm certain they can and do. But we do not need to helplessly wait for them to step in. We can create the change we want to see.

Prayer as Devotion

Prayer as magic, petition, or invocation of personal divinity are not the only reasons to pray. For many Witches, prayer isn't just about power or magic. It can also be a devotional act. Whether we work with or worship our deities, prayer can be a powerful way of strengthening the sacred relationship and showing gratitude for their impact in our life, whether that be magical or even just connecting us to our culture.

One really interesting study found that prayer lights up the same areas in the brain as socialising.[98] When we communicate with a deity we truly believe in, our brain seems to recognise it as social communication. We can build a sacred relationship with our deities by using this form of communication that even our bodies recognise as valid.

One aspect of prayer that made it difficult for me to connect was the idea that God was always watching me. Why talk to someone about your day, your concerns, your successes when they already know all about them? This idea doesn't translate into Witchcraft. Our gods have better things to do than

....

98. Uffe Schjoedt, Hans Stødkilde-Jørgensen, Armin W. Geertz, and Andreas Roepstorff, "Highly Religious Participants Recruit Areas of Social Cognition in Personal Prayer," *Social Cognitive and Affective Neuroscience* 4, no. 2 (June 2009): 199–207, https://doi.org/10.1093/scan/nsn050.

constantly watch us. Therefore, when we take the time to talk to them, to share our thoughts, feelings, and concerns, it can build a powerful bond. This, in turn, can help when we invite the Divine to work magic with us. But there is more than just prayer to create a reciprocal relationship with divinity. We have more to offer.

Sacrifice and Offerings

In the cult, I was never doing enough. No matter what, I should always have done more: more hours preaching, more hours studying, more money donated. My worth as a person was dependent on how much I had done for God that day. Nothing else mattered. If I wasn't sacrificing enough, I didn't matter.

Sacrifice is another one of those concepts that bridges the gap between my old faith and the new. While the gods of Witchcraft do not demand offerings or sacrifice, they are a helpful part of establishing a working relationship with them. In fact, it is not only the gods who appreciate offerings, but any energies and spirits you might work with. Having at least a surface knowledge of sacrifice was a great help to me.

Sacrifice and offerings are related concepts but slightly different. There is an old fable that illustrates this point.

> *A chicken and a pig are walking along when they pass a charity event selling breakfast. "Ham and eggs for sale, all proceeds to a good cause," the sign reads. The chicken, being a kind and generous soul, decides they should do something to help.*
>
> *"Let's donate some ham and eggs," he cries.*
>
> *"Not so fast," says the pig, "For you that's an offering, but for me it's a sacrifice."*

It's only a short fable but makes its point very well. An offering is something we give that may cost us a little. A sacrifice is a commitment that asks us to give something up at great personal cost. We give up something we know we will miss, something we don't want to give up.

Within Witchcraft, the relationship we have with our gods (if any) is joyful and celebratory, not some strange form of egotistical appeasement, where they get angry at us if we don't praise them enough. The gods have their own lives and know that we do too.

Therefore, in my experience, the Witches of the modern world give offerings far more often than we make sacrifices. We are in a symbiotic relationship with the energies we work with. It's a give and take. Of course, this varies greatly depending on the gods you acknowledge and the kind of relationship you have with them.

An offering can be many things: Some food for the local wildlife, some sweet-smelling incense smoke, or even poetry or prayer. Cleaning up litter from your working area can be an offering. Even singing to the spirits of the place can work very well. The idea of giving your gods something, be that sacrifice or offering, was nothing new to me. I gave twenty years to the god of the cult. However, I was able to incorporate this idea into my practice with the energies I worked with, albeit in a less intense way.

I like to think of this through the lens of how we show people we love them. There are many recognised ways we express affection, and each of us is likely to do it in a slightly different way. One way is by gift-giving. I personally love to show my affection for someone by picking out a gift I think they'll truly appreciate, be it something physical or an experience. It's something we all do quite naturally. We gift something to those we love to show them how well we know them and to make them happy. Who doesn't love the smile on a close friend's face when you hand them the perfect gift? Offerings to the gods, in my opinion, are very similar. When we work out what they really like and offer it to them, it can bring us as much joy as it brings them. Often it will move them to want to reciprocate. That is not the point of the gift, however. The offering is to work on the relationship; anything we get back is a product of that relationship. It's not like a vending machine where you insert your offering and get a reward. It's a far more personal process of building a relationship with a being you care about.

An Altar as Sacred Space

Most spiritual traditions have some concept of an altar. This is physical space to interact with the gods, to invite them to share in our magic and present them with offerings. I find it helpful to think of an altar as the bedside table of a deity. If someone gives you a bedside table within their space, it is a symbol of intimacy.

We would never give that space to someone we're not close with. It doesn't mean you live there, but the person wants you to feel comfortable. People would be able to learn something about you from what you choose to place on it. It represents you, and whenever you are there, it makes you feel at ease.

If someone walked into my bedroom and saw my bedside table, they would learn that I like to play on my Switch. They would see what books I'm currently reading, the skincare products I use, and the little trinkets that mean something to me. From that information, they could make some fairly accurate guesses about my personality. I believe the same can be said for altars. A good altar will say something about the deity it is dedicated to. It will make them feel comfortable in the space. The altar is not where the god lives, but it is where you call to them in order to praise them or invite them to join you in ritual work or magic. Therefore, you want it to be somewhere they feel at home.

Within many streams of Christianity, the idea of an altar is usually something exclusive to a church. However, in Witchcraft, altars are usually within your home. When we go into nature to work ritual, an altar is less necessary, as the gods are already there, though a smaller devotional space may also be set up even then.

The idea of an altar within the home has a long precedent. The altars that have survived from ancient Roman religion were mostly household or personal ones rather than those dedicated at temples. There is even evidence that these altars would have been portable so you could bring the gods with you wherever you went.[99]

The concept of an altar was completely alien to me when I first became a Witch. To the cult, this would have been idolatry. The joyless, fundamentalist God would rage at any images or trinkets made in his honour. To do so was a sin worthy of death. The gods of Witchcraft are far more appreciative and joyous. To dedicate a space to them in your home is a great way to connect with divinity and add something spiritual into the everyday. My personal altar is under the bedroom mirror so that when I get ready in the morning, I can take a moment of reverence for the gods I work with.

....

99. Anthony King, "Carrying the Gods with Them? Provenance and Portability of Altars to Romano-Celtic Deities in Britain," in *Celtic Religions in the Roman Period: Personal, Local, and Global*, eds. Ralph Haeussler and Anthony King (Aberystwyth, Ceredigion, Wales: Celtic Studies Publications, 2017), 119–50.

Divinity isn't the only thing allowed an altar in Witchcraft. An altar can act as a focal point to connect with any kind of spirit life. I have an altar to the household spirit where I regularly leave offerings of sweetened milk. It is a sacred space within my home, reserved for spirit communication and building reciprocal relationships. In many ways, an altar is a microcosmic expression of your relationship with the spirits you dedicate it to.

Exercise: Planning and Constructing an Altar

Now that we've discussed a little about altars, it's time to have a go, or at least plan how you might go about it when you're ready. An altar is not necessarily about Witchcraft, nor is it necessarily about worship. It can be a powerful way to honour yourself, your ancestors, or any other beings you may wish to. This exercise will also be helpful if you continue to walk this path, allowing you to take the first step in honouring any deities you may feel called to. If you are not ready to construct an altar, then this is a good opportunity to journal about it and better understand your own feelings.

Materials:
• Your Llyfr Cyfrin or other journal
• A pen
• The items you feel called to include

Directions:
This is part journaling and part practical. First, you have to figure out what represents the deities or spirits you want to work with, and then you can put those things into action. Take a moment to think about that. Is there a certain divinity you would like to work with? Or some deity you believe has been reaching out to you?

If nothing springs to mind or you're uncomfortable with the idea of gods, constructing an altar to the household spirit can be a powerful way to connect with the sacred in your home.

Now take a moment to tune in to your intuition. What colours represent the deity you have chosen? Perhaps choose an altar cloth of that colour. Do they have any correspondences that immediately come to mind? For example, the goddess Rhiannon is represented by horses, and a depiction of a horse would be a great way to invite her into the space. If you are working with a deity from antiquity, like Aphrodite or Odin, it may be worth researching how they were depicted on historic altars and what devotional statues may have been dedicated to them. This can be a powerful way to connect with them.

Ultimately, there is no wrong way to construct an altar. As long as you put some thought into it and make it a meaningful representation of your relationship with the Divine or with yourself, you will get powerful results.

The Gods Need Us and We Need Them

The gods don't need our worship. They do, however, need their stories to be told. In a very real way, divinity flows through the tales; for if the stories die, the gods fade with them.

Witches do not expect their gods to be perfect. In fact, we're very aware of the fact they aren't. They can't fix everything for us, and we shouldn't expect them to. If you believe that some divinity is going to fix everything, you stop trying to make anything better. You just start "waiting on God." Why do anything when he's going to step in and remake the earth anyway? Why waste time doing something unnecessary? An almighty saviour god absolves you of all responsibility. Why better the world when he's going to do it anyway? This is incredibly dangerous thinking. The gods need us to save ourselves. If there is no world and there are no people, then there are no gods.

Sometimes, gods may come into existence because we need them. They fill some void or call us back to something we are in danger of forgetting. After all, if they were irrelevant, they would simply fade away. The gods of Witchcraft are not about salvation. They are not literally going to save us. But in my opinion, they do serve an important function.

I think one of the most important aspects of divinity is to enchant us with the mystery. They exist to remind us we don't know everything—that we can't know everything. They reveal pieces of themselves but never all that they are; then they challenge us to comprehend them. We pick at what it could all mean, dissect it, debate it, and all the while fall deeper in love with the mystery of existence. Perhaps the gods aren't meant to be understood. Perhaps they are meant to be adored. Perhaps their role is to embody the mystery and lead us back to where we're meant to be.

As well as mystery, the gods embody paradox and liminality. We receive conflicting information about them that we must somehow reconcile. They challenge us to broaden our understanding, to sustain the many versions of them that exist. In this way, they help us to understand magic and the spiritual side of life, where there are no easy answers, and many things can all be true. Regardless of whether they are literally real or not, they still challenge us to do that most important of things: think.

Chapter 11
Embodying the Witch Within

The person I was at eighteen would hate the person I am today. An openly gay Witch was about the most dangerous, heretical thing he could imagine. I would have been truly terrified of myself, and nothing makes me prouder. At least it means I'm doing the Witchcraft thing right.

The funny thing is, that eighteen-year-old version of me already had the seeds of Witchcraft within him. He already had the power. We all do; most just don't recognise it. He had already filled his mind with fantastic worlds of imagination and fantasy, both powerful tools in the arsenal of a Witch. And he understood some spiritual concepts, even if they were distorted by the doctrine of fear and control. The point is that the Witch I am today already lived in that scared teenager.

Finding that inner Witch, however, would take many years. I had to deconstruct my old belief system and unlearn all the lies I had been taught about the magical side of life. I had to clear away the remnants of indoctrination and discover who I truly was at my core.

This book exists because I did just that. The amazing people in my life, the authors who put inspirational books out there, the many people sharing their stories—these all helped me to find my way into my practice and helped reveal who I was always meant to be.

Anyone Can Be a Witch

To be a Witch is not a matter of birth or heredity. It is not about DNA. It is an acknowledgment of a power anyone can possess and adopting a worldview most seem to miss. Every day you wake up and become the Witch. Every person has the potential to be a Witch; it is whether they choose to act on that potential or not.

The path of Witchcraft is never finished. If you choose to, it is something you can continue to walk your entire life. My practice evolves daily. Writing this book changed the way I Witch. Those changes may be subtle and long-term, or they may be seismic and sudden, like joining a new coven or tradition. Either way, every moment, every version of you, will have a slightly different version of the Craft. It's why I believe continuing to learn is so important. A book gives a glimpse into someone's practice at the moment of writing. But that practice will change. Witchcraft will change, the same way that life will change you. Every day that passes leaves a little mark on your identity. If you choose to continue this journey beyond this book, be open to that change. Do not feel that you must commit to one way of doing things; all doors are open to you. Take joy in what you find.

Bring Back the Sacred

If you are leaving one faith for another, one of the most difficult things can be making space for the sacred. Everything you ever held dear, everything you believed and found value in, is up in the air. It's important to take some time to reconnect with the idea of sanctity and bring some form of it back into your life. Regardless of whether you continue walking this path, making a little space for the sacred in your life can be a profoundly joyous thing. I will briefly discuss three ways the sacred can be woven into the practice of Witchcraft, but I believe these principles can find a home in any spiritual path.

Sacred Time

The concept of sacred time is important in constructing a working practice. The idea of sanctifying water was something we discussed earlier in the form of moon water, but we can also sanctify our time. Essentially, this means setting it apart as holy or for a spiritual purpose. Any time we dedicate to our Craft is sacred time. But an important aspect of this is presence. When you fully immerse yourself in spellwork, in ritual, in research, or in any other part of your Craft, you will tap into the flow. You will become so present in the moment, it is as if you become completely unaware of time, carried in the stream of spirit. You may have experienced this yourself already and know exactly what I'm talking about, or it may be an experience in your future. You will know it when it happens.

With so many people sharing their practices online, it's easy to feel like you're doing it wrong, that you need all the bells and whistles to be a real Witch. But if you can set aside sacred time, you're already halfway there. Magic shared on social media is not magic practiced in sacred time. It is designed to look aesthetic and beautiful. It is designed to be shared. However, the act of filming it rips you out of presence. It isn't there for you to experience. Sacred time is pure experience. Don't worry about what other people are doing or posting. Be in the moment and the magic will follow.

This is quite easy to observe during group ritual. Those who can be present and immerse themselves in it will have a profound experience. You have to allow yourself to be lost in it, to bring that state of mind. If you watch people after ritual, you will see those who look as if they have come back from another time. They've had an intense, emotional, spiritual experience because they brought presence to the ritual. They made that time sacred. No one can do that for you.

Interestingly, if we look at much of the lore we have about the otherworld, time often moves differently there. When you return, you believe a few moments have passed when it may be years, or you may have been gone for years and find it was only a few moments. Time is distorted and stretched in the world beyond ours. This ties sacred time and space together quite nicely.

Sacred Space

As well as sacred time, the practice of a Witch incorporates sacred space. Most traditions have some form of ritual that dedicates a space to work magic. The famous example that is commonly used is casting a circle. This creates a symbolic boundary between the magical and mundane spaces. Other people may simply use their altar for this purpose or have some other space that is sacred to them somehow.

Sacred space is usually liminal in nature. This is a word you'll probably hear a lot in reference to Witchcraft, and it essentially refers to an in-between space: The threshold of a doorway, when you are neither in one room nor another. The moment of midnight, when you stand with one foot in yesterday and the other in tomorrow. The edge of a forest, when you are neither among the trees nor in the meadow. These are all liminal spaces and all powerful for working magic.

Exercise: Experiencing Liminality

This exercise is about shifting your state of mind slightly. It can be done very simply. I like to do it stood on the edge of a forest, but it can be done on any boundary. A doorway is great, anywhere you can stand with one foot on either side of the boundary.

Materials:
- Your body
- A boundary space, like a doorway

Directions:
Once you are in the in-between space, bring your attention to it. If you are in a doorway, acknowledge you are neither in one room nor the other. How does it feel to be in a space of transition, neither quite here nor there? It might be a little uncomfortable when you first bring your attention to it so intensely. Usually, when we cross a liminal threshold, we do so without paying any attention to it. Try and persevere in the experience for a few moments, then think about these questions. Perhaps write about them in your Llyfr Cyfrin.

- How does it feel to be in the in-between space?
- Did it make you feel uncomfortable or bring up any other sensations?
- Did you feel like it was a space you shouldn't be in but should instead just pass through?

Within the tradition of the coven, we call this the *space between space* and invoke it whenever we perform ritual. Our first act is to sanctify the space and set it apart. Within some historic traditions, enclosed spaces were seen as sacred, and we symbolically enclose our space, creating a bubble world where magic can be worked.[100] This becomes a space

100. Claude Lecouteux, *Demons and Spirits of the Land: Ancestral Lore and Practices* (Rochester, VT: Inner Traditions, 2015), 108–12.

somewhere between this world and the otherworld, allowing us to tap into both simultaneously. It is through this fusion of sacred time and sacred space that ritual is powered. However, there is one more vital component to consider.

Sacred Relationships

Throughout this book you have read about the many relationships that inform the life of a Witch: relationship to self, to spirits, to nature, to community, to culture, and far more. These points of connection are also powerful components of Witchcraft. In *The Book of Celtic Magic*, Kristoffer Hughes describes magic as pulling on the strands of a web that weaves together all realities. Since everything is inherently connected, when we influence one point, that can ripple out and change another part of the web.[101] While I have given my personal definition of magic earlier, I still think this is a very helpful way to visualise it. To the animistic Witch, everything is fundamentally connected, and there is power in that connection, both seen and unseen. But there is far more to sacred relationships than simply a source of power.

Realising our place in the web can grant us a deep sense of connection. We become less lonely, less afraid. When we gather with like-minded people, it isn't just a social event. It is spending time with others who see the web beneath all things. It is strengthening our ties to ourselves, our friends, our community, and even the wider universe. The relationships we have position us in the world and grant us a foundation from which to change it. Most of what I have discussed in this book incorporates sacred relationships of some kind, whether through correspondences or working with your community.

These relationships stretch deep into the land and into the past, while also propelling us into the future. They are the foundation of what we do as Witches. Recognising that means nurturing those relationships. We form bonds with our land, with the spirits around us, with our community, and with any gods we recognise. They are not a resource we draw upon when we need it, but a part of the whole that we must connect with. This is where authenticity is once again

101. Hughes, *The Book of Celtic Magic*, 3.

important. When we authentically connect with the many beings around us, we build the sacred relationships that are integral to the Craft.

Forge Your Own Path

Throughout this book, I have mentioned both Welsh and German charms, both learned magic and folk magic. I have mentioned different traditions of modern Witchcraft as well as other magical paths. All these elements combine to influence and create my own unique practice. Within the coven, we have practitioners who work with different pantheons of gods; we have practitioners from different cultural backgrounds. While the main expression of our Witchcraft is focused through Welsh lore and culture, there is room for everyone to bring a piece of themselves to it. In fact, this only serves to make the tradition richer and more satisfying. It allows every individual to find themselves in it, which in turn makes the magic more powerful.

In the opening chapter, I discussed Witchcraft as a series of streams, each with different sources but running toward the same sea. The syncretism and eclecticism of Witchcraft exists because everyone will have a different mix of sources adding to their stream. This doesn't make one better than the other; it just makes every practice unique to the practitioner, even if only in small ways.

Inspiration and Passion

As a result, the secret ingredient in any Witchcraft practice is inspiration. Your path has to spark passion in your soul if it's going to work for you. The world of magic is the world of emotion, of intuition, of spirit. If your path doesn't tap into those in some way, it's unlikely to work for you. For some people, that will mean connecting to an established tradition and practicing exactly as that tradition expects. That's completely valid as long as it gives you that sense of connection you need. For many people, it's a great starting point. However, you may feel the desire for something else. You may desire something that connects you to where you are and the people around you, or something that connects you to your ancestry and heritage. Whatever you are seeking, it's okay to build your Witchcraft practice around that.

Of course, as we have discussed, this does come with some caveats. Your practice is *your* practice; dictating that other people should do things the way you do is not okay. It's fine to teach your methods and point out why you believe they work, but insisting on them is not the way. Remember, Witchcraft is not about salvation. It doesn't affect you in the slightest how someone else chooses to be a Witch.

The Power of Imagination

Building on this, it is also worth mentioning creative imagination as an incredibly powerful force. For many people, this simply means fantasy, but I think that view is a little shortsighted. Imagination is the spark of all creation. If we cannot first conceive of something, then we cannot birth it into the world. This is true both physically and spiritually. A strong imagination is the beginning of a strong magical practice.

In many occult streams of thought, it is believed that the creative imagination gives us direct access to higher or different levels of reality.[102] This is something we have touched on in discussing the power of myth. These imaginative, emotive stories are channelled from another reality and contain truths and lessons hidden in the narrative. This is true across many beliefs, and in Welsh culture, it is embodied in the idea of channelling the Awen. When our imagination is truly fired up and we feel the passion surge through our bodies, we can almost taste the Divine. In the combination of inspiration, imagination, and emotion, we can find an incredibly powerful magic.

Again, it is worth reinforcing the point that you need not be restricted by what already exists, nor limited by any one tradition. Of course, if an established tradition is what speaks to you, there is nothing at all wrong with it. But if, as you read into your culture, you find practices and customs that resonate deeply, you can use creative imagination to weave them into your practice today and create a new stream of your own.

Beware of Cultural Appropriation

There is also the issue of cultural appropriation. This is where the way you Witch does start to affect other people. If your practice harms another group of people or culture, expect to be called out on it. This is not an act of judgment, but of

....
102. Antoine Faivre, "The Imagination … You Mean Fantasy, Right?" in *Hermes Explains: Thirty Questions about Western Esotericism*, ed. Wouter Hanegraaff, Peter Forshaw, and Marco Pasi (Amsterdam, The Netherlands: Amsterdam University Press, 2019), 80–87.

respect for the culture and an attempt to preserve it. Freedom is not the same thing as anarchy, and the basic rules of being a decent human still apply. Being respectful to culture and community is an important part of Witchcraft, especially since there are so many different sources and streams of magic you can draw upon.

Beyond that, have fun. Explore and see what works. There is a rich variety of magical and spiritual practices out there waiting to be discovered. Look into the practices of your land and heritage, and you are sure to find many magical delights.

Building Your Practice

Finding a source for your practice can be really helpful, like looking into what your ancestors did as a springboard into your own workings. However, Witchcraft and academia are not the same thing, and we do not need to be glued to what is written in old books to justify our path. An enormously important part of any spirituality is direct personal experience with the spirits. What we learn from this experience will influence our practice. To disregard spiritual experience is to rip the magical heart right out of the Craft.

UPG

If you are active in the Witchcraft community, you have probably heard this direct experience referred to as *UPG*, or *unverified personal gnosis*. This is a catch-all term for the elements of your practice that are not taken from scholarly knowledge or from a passed-down tradition. They are the truths that have been revealed to you and you alone and therefore cannot be verified by anyone else. But that doesn't make them any less valid. Your practice does not need verification or validation from anyone else. I personally dislike the term *UPG* and much prefer *personal gnosis*. Adding the word *unverified* simply seems disparaging. In a culture heavily influenced by the revealed religions with a central doctrine or text that all beliefs can be checked against, an unverified belief is looked upon with judgment. I have personally spoken to many people agonising over the fact their practice contains "unverified" elements, as if direct revelation from the spirit realm were somehow lesser than if it were recorded in a book.

There is a balance to be struck, however. Where this balance lands is down to each person, but all will decide how much of their Craft is scholarly and handed-down knowledge and how much is personal gnosis. In a decentralised belief system, only the individual can make this decision for themselves. That being said, there are some things to be aware of. Personal gnosis is never an excuse for hate or exclusionary ideologies and practices, or for adding elements to your Craft that harm another person. There is also a need to be respectful of culturally sensitive practices and beliefs. Personal gnosis does not entitle you to take something that doesn't belong to you. It is also important to understand that personal gnosis is not doctrine. What is revealed to you is revealed to you and is for you. There is no harm in sharing that and seeing if anyone else is inspired by it, but the moment you attempt to enforce it, you have crushed the spirit out of it.

Reconstruction or Reinvention

An ongoing debate in many Pagan and Witchcraft communities is whether we should reconstruct practices from the past using the material we have available today, or whether we should reinvent them for the modern day. Essentially, are we trying to practice *exactly* as our ancestors did or as close as we can possibly get, or can we pick from what is preserved in lore and history to create something new for the modern day? If you choose to continue walking this path, it is likely a question you too will ponder. It should come as no surprise that I am firmly in the camp of reinvention, but with a respect for the recorded lore.

The way I see it, we don't need to reinvent the wheel, but we can come up with new ways to use it. The cars of today are certainly ancestors of the carts and carriages of the ancient world. They serve a similar function, and they have wheels and axles. But cars have been reinvented for modern use. The pieces that work haven't been changed. There is a core stretching back millennia. But that doesn't mean we're all riding around in carts and carriages today. We take what is useful from the past but make it work for today.

My philosophy on Witchcraft is very similar. There are core parts of the Craft that we will take from history, but the Craft has to work for today. A modern practice must solve modern problems, most of which our ancestors couldn't conceive of. How much of your practice borrows from older techniques is up to you, and everyone has to find their own balance. But in my opinion, even if there were such a thing as an ancient Witch religion, the job of a modern practitioner is not to reconstruct that. We reinvent it into something that works for the here and now.

A great example is the cruelty to animals that can be found in many folk charms or the casting of sigils in precious metals. These inhumane or impractical aspects of the Craft don't really have a place in modern practice, and leaving them in the past is probably best. Reinventing them and finding alternatives is the best way forward. Again, the way these are reinvented can be a personal thing. As always, your path is your own.

Trust Your Intuition

Perhaps one of the most difficult parts of becoming a Witch is learning to trust your intuition, especially after leaving a cult. For years I was told that the heart is treacherous, I couldn't trust myself, and I should just let others tell me what to do. But the Witch knows to trust their intuition and works to train it. We don't take our instructions from anyone else.

The first step is to trust your feelings when it comes to magic. If you feel something is working for you, trust that it is. If you feel it isn't, let it go. It doesn't matter what everyone else is doing; your practice has to work for you. This also translates into divination. I strongly encourage you to try a wide variety of different divinatory practices and see how each of them feels. Do they help you tap into your intuition? A daily divination practice helped me start to trust myself again.

A big part of intuition is being present, being 100 percent in the flow of the moment. A regular practice of meditation can be a powerful way of achieving that. Presence can also help stop your intuition from being overwhelmed by anxiety.

Synchronicity

Synchronicity is another really interesting concept. It was first described by the psychologist Carl Jung and can essentially be boiled down to meaningful coincidence. It's quite similar to the idea of magic, in that it suggests two events can be connected without a clear cause and effect. It's important to state that this theory is not really accepted by modern science; however, science also doesn't dictate spirituality. An example Carl Jung gave was dreaming that you're going to receive a letter from someone, then receiving a letter from them in the next post.[103] Those events aren't physically related, but they are bound together by

....

103. Carl Jung, *Synchronicity: An Acausal Connecting Principle*, trans. R. F. C. Hull, vol. 8, *The Collected Works of C. G. Jung*, Bollingen Series 20 (Princeton, NJ: Princeton University Press, 2010), 28.

synchronicity. The coincidence has a meaning to you; it makes you stop and think. It seems like there's something a little odd going on.

As you begin your witchy path, you're likely to notice more synchronicity in your life. That doesn't mean you should be looking for it. Forcing coincidence isn't really what we're talking about. But being more open to the spiritual side of life is likely to cause subtle changes that you will notice.

I'd like to share a powerful example of this that I personally experienced that still makes me emotional to this day. After I had decided to immerse myself deeper in the world of Witchcraft and found my coven, I wanted to start attending Witchcraft events. If you've stuck with me so far, you'll probably have realised Terry Pratchett was a profound influence on me growing up. As mentioned earlier, I credit his writing with helping me leave a cult and find Witchcraft in the first place. Anyway, I arranged to attend a Witchfest event with my coven and was excited to hear Professor Ronald Hutton was going to be speaking. I'd listened to some of his talks online and knew he was a great speaker. The subject of the talk wasn't immediately revealed though.

A few weeks before I was due to attend, it was announced. Ronald Hutton was delivering a talk about Terry Pratchett. In that moment, I knew I was exactly where I was meant to be. On the day of the talk, I sat in the front row and desperately tried to hold in my tears. I failed. I must have looked so strange to everyone around me, almost sobbing as the history of Terry Pratchett's life was recounted. It wasn't a particularly emotional or meaningful talk, but it meant everything to me.

Be open to the universe speaking to you through these meaningful coincidences. You will know when you're on the right path.

Next Steps

So, where does this all leave us? I hope I've given you some idea of why I celebrate Witchcraft as a space of joy and freedom. Of course, it isn't perfect. Nowhere is. But the ecstatic celebration and acceptance of the Craft make it a wonderful place to explore your spirituality and take power in your otherness.

As I've said before, I'm not interested in recruiting anyone to the Witchcraft side. We may have cookies, but they're only here for those that want them. I've done more than enough preaching in my lifetime. If Witchcraft is not for you, then feel free to put this book down and walk away. Cut the cord that we dedicated in chapter 5 and don't look back. There are absolutely no consequences. No one will shun you, you won't burn in hell, and you won't miss out on salvation. However, if what I've written has intrigued you, then feel free to explore this path further.

One book can never show you everything that makes up the wide world of Witchcraft. As we discussed, there are countless streams and sources that inform the many traditions. This book is just a taste through the lens of my own journey and experiences. The fun bit is what comes next. Look at what else is available out there. Look to history but also to the practitioners of today. We're in a golden age of Witchcraft, and people are sharing their practices on social media, on YouTube, in podcasts—anywhere you can imagine. Go see what's out there and if any of it speaks to you. I hope to follow this book with another that explores my own practice and magical philosophy as a Bardic Witch, and if what you've read so far intrigues you, please keep an eye out for that. Until that time, however, there are many wonderful authors and teachers in the Witchcraft community today. You will find some of them in the suggested reading list at the end of the book, and I highly recommend you at least look at what they do to see if it resonates.

At the outset of this book, we dedicated a Llyfr Cyfrin. Throughout, you have had opportunities to add to it by journaling prompts or reflection, or simply by adding in the exercises you felt worked for you. That book serves as a great starting point for your continued exploration of this path. Find new ways to add to it, new streams of magic that call to you. Once your first book is filled, start another. One day you will look back and see your journey mapped out, the many twists and turns of your personal stream recorded as a history of your path of Witchcraft.

Conclusion
The End and the Beginning

We have finally reached the end of our journey together. However, this is only one step of your larger path, and I'm grateful you let me walk it with you. Before we part ways, I have a couple of things to say if you wish to continue exploring the joyous path of the Witch.

Exploring this path is fun, and there's no harm in being anonymous. However, if it is safe for you to do so and you choose to continue on this path, coming out of the broom closet can be a really powerful thing. We all deserve to live an authentic life.

The world we live in often marginalizes people. By coming out of the broom closet and publicly identifying as a Witch or Pagan, we add another voice to the chorus that sees Witchcraft as a valid and healthy magical and spiritual path. We contribute to the community of the Craft and help make it more visible. We contribute to breaking down stigma and stereotypes. Unfortunately, we live in a world where visibility is often the first step to progress. When we step out of the broom closet and proudly claim our space as a Witch, we help to make this magical and spiritual practice more visible. This, in turn, makes it a safer space for all of us.

The nature spirituality church Circle Sanctuary is a great example of this. Founded In 1974 by Selena Fox, Circle Sanctuary has campaigned on a range of Pagan issues. In 2007, after a decade of work alongside many other organisations, they won the legal right for Pagan veterans to be buried with a pentacle, or encircled pentagram, on their gravestone.[104] These kinds of freedoms

---

104. Selena Fox, "Success in the Veteran Pentacle Quest!" Circle Sanctuary, accessed June 28, 2023, https://circlesanctuary.org/lll/Success-in-the-Veteran-Pentacle-Quest!.

and victories wouldn't be possible without the visibility that leaving the broom closet brings.

As well as helping with visibility, coming out of the broom closet can help you find community. After leaving a cult, I had no one. Though the experience may not be as extreme for everyone, many people stepping into Witchcraft have also struggled to find acceptance and community. A powerful part of the Craft is the way it connects you with like-minded people who can often understand the difficult experiences you may have gone through. The found family of the Craft can be as powerful as any magic you might work. In putting myself out there as someone who left fundamentalist Christianity and became a Witch, I have spoken to countless people who have gone through a similar thing. I have made lifelong friends who understand my experience, even if we don't often directly talk about it. That knowledge brings me great comfort. If you continue to walk the path of Witchcraft, you will find your people.

All that remains now is to thank you for joining me on this journey and wish you well wherever yours takes you next. May you always find joy, spirit, connection, and empowerment on your path. Your heart is not treacherous; it can guide you well if you learn to trust it. The spark of divinity is already within you. Nurture it, and may your inspiration never run dry.

My story did not end in a cult. Once upon a time, I was a young man terrified that the cage of Christianity was all there would ever be for me. I couldn't see beyond it. I certainly couldn't imagine where I would be today. My life has changed in more ways than I could ever count, and I'm sure in ten years' time it will have changed again. The point I'm trying to make is that if I froze myself as that young man in a cult, I never would have found my path. I am not him anymore. I'm grateful that I once was and that I had the strength to get through everything I did. But I also accept that the river of life has carried me away to new shores. I could sit and judge myself for being fooled and trapped for so long but doing that would freeze me as that young man forever. I had to accept I could change and then go out and live that change.

Wherever you are in life right now, you don't have to be defined by it. If you choose to be a practicing Witch, if you choose to dabble, or if you decide this isn't for you, that doesn't define you. You can be whatever you want to be; every single moment is an entirely new reality. The only thing that defines you is who you choose to be next. Whatever path you follow, choose to be kind. Choose to treat others with respect and tolerance. Choose to show them the same acceptance you desire for yourself. Regardless of the path you follow, those choices will ensure you live a good life. And if you choose to practice Witchcraft every now and then, well that's just part of the fun.

Recommended Reading

The purpose of this book is to introduce you to the joyous and freeing practice that Witchcraft can be. As such, a list of resources to go a little deeper is provided here. I've broken them down by chapter to help you access any areas of particular interest. If you choose to continue the path of Witchcraft, I know that these will be helpful. They helped me find my own way too.

Chapter 1—Finding Witchcraft

This chapter discussed some myths about Witchcraft and clarified what it means to be a Witch today. The suggested reading builds on that, showcasing a range of current, lived Witchcraft practices. Each book takes a slightly different perspective, showcasing different ways of working magic and interacting with spirits.

Welsh Witchcraft: A Guide to the Spirits, Lore, and Magic of Wales by Mhara Starling (Woodbury, MN: Llewellyn Publications, 2022)

This book is very influential on my Craft and written by my coven leader. It introduces Witchcraft from a Welsh folk magical perspective, but these lessons can be taken and applied to any region. It's a great example of a current, working folk Witchcraft practice.

Psychic Witch: A Metaphysical Guide to Meditation, Magick & Manifestation by Mat Auryn (Woodbury, MN: Llewellyn Publications, 2020)

This hugely successful book showcases Witchcraft from a psychic perspective, utilising concepts such as your inner divinity to create change in the world. It presents an empowering way of working Witchcraft that has resonated with many people the world over.

The Crooked Path: An Introduction to Traditional Witchcraft by Kelden (Woodbury, MN: Llewellyn Publications, 2020)

This book presents an introduction to Traditional Witchcraft that has also been influential in my journey. Again, it presents a slightly different perspective on the Craft, but it will help you grasp complex magical concepts in an approachable and easy-to-understand way.

Chapter 2—How to Leave a Cult

This chapter discussed the harmful way cults may operate and some useful tips for escaping from controlling situations. The suggested reading builds on that, taking it deeper.

Combatting Cult Mind Control: The #1 Best-Selling Guide to Protection, Rescue, and Recovery from Destructive Cults by Steven Hassan, 30th Anniversary Edition (Newton, MA: Freedom of Mind Press, 2018)

This book is by Steven Hassan, who created the BITE model of cult influence this chapter discusses. In this work, he dives into the discussion in far greater depth than me. This book and the following are the best resources that I can recommend on the subject.

Freedom of Mind: Helping Loved Ones Leave Controlling People, Cults, and Beliefs by Steven Hassan (Newton, MA: Freedom of Mind Press, 2022)

This is yet another book by Steven Hassan that addresses the BITE model in depth.

Chapter 3—Discovering Magic

This chapter introduced the topic of magic, providing my personal definition and some ways to interact with this spiritual force. The recommended reading builds on this, continuing the discussion of magic.

The Book of Celtic Magic: Transformative Teachings from the Cauldron of Awen by Kristoffer Hughes (Woodbury, MN: Llewellyn Publications, 2014)

As head of the Anglesey Druid Order, Kristoffer Hughes has a deep understanding of magic that he shares in this wonderful book. Again tackling magic from a Welsh perspective, it introduces important concepts for anyone wanting to further explore this path.

Path of the Moonlit Hedge: Discovering the Magick of Animistic Witchcraft by Nathan M. Hall (Woodbury, MN: Llewellyn Publications, 2023)

This wonderful book approaches magic from an animistic perspective, taking the discussion to great depth and helping readers understand how the living world around us contributes to any magical working we attempt.

Chapter 4—Connecting to Culture

The suggested reading for this chapter opens up the discussion of culture, introducing practices of Witchcraft built around specific cultural expressions.

From the Cauldron Born: Exploring the Magic of Welsh Legend & Lore by Kristoffer Hughes (Woodbury, MN: Llewellyn Publications, 2012)

Another offering by Kristoffer Hughes (honestly, I recommend all his works), this book explores Welsh culture, with a specific focus on the figure of Taliesin. It contains some superb retellings of the *Ystoria Taliesin*—the tale of Ceridwen and Taliesin.

Baba Yaga's Book of Witchcraft: Slavic Magic from the Witch of the Woods by Madame Pamita (Woodbury, MN: Llewellyn Publications, 2022)

This treasure trove of magic explores Witchcraft from a Slavic cultural perspective, with extensive research and personal experience informing each and every page. A delightful book to explore how cultural Witchcraft can be.

Traditional Witchcraft: A Cornish Book of Ways by Gemma Gary (Cornwall, UK: Troy Books, 2008)

This book explores Witchcraft from a Cornish perspective and has been very influential on many practitioners all over the world. Wonderfully practical, you'll definitely find lots here that will inform the way you practice magic going forward.

Chapter 5—Coven and Community

This chapter explores the community aspects of Witchcraft, exploring the joys but also giving a warning of potential dangers.

Weave the Liminal: Living Modern Traditional Witchcraft by Laura Tempest Zakroff (Woodbury, MN: Llewellyn Publications, 2019)

I adore this book and recommend you read it cover to cover. However, I consider the sections on community and breaking oaths essential reading. This adds a great deal to the discussion started in this chapter.

The Everyday Witch's Coven: Rituals and Magic for Two or More by Deborah Blake (Woodbury, MN: Llewellyn Publications, 2023)

A brilliant and accessible book about working magic with a group. A fantastic read if you want to practice magic with other people.

Chapter 6—The World of Spirits

This chapter explored the wide world of spirit life that Witches interact with, and the suggested reading builds on that.

The Four Elements of the Wise: Working with the Magickal Powers of Earth, Air, Water, Fire by Ivo Dominguez Jr. (Newburyport, MA: Weiser Books, 2021)

A brilliant discussion of the four elements and the ways they can be incorporated into a practice, which continues the brief exploration started in this chapter.

Cunning Folk and Familiar Spirits: Shamanistic Visionary Traditions in Early Modern British Witchcraft and Magic by Emma Wilby (ISBS, 2005)

This is an academic book and not a practical Witchcraft guide, but I wanted to include it as it provides great context. It's a wonderful exploration of familiar spirit beliefs from an academic perspective.

The Wakeful World: Animism, Mind and the Self in Nature by Emma Restall Orr (Winchester, UK: Moon Books, 2012)

This is a wonderful discussion of animism, and it opens up a wonderful conversation about what it means to live in a world filled with spirits. I love Emma Restall Orr's work, and it has definitely influenced my personal practice.

Chapter 7—A Nature-Based Faith

This chapter discussed how a reverence and respect for nature are central to Witchcraft. The suggested reading continues this discussion.

Unveiling the Green: Working Astrologically, Alchemically & Psychologically with Plants by Sian Sibley (Bembridge, IOW: Black Lodge Publishing, 2022)

Sian Sibley is an incredible and inspirational Witch, and her philosophy on the natural world has hugely influenced my approach toward ethics. This book is a treasure trove, and you will come away feeling inspired and enthused to do all you can to protect this wonderful planet we call home.

Natural Magic by Doreen Valiente (New York: St. Martin's Press, 1975)

A classic of modern Witchcraft that discusses how natural forces can be incorporated into Witchcraft.

Under the Sacred Canopy: Working Magick with the Mystical Trees of the World by JD Walker (Woodbury, MN: Llewellyn Publications, 2023)

A wonderful examination of the role trees play in spirituality and how much we have to learn from them.

Animism: Respecting the Living World by Graham Harvey (New York: Columbia University Press, 2006)

Another academic text, this time by Professor Graham Harvey, this book takes the discussion on animism into far greater depth.

Chapter 8—The Queerness of Witchcraft

This chapter discussed how Witchcraft is inherently queer and what that might mean for the way we practice. The suggested reading opens up the discussion about the queerness of this space.

Queering Your Craft: Witchcraft from the Margins by Cassandra Snow (Newburyport, MA: Weiser Books, 2020)

A brilliant, practical book that will immediately allow you to incorporate the inherent queerness of the Craft into a working practice.

Bending the Binary: Polarity Magic in a Nonbinary World by Deborah Lipp (Woodbury, MN: Llewellyn Publications, 2023)

This important book dives into the polarity of Witchcraft, a discussion touched upon in this chapter. It helps approach Witchcraft from a more inclusive perspective.

Sacred Gender: Create Trans and Nonbinary Spiritual Connections by Ariana Serpentine (Woodbury, MN: Llewellyn Publications, 2022)

Another important book that dives into the role of gender in Witchcraft and how we can make this an ever more inclusive space. A great example of moving with the stream of magic and creating spirituality that works for today.

Chapter 9—Reclaiming the Devil

This chapter discussed the figure of the devil and his role in modern Witchcraft, as well as the way fundamentalist Christian teachings use the devil as a tool of fear and control.

The Horned God of the Witches by Jason Mankey (Woodbury, MN: Llewellyn Publications, 2021)

A great discussion of the figure of the Horned God and his association with the devil.

The Devil's Supper by Shani Oates (Gatineau, Canada: Anathema Publishing, 2017)

An insightful discussion of the devil and his lore by a practitioner with vast experience, this book builds beautifully on the discussions in this chapter.

The Witch at the Forest's Edge: Thirteen Keys to Modern Traditional Witchcraft by Christine Grace (Newburyport, MA: Weiser Books, 2021)

Another fantastic book from cover to cover; however, the chapter on ethics particularly builds on themes discussed here.

Chapter 10—Contemplating the Divine

This chapter discussed the nature of divinity and the ways Witches may interact with the Divine.

A Book of Pagan Prayer by Ceisiwr Serith (Newburyport, MA: Weiser Books, 2018)

This book helped me open up to the idea of prayer again after leaving the cult, and I highly recommend it. It is a gorgeous discussion of the role prayer can play in Pagan practice.

Cerridwen: Celtic Goddess of Inspiration by Kristoffer Hughes (Woodbury, MN: Llewellyn Publications, 2021)

A personal account of the goddess Cerridwen, this book is great for understanding the role divinity does play in modern practice.

Queen of All Witcheries: A Biography of the Goddess by Jack Chanek (Woodbury, MN: Llewellyn Publications, 2023)

An insightful book centred on the goddess, this again helps showcase the role divine beings continue to play within many streams of Witchcraft.

Chapter 11—Embodying the Witch Within

This chapter helped bring it all together, introducing important concepts for taking the next step if you choose to continue practicing. As such, the suggested reading is about advancing your Witchcraft practice to the next level.

The Witch's Path: Advancing Your Path at Every Level by Thorn Mooney (Woodbury, MN: Llewellyn Publications, 2021)

I love this book. It's a fantastic discussion of how to advance your Craft, but with an eye on accessibility and making space for everyone on the path.

Mastering Magick: A Course in Spellcasting for the Psychic Witch by Mat Auryn (Woodbury, MN: Llewellyn Publications, 2022)

The follow-up to *Psychic Witch*, this book builds on the concepts introduced, again serving as a guide to take your practice to the next level.

Witchery: Embrace the Witch Within by Juliet Diaz (London: Hay House, 2019)

This is an empowering book that will help you stay on this path if you have chosen to walk it. A glorious celebration of the power and joy of Witchcraft.

Resources

Leaving a cult or high-control group is a terrifying experience, and the first stages are often filled with uncertainty. However, there are many resources available to help with any stage of the transition. The following are a handful of online resources that I have found helpful on my journey. The ones I have chosen to include are broad so as to be useful to the greatest number of people; however, if you have left a cult or are leaving one, I encourage you to search up resources specific for the group you are leaving. For example, I found the r/exjw subreddit and certain Facebook groups helpful; however, these would be less useful to someone leaving a different denomination. It is likely that communities exist for whichever group you have left or are leaving, and a quick internet search is likely to point you in the right direction.

igotout: igotout.org

This is a great website that has also pushed the hashtag #igotout, encouraging survivors of cults to share their experiences online. Searching that hashtag on social media can also help you find people to connect with. The purpose of igotout is to help and empower survivors to tell their stories, thereby helping others in the community.

Freedom of Mind Resource Center: freedomofmind.com

This is the website of Dr. Steven Hassan, whose books are also extremely helpful and have been previously cited. It's a great website by one of the world's leading cult experts, filled with resources for wherever you are on your journey.

Dare to Doubt: daretodoubt.org

This is a fantastic resource that gives you permission to question your belief system, celebrating the courage that the simple act of doubt requires. A wide range of belief systems are represented, and the layout of the website makes navigating it easy. The purpose of this site is to provide a safe space for anyone who may be questioning their faith.

Janja Lalich: janjalalich.com

Dr. Janja Lalich is another renowned cult expert, and her work has been hugely influential and helped many people. Her website signposts her services but also hosts some great resources. I found her TED-Ed talk on why people join cults especially helpful in understanding my own experience.

These are only a handful out of countless resources available, but they cover a broad range of faiths and denominations, making them particularly useful to anyone. They are a great starting point for anyone leaving a high-control group and are likely to continue to be useful along the journey. They are also a great stepping stone to finding resources specific to the faith or religion someone might be leaving.

Glossary and Pronunciation Guide

animism: The belief that all things on earth contain an animating spirit and so are nonhuman persons we can interact with.

apostate: Someone who has renounced their faith. Often reinterpreted by cults to slander anyone who leaves.

apotheosis: The process of becoming divine.

Aradia: A goddess in the lore of Witchcraft, featured prominently in a book by Charles Godfrey Leland in the nineteenth century.

bardic tradition: An ongoing part of Welsh society stretching back centuries. The bardic tradition originates from an order of poets who inspired the story of the wizard Merlin. These poets would compose for kings, cementing their status as rulers.

Book of Shadows: A book in which magical workings and rituals are recorded, mostly associated with the Wiccan tradition.

charm(s): A name given to magical workings, usually written and carried by a person for their magic to work.

coven: A formal group of magical practitioners, usually Witches, who share a magical philosophy.

crossing the hedge: Also known as spirit flight—that is, leaving your body and travelling in spirit form.

cultural appropriation: Taking sacred practices from marginalised cultures and using them without their original context, often causing harm to their culture of origin.

decentralised: A faith without a set of rules or holy book around which to build itself and with which to police itself.

familiar spirits: Spirits that could take various forms and helped Witches with their magic.

folk magic: Historically, magic of the everyday people.

genius loci: The spirit of place.

Horned God: A common name for the God of the Witches.

initiation: A ritualised commitment to a certain group or tradition and often a requirement of joining.

moot: A gathering of Witches and Pagans

myth(s): Sacred and symbolic stories of gods and supernatural events.

Pan: The Greek god of the wild and a prominent part of the lore of the Horned God.

pentagram: A five-pointed star drawn from one continuous line and a prominent symbol of Paganism.

poppet: An effigy of a person used to work magic upon them.

ritual: A formal and structured way of working magic.

UPG, unverified personal gnosis: Truths you have learned from the spirit world that cannot be verified by others.

Welsh Marches: The border region between Wales and England, which contains a distinct and hybridised culture.

Wicca: The oldest public tradition of Witchcraft, founded by Gerald Gardner and Doreen Valiente in the twentieth century.

Welsh Glossary and Pronunciation Guide

"Angar Kyfundawt" (*ahng-ARR KUV-in-doubt*): A middle Welsh poem recorded in the Book of Taliesin.

Annwfn (*ANN-ooh-vuhn*): The Welsh otherworld.

Awen (*AH-when*): Divine inspiration in Welsh lore, mythology, and poetry.

Ceridwen (*care-RID-when*): A figure from Welsh mythology, today venerated as a goddess of magic.

Gwion Bach (*gwee-ONN bah-ch*): The boy who became Taliesin, who stirred the cauldron of Ceridwen.

Gwyn ap Nudd (*GOO-IN app NEE-dd*): A figure from Welsh mythology, today venerated as a god, and occasionally a form of the Horned God.

Hafren (*Sabrina*) (*have-WREN*): The goddess of the River Severn.

Llyfr Cyfrin (*llee-VUHR KUV-reen*): The Welsh term for the secret book of a magical practitioner.

Myrddin (*MURR-theen*): The Welsh name for Merlin and also a bard in Welsh lore.

"Preiddeu Annwn" (*PRAY-they ANN-oohn*): Another middle Welsh poem from the Book of Taliesin

Sarffes Goch (*SARR-fess GAW-ch*): The name of the coven I belong to, translating as *red serpent*.

tair ysbrydnos (*TYRE us-BRUD-noss*): The tair ysbrydnos are the three spirit nights of the Welsh calendar—magical dates when spirit interaction is thought to be a little easier. They are:

- *Nos Galan Gaeaf (NOSS cah-LAHN gay-av)* occurring around Halloween.
- *Nos Galan Haf (NOSS cah-LAHN hahf)* corresponding to Beltane.
- *Gwyl Ifan (GOO-ill EVE-ann)* corresponding to midsummer.

Taliesin (*tahl-EE-YES-in*): The archetypal poet and magician in Welsh lore.

Bibliography

Abram, David. *The Spell of the Sensuous: Perception and Language in a More-Than-Human World*. New York: Vintage, 2012.

Auryn, Mat. *Psychic Witch: A Metaphysical Guide to Meditation, Magick & Manifestation*. Woodbury, MN: Llewellyn Worldwide, 2020.

Behringer, Wolfgang. *Shaman of Oberstdorf: Chonrad Stoeckhlin and the Phantoms of the Night*. Charlottesville, VA: University of Virginia Press, 1998.

———. *Witches and Witch-Hunts: A Global History*. Cambridge, UK: Polity Press, 2004.

Bollard, John K. "The Earliest Myrddin Poems." In *Arthur in the Celtic Languages: The Arthurian Legend in Celtic Literatures and Traditions*, edited by Ceridwen Lloyd-Morgan and Erich Poppe, 35–50. Cardiff: University of Wales Press, 2019.

Bosse-Griffiths, Kate. *Byd y Dyn Hysbys: Swyngyfaredd yng Nghymru*. Talybont, Wales: Y Lolfa, 1977.

Briggs, Robin. *Witches & Neighbours: The Social and Cultural Context of European Witchcraft*. 2nd ed. Oxford, UK: Blackwell Publishing, 2002.

Brown, Adelia. "Hook, Ursula, and Elsa: Disney and Queer-Coding from the 1950s to the 2010s." *The Macksey Journal*, 2, no. 43 (2021): 1–14. https://mackseyjournal.scholasticahq.com/article/27887-hook-ursula-and-elsa-disney-and-queer-coding-from-the-1950s-to-the-2010s.

Buecker, Susanne, Marcus Mund, Sandy Chwastek, Melina Sostmann, and Maike Luhmann. "Is Loneliness in Emerging Adults Increasing Over Time? A Preregistered Cross-Temporal Meta-Analysis and Systematic Review." *Psychological Bulletin* 147, no. 8 (2021): 787–805. https://doi.org/10.1037/bul0000332.

Cacioppo, John T., and Stephanie Cacioppo. "The Growing Problem of Loneliness." *The Lancet* 391, no. 10119 (February 2018): 426. https://doi.org/10.1016/S0140-6736(18)30142-9.

Chambers, Robert. *Popular Rhymes, Fireside Stories, and Amusements of Scotland*. Edinburgh: William and Robert Chambers, 1842.

Clark, Stuart. *Thinking with Demons: The Idea of Witchcraft in Early Modern Europe*. Oxford, UK: Oxford University Press, 1999.

Copenhaver, Brian. *The Book of Magic: From Antiquity to the Enlightenment*. Bungay, England: Penguin UK, 2015.

Coy, Jason Philip. *The Devil's Art: Divination and Discipline in Early Modern Germany*. Charlottesville, VA: University of Virginia Press, 2020.

Crowley, Vivianne. *Phoenix from the Flame: Pagan Spirituality in the Western World*. London: Thorsons, 1995.

Davies, Owen. *Grimoires: A History of Magic Books*. Oxford, UK: Oxford University Press, 2010.

Dillinger, Johannes. "Germany—'The Mother of the Witches.'" In *The Routledge History of Witchcraft*, edited by Johannes Dillinger, 94–112. London: Routledge, 2021.

———. *Magical Treasure Hunting in Europe and North America: A History*. Hampshire, UK: Macmillan, 2012.

Downie, Alison. "Christian Shame and Religious Trauma." *Religions* 13, no. 10 (2022): 925. https://doi.org/10.3390/rel13100925.

Eliade, Mircea. *Rites and Symbols of Initiation: The Mysteries of Birth and Rebirth*. Translated by Willard R. Trask. London: Harvill Press, 1958.

Faivre, Antoine. "The Imagination ... You Mean Fantasy, Right?" In *Hermes Explains: Thirty Questions about Western Esotericism*, edited by Wouter Hanegraaff, Peter Forshaw, and Marco Pasi, 80–87. Amsterdam, The Netherlands: Amsterdam University Press, 2019.

Farrar, Stewart. *What Witches Do.* Suffolk, UK: Book Club Associates, 1992.

Fleming, Andrew, dir. *The Craft.* 1996; Culver City, CA: Columbia Pictures.

Ford, Patrick K. *The Celtic Poets: Songs and Tales from Early Ireland and Wales.* Belmont, MA: Ford & Bailie, 1999.

———. "The Death of Merlin in the Chronicle of Elis Gruffydd." *Viator* 7 (1976): 379–390. https://doi.org/10.1525/9780520331952-014.

Fortson, Benjamin W. IV. *Indo-European Language and Culture: An Introduction.* Oxford, UK: John Wiley & Sons, 2011.

Franklin, Anna. *Pagan Ritual: The Path of the Priestess and Priest.* Earl Shilton, UK: Lear Books, 2008.

Gardner, Gerald Brosseau. *Witchcraft Today.* Secaucus, NJ: Citadel Press, 1954.

Gary, Gemma. *The Devil's Dozen: Thirteen Craft Rites of the Old One.* Cornwall, UK: Troy Books, 2015.

Ginzburg, Carlo. *The Night Battles: Witchcraft and Agrarian Cults in the Sixteenth and Seventeenth Centuries.* Translated by John Tedeschi and Anne C. Tedeschi. Baltimore, MA: The Johns Hopkins University Press, 2013.

Goethe, Johann Wolfgang von. *Goethe's Faust.* Parts 1 and 2. Translated by Albert G. Latham. London: J. M. Dent & Sons, 1912.

Grace, Christine. *The Witch at the Forest's Edge: Thirteen Keys to Modern Traditional Witchcraft.* Newburyport, MA: Weiser Books, 2021.

Grey, Peter. *Apocalyptic Witchcraft.* London: Scarlet Imprint, 2013.

Grimm, Jacob. *Teutonic Mythology.* Vol. 3. 4th ed. Translated by James Steven Stallybrass. London: George Bell and Sons, 1883.

Harvey, Graham. *Animism: Respecting the Living World*. New York: Columbia University Press, 2005.

Hassan, Steven. *Combatting Cult Mind Control: The #1 Best-Selling Guide to Protection, Rescue, and Recovery from Destructive Cults*. 30th anniversary edition. Newton, MA: Freedom of Mind Press, 2018.

Haycock, Marged. *Legendary Poems from the Book of Taliesin*. Aberystwyth, Wales: CMCS Publications, 2007.

———. "'Preiddeu Annwn' and the Figure of Taliesin." *Studia Celtica* 18 (1983): 52–78.

Henningsen, Gustav. "'The Ladies from Outside': An Archaic Pattern of the Witches' Sabbath." In *Early Modern European Witchcraft: Centres and Peripheries*, edited by Bengt Ankarloo and Gustav Henningsen, 191–215. Oxford: Clarendon Press, 2001

Hughes, Kristoffer. *The Book of Celtic Magic: Transformative Teachings from the Cauldron of Awen*. Woodbury, MN: Llewellyn Publications, 2014.

———. *From the Cauldron Born: Exploring the Magic of Welsh Legend & Lore*. Woodbury, MN: Llewellyn Publications, 2012.

Hutton, Ronald. *The Triumph of the Moon: A History of Modern Pagan Witchcraft*. Oxford, UK: Oxford University Press, 2001.

Jahn, Ulrich. *Hexenwesen und Zauberei in Pommern*. Breslau, Germany: W. Koebner, 1886.

Jung, Carl. *Synchronicity: An Acausal Connecting Principle*. Translated by R. F. C. Hull. Vol. 8, *The Collected Works of C. G. Jung*, Bollingen Series 20. Princeton, NJ: Princeton University Press, 2010.

Kelden. *The Crooked Path: An Introduction to Traditional Witchcraft*. Woodbury, MN: Llewellyn Publications, 2020.

King, Anthony. "Carrying the Gods with Them? Provenance and Portability of Altars to Romano-Celtic Deities in Britain." In *Celtic Religions in the Roman*

Period: Personal, Local, and Global. Edited by Ralph Haeussler and Anthony King. Aberystwyth, Ceredigion, Wales: Celtic Studies Publications, 2017.

Lecouteux, Claude. *Demons and Spirits of the Land: Ancestral Lore and Practices.* Rochester, VT: Inner Traditions, 2015.

Leland, Charles Godfrey. *Aradia, Or, The Gospel of the Witches.* London: David Nutt, 1899.

MacGregor, Neil. *Living with the Gods: On Beliefs and Peoples.* New York: Alfred A. Knopf, 2018.

Marková, Ivana. *The Dialogical Mind: Common Sense and Ethics.* Cambridge, UK: Cambridge University Press, 2016.

Miller, Jason. *Consorting with Spirits: Your Guide to Working with Invisible Allies.* Newburyport, MA: Weiser Books, 2022.

Napier, Gordon. *Maleficium: Witchcraft and Witch Hunting in the West.* Stroud, UK: Amberley Publishing Limited, 2017.

Nejade, Rachel M., Daniel Grace, and Leigh R. Bowman. "What Is the Impact of Nature on Human Health? A Scoping Review of the Literature." *Journal of Global Health* 12 (2022): https://www.doi.org/10.7189/jogh.12.04099.

Northcott, Kenneth. "An Interpretation of the Second Merseburg Charm." *The Modern Language Review* 54, no. 1 (January 1959): 45–50, https://doi.org /10.2307/3720832.

Ogden, Daniel. "Part 1: Binding Spells: Curse Tablets and Voodoo Dolls in the Greek and Roman Worlds." In *Witchcraft and Magic in Europe: Ancient Greece and Rome,* by Valerie Flint, Richard Gordon, Georg Luck, and Daniel Ogden, 1–90. London: Athlone Press, 2000.

Otto, Bernd-Christian, and Michael Stausberg, eds. "Plotinus." In *Defining Magic: A Reader.* Critical Categories in the Study of Religion, 28–32. Milton Park, UK: Acumen Publishing, 2013.

Peel, Edgar, and Pat Southern. *The Trials of the Lancashire Witches: A Study of Seventeenth-Century Witchcraft.* Nelson, UK: Hendon Publishing, 1985.

Plato. *Plato's Phaedo*. Edited by John Burnet. Oxford: Clarendon Press, 1911.

Pratchett, Terry. *Monstrous Regiment*. London: Corgi Books, 2014.

———. *Small Gods: A Novel of Discworld*. New York: Random House, 2008.

Purkiss, Diane. *Troublesome Things: A History of Fairies and Fairy Stories*. London: Allen Lane, 2000.

Schjoedt, Uffe, Hans Stødkilde-Jørgensen, Armin W. Geertz, and Andreas Roepstorff. "Highly Religious Participants Recruit Areas of Social Cognition in Personal Prayer." *Social Cognitive and Affective Neuroscience* 4, no. 2 (June 2009): 199–207. https://doi.org/10.1093/scan/nsn050.

Shakespeare, William. *Macbeth*. Wordsworth Classics. Ware, England: Wordsworth Editions, 1992.

Starling, Mhara. *Welsh Witchcraft: A Guide to the Spirits, Lore, and Magic of Wales*. Woodbury, MN: Llewellyn Publications, 2022.

Suggett, Richard. *A History of Magic and Witchcraft in Wales: Cunningmen, Cursing Wells, Witches and Warlocks in Wales*. Stroud: History Press, 2008.

Valiente, Doreen. *The Charge of the Goddess: The Poetry of Doreen Valiente*. Expanded ed. The Doreen Valiente Foundation, 2014.

———. *The Rebirth of Witchcraft*. Ramsbury, UK: The Crowood Press, 2016.

———. *Witchcraft for Tomorrow*. London: R. Hale, 1978.

Wilby, Emma. *Cunning Folk and Familiar Spirits: Shamanistic Visionary Traditions in Early Modern British Witchcraft and Magic*. Eastbourne, UK: Sussex Academic Press, 2005.

———. *The Visions of Isobel Gowdie: Magic, Witchcraft and Dark Shamanism in Seventeenth-Century Scotland*. Eastbourne, UK: Sussex Academic Press, 2010.

Williams, Ifor, ed. *Canu Taliesin*. Gwasg Prifysgol Cymru, 1960.

Zakroff, Laura Tempest. *Weave the Liminal: Living Modern Traditional Witchcraft*. Woodbury, MN: Llewellyn Publications, 2019.

Online Resources

Fox, Selena. "Success in the Veteran Pentacle Quest!" Circle Sanctuary. Accessed June 28, 2023. https://circlesanctuary.org/lll/Success-in-the-Veteran-Pentacle-Quest!.

"The Lion Man: An Ice Age Masterpiece." The British Museum. October 10, 2017. https://www.britishmuseum.org/blog/lion-man-ice-age-masterpiece.

"Religion, England and Wales: Census 2021." Office for National Statistics. November 29, 2022. https://www.ons.gov.uk/peoplepopulationandcommunity/culturalidentity/religion/bulletins/religionenglandandwales/census2021.

"Worship." Cambridge Dictionary. Accessed June 28, 2023. https://dictionary.cambridge.org/dictionary/english/worship.